1/19
THT
NOW1·19

MARLENE
my friend

Other titles by David Bret published by Robson Books

The Piaf Legend
The Mistinguett Legend
Maurice Chevalier

MARLENE

my friend

AN INTIMATE BIOGRAPHY
DAVID BRET

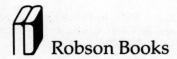

Robson Books

This book is in memory of
Frank Elliss and Les Enfants
de Novembre

First published in Great Britain in 1993 by Robson Books Ltd,
Bolsover House, 5–6 Clipstone Street, London W1P 7EB

Copyright © 1993 David Bret

The right of David Bret to be identified as author of this work
has been asserted by him in accordance with the Copyright,
Designs and Patents Act 1988

British Library Cataloguing in Publication Data
A catalogue record for this book is available from the British
Library

The author is grateful to Marlene Dietrich for supplying the
photographs reproduced in this book, which are included at
her express request.

ISBN 0 86051 844 2

Photoset in North Wales by Derek Doyle & Associates, Mold,
Clwyd. Printed in Great Britain by St Edmundsbury Press,
Bury St Edmunds, Suffolk.

It isn't enough, just saying that you're unique ... your art is nothing short of a masterpiece of precision and perfection

You write what is inside your heart and you never misunderstand me ... this is why our relationship means so much to me

Contents

Acknowledgements

The author would like to thank the following for the extracts used in this book:

SECKER & WARBURG, London: Josef von Sternberg: Fun in a Chinese Laundry (1965).
EDITIONS GRASSET, Paris: Marlene Dietrich: Marlene D (French language version re MD's request, 1984).
MACMILLAN, London: Memo from David O. Selznick (edited by Rudy Behlmer, 1972).
The staff of the *New York Times*.
UNGAR, New York: Marlene Dietrich: Marlene Dietrich's ABC, 1961.
PETER MAURICE LTD., London: For the songs 'Lili Marlene', 'Where have all the flowers gone?', 'Illusions'.
Der Montag Morgen and *Soundwave Illustrated*.
EDITIONS PAUL BEUSCHER, Paris: For the songs 'Un coin tout bleu', 'La légende des étoiles'.
The Staff of *The Times* and the *Sunday Times*.
NOEL GAY LTD: For 'When the world was young'.
Gilbert Adair of the *Independent*.
John Sweeney of the *Observer*.
The Estate of Ferdinand Freilgrath.

Especial thanks to Joan Hirst and Graham Payne of The Noël Coward Estate for the Café de Paris introduction of 1954.
The Staff of the *Bunte*, particularly Hans Gerwiess of Munich.

Ryszard Straszewski and Hanna Szymonovska of Warsaw, and
  Julius Wilbur Garztecki, my Polish agent.
Monica Solash of The British Theatre Museum.
Mark Furness, Terry Sanderson, Keith Porteous-Wood, Jacqueline
  Danno, Romuald Colson, Betty Paillard, Marc Ringo, François
  and Madeleine Vals, André Bernard, René and Lucette
  Chevalier, Michael Guyarmathy, Piers Ford and John for their
  much appreciated words of comfort and messages of
  condolence.
The Staff of Robson Books, particularly Jeremy Robson, Louise
  Dixon and Cheryll Roberts, for putting up with me in general.
Barbara, and Renate and Gottfried Helnwein, for inspiration . . .
  and Renate in particular for talking me through some of my
  worst experiences.
Heartfelt thanks to David and Sally Bolt, without whose help I
  would not have pulled through. Likewise my best friend Roger
  Normand, who helped me through the aftermath of Marlene's
  death.
My wife Jeanne, who is the keeper of my soul.
And finally to Marlene, who will eternally remain the life-blood of
  my existence. God bless you, Mama, wherever you are!

Preface

'I have called to say goodbye. I am telling you that I love you, and that now I may die . . .'

This was Marlene Dietrich's very last call to me, on Monday 4 May 1992, at 7.45 p.m. precisely – ironic, for in our early days she had always called at this time.

It was a final, absolute statement, and one that I had anticipated for almost two years. One week earlier she had called, and we had chatted normally as though there had been nothing untoward. Marlene had given no indication to me that she might have been feeling tired.

A few days later she contacted her family. Her wishes were that she should die in her bed – her church and her island of solitude for as far back as I could remember – but when her grandson arrived, he carried her to the sofa in her living room. Here, surrounded by her most cherished personal effects – photographs, books, and the letter she had received from General de Gaulle after the war – she closed her eyes for the last time. It was the eve of the Cannes Film Festival and the sponsors had adopted her famous photograph from *Shanghai Express* as their official emblem. Outside in the avenue Montaigne, the sun was shining.

Now, there is only darkness, though I do not doubt that when the skies finally clear we will observe that the brightest star in the firmament will be named MARLENE.

N'oublie pas, mon ange. La vie sans amies c'est comme un jardin sans fleurs . . .

David Bret

Introduction

'After I've Gone and Left You Crying'

It's easier, opening your heart to a person you don't have to see every day. It's easier, letting yourself go.

In May 1973 Marlene Dietrich flew into London to begin a five-venue tour of the country. Towards the end of that month she gave a series of concerts in Southport and my wife, Jeanne, and I were indeed fortunate in acquiring seats for the première. It is an evening that I shall never forget as long as I live . . . Sixteen years or so later speaking about it would open the gates to a friendship which, though clandestine and sometimes more than a little odd, would endure the rest of Marlene's life.

Bizarre our relationship may have been, yet it is something which Marlene treasured, otherwise she would not have given me her personal telephone number and made the supreme effort to stay in touch, in spite of one or two arguments and mutual bouts of temper and rudeness.

It was during my research for my book *The Piaf Legend* in 1988 that I found myself writing to the French magazine *Paris-Match*, asking their permission to publish an extract which they had quoted from Marlene's 1984 biography, *Marlene D*. The lengthy piece had borne the subtitle 'Marlene: my men and I', and figuring

1

prominently amongst her 'men' had been Edith Piaf. The magazine then put me in touch with Marlene's French publisher and a few weeks later I was furnished with details of how to contact her, and told that I should brook no delay in doing so. This took no ordinary amount of courage. I dispatched my very first letter to her on 12 August 1988, seven weeks before *The Piaf Legend* was due to be published so, even if she had objected to the extract being used in my book, she would have been too late.

Dear Miss Dietrich,
    It will be twenty-five years in October since Edith Piaf left us, and so many horrible things have been said about her that I wanted to show the world how much one man cared about this wonderful woman.
    I have referred to you many times in my book. You were such a kind friend to Edith. You helped her when she needed help during the worst of her many tragedies, and I for one always shall be grateful for that. In my book I am including a picture of you and Edith at her wedding in 1952, and I have included the brief translation from your book.
    Life is often filled with broken dreams, empty promises, unrealized ambitions and regrets. My regret is that I never saw Piaf, and that I never met you properly. My wife and I come to Paris regularly. We hope to come in October, and when we do I shall bring you flowers. It is a small price to pay for the warmth which you have brought to all our hearts . . .

Sime time later, when I had become accustomed to Marlene's peculiar sense of humour – the fact that the tone of her voice made me howl with laughter when all the time she was being deadly serious – she would remember my first letter, and our very first telephone conversation.

'How can I ever forget that letter, or the first time we ever spoke? I only rang to put you straight on a few points. That's because I thought you were a journalist. Okay, so I was very off-hand with you. But if you'd have met some of the people that I've met, you would understand why. And you ask why you can hear paper rattling? I'm making notes, dear! What's so strange about that? When I'm dead nobody will believe we had this conversation . . . or any of the others. Then again, maybe they'll find something. I get

Norma to photocopy everything. And I've kept all your letters –
even the first one!'

I asked Marlene what was so special about my first letter and she
replied, 'I thought it was just another fan letter, so I put it in the bin
– and in any case, it was the kind of letter that made me want to
throw up. The cleaning-woman didn't come in that day, though,
and by the time you wrote to me again I'd found the first letter. I'm
glad I did. Our relationship means a lot to me, now. You never
misunderstand the things I say, like everyone else does.'

In January 1989 I sent Marlene an autographed copy of my
book, not that she bothered replying to any of my letters, of which
there had now been five. Mutual friends in Paris informed me that
since refurbishing her sumptuous apartment on the avenue
Montaigne, Marlene had become a virtual recluse. I also heard, on
the grapevine, that her memoirs were about to be published in
England. This put paid to any plans I had had in following *Piaf*
with a biography of Marlene.

By the summer of 1989 there had still been no reply to my letters
. . . no indication at all, so far as I thought in my desperation, that
Marlene was still alive. I had just finished the first draft of my
book, *The Mistinguett Legend*, and had decided that my next
project would be about female stars of the French music-hall only,
under the title *Les grandes dames de la chanson*. I got to thinking
of all the 'foreign' stars who had invaded Paris over the last sixty
years and naturally Marlene's name headed my list. I wrote to her,
informing her of this, then promptly flung myself headlong into
my work.

The script for *Mistinguett* was well under way when, on 16
August, I received a typewritten airmail envelope. On the back of
this, in a large scrawl, were the initials MD and her address. This
letter had been typed by Ramon, the young receptionist at
Marlene's apartment block on the avenue Montaigne. What
amused me most about the letter were the postage stamps – three
times the value they should have been, and all stuck on
upside-down! The date on that first single sheet of paper was 14
August.

And then, on 16 September 1989, when I was in a foul mood
because that afternoon my electronic typewriter had broken
down, Jeanne came into the study to inform me that 'Miss

Dietrich' was waiting to speak to me on the telephone. Our extraordinary liaison had begun.

Initially, her tone was severe. It took her a while to trust me not to rush off to the nearest radio station or newspaper to blurt out some of the things she had said. After a while, she would address me as if she had known me all her life, though this did not change her moods if I said anything which she thought to be stupid . . . or worse still, if I forgot anything. Marlene never minced words.

That she actually cared about her friends and loved ones goes without saying. When my wife was taken ill in June 1990 Marlene tried to call the hospital – when she could not get through, she rang me and began crying. When Jeanne's father died, eight days before the Christmas of 1991, she sent a message to the funeral. Her 'taboos' were the war, Germany, one or two of her songs and most of her films, homosexuals, talking about one's health, the weather, and pop music. Initially, I shied away from every one of these subjects. Then, when I learned from experience that she loved nothing more than a really good argument – providing she was always allowed to win, of course – I often tried to steer our conversations in the 'wrong' direction.

Half-way through *Les grandes dames de la chanson* – when I had dispatched to her the chapter entitled 'Les visiteurs du soir' – I plucked up the courage to ask Marlene if I could write a book about her.

Surprisingly, she did not snap my head off.

'Why do you want to write a book about me, for God's sake? Too much has been written about me already. Why should your book be different? And how do I know you won't tell lies about me, like everybody else?'

I promised Marlene that if I did write a book about her, that I would never do it without her permission and that I would sign a document promising her that I would let her read my script before anyone else ever saw it. Her response to this was, 'You won't have to ask for my permission, David! If I want you to write about me, I'll say so!'

Leaving me with that one little ray of hope, Marlene hung up. During the course of the next few weeks, each time she rang I always tried to work our conversation around to discussing the book, without success. Eventually I began dismissing the project altogether. She had agreed to the chapter in *Les grandes dames de la chanson*, and had even promised to go through the text with me. I asked her for a list of her favourite entertainers, and she complied at once, adding that there would be no more than four or five French ones, if that. I knew already that she would pick Piaf as her favourite entertainer of all time, though what she eventually said about some of the others did astonish me. For example, when I mentioned the chanteuse who had collaborated with the Germans during the occupation of Paris, I half expected the telephone wires to melt.

> Then, one evening whilst we were going through one of my music-hall scripts, she began chuckling to herself. 'You're making all these notes about me, and I'm writing things down and keeping a file about you. Perhaps we should write a book about one another! I should imagine that you've told me things about yourself that you'd never tell anyone else?'
>
> I explained that this was perfectly true, and added, 'If only you were serious about me writing a book about you, though.'
>
> 'Then do it!' Marlene exclaimed. 'Providing that your book comes out only after I'm dead, and not before, do it! You're sure to make a great deal of money out of it after I'm gone – there's no sense in doing it whilst I'm still alive. And I would have to tell you what to write, so that it wouldn't be just one more boring biography. There are too many of those already, for God's sake.'
>
> 'So what would you want me to write?' I asked, still reeling from the shock. 'Personal recollections?'
>
> Marlene chuckled again. 'Anything, sweetheart. So long as it's the truth . . .'

Writing such a book, of course, would have been far from easy on account of Marlene's unusual lifestyle. At that time I did not have her telephone number, and if she rang me in response to my letters and queries, she merely added that she had received my letter before promptly discussing something else. On the other hand, if I persisted she would make some excuse to hang up. Worse still she would slam down the receiver and sometimes it would be weeks before she called again. Then one evening, when she was yelling at me because one of my packages had gone astray I yelled back. Ten minutes later she had given me her number, and from then on our conversations became more intense, more personal than I could have imagined. I found myself entering the cocoon which she had woven about herself.

To a certain extent, Marlene approved of my chapter for *Les grandes dames de la chanson*, though she was not too keen on the rest of the book.

> 'You seem to know what you're talking about, but you still haven't said enough about me. But your work shows promise, and I guess you're doing a good job keeping me separate from all those other women. Do it again, sweetheart, and bring it to the apartment. I'll be going to Switzerland in a few days' time. If I'm back, I'll see you. If not there's always someone at reception. And make sure you stick everything down.'

'Going to Switzerland' was an old ruse. She had repeated the phrase dozens of times before, when all the time she had been sitting alone – and I suspect feeling pretty miserable – in her apartment. Even so, she had asked us to drop in and see her and this is exactly what we did. That morning, Manuel was on duty on the reception desk. He told us that Marlene no longer lived in the block, though as soon as I produced my 'password' he changed his mind and admitted that she was in Gstaad. Therefore I did as I had been told, tucking my message inside the second volume of *Piaf* which Marlene had requested for her daughter, and sealing this inside a thick brown envelope. A few days after our return to England, Marlene rang:

> 'I gather you had some difficulty trying to convince Manuel who you were? The afternoon receptionist is a nice young man – his name is Ramon. You should have come back and had a word with him. And you also seem to have the impression that I'm a miserable so-and-so who never wants to see anybody. In your letter you said that I was almost impossible to get hold of. That isn't true – not as far as you're concerned!'
>
> 'I merely meant that you're hard to locate when you're not in Paris,' I tried to explain. 'Are you trying to tell me now that you've never been inaccessible?'
>
> 'No, at least not like that other woman you mentioned in your letter,' came the almost irate reply. She meant Garbo, of course. 'I don't even want to talk about her. Okay, so we both arrived in

America without knowing much about Hollywood, and we both had a hard time, adapting to their way of doing things. So why did you write, asking me to talk about her? She never talks about me. Come to think of it, she never talks about anything.'

'But you have been accused of being inaccessible, like Garbo,' I argued gently, remembering what I had been told, secondhand albeit, by my friend, Roger Normand, who had visited her regularly during the Sixties, when she had performed one of his songs in her recitals at the Olympia. 'Somebody once said that whenever you wanted anything from a shop, you always wrote a letter to the cleaning-lady, and that you shoved it under the door . . .'

'I know,' Marlene laughed. 'And I haven't seen my secretary for years and years! They leave the groceries outside my door, and I wait until they're gone before going outside to drag everything into the kitchen. If you believe that, you'll believe anything. It's all a lot of balls! I won't give anyone my telephone number, naturally – you are one of the few people in England who has it, if not the only one. But if people write to me something that I find interesting, then I'll call them. No, sweetheart, I'm not inaccessible. But just you wait! Just you wait and see what they're going to say about me. That I live alone, and that I'm into solidarity! Solitude! God in heaven, so-li-too-ood!' But I see all my friends. They come here and I organize dinner, but naturally I see all my friends only. There's Louis Bouzon who's a great, great friend of mine. And Madame Mario who lives at Number Sixteen. I see all my friends, but never strangers. Why should I see strangers, David? I never did.'

'Maybe people tend to think that because you're so famous, you shouldn't have a private life,' I suggested.

'But sweetheart, if I were to see all the people who write to me, who say: "I would like to come and see you!" Can you imagine that? They bring flowers here. Flowers, flowers, flowers that I send on to friends. They all expect me to receive strangers, but in my entire life I've never received strangers. And why? Because they only make conversation! They say how it rains, how the weather is. The English in particular are like that. "Ha-ha-ha! Let's talk about the weather!" And they point at the window as if I didn't know that it was raining outside. They're stupid! Most people are stupid, David, believe me! But there's also one other reason why I see only my friends. You see, since I broke my leg for the sixth time – the same leg – I finally gave up having it always in plaster. No, I wasn't going to do that again. So I just lay down on the bed, and I've been here ever since.'

'But you do still get around?' I pressed, harking back to the alleged visits to Switzerland, or Neuilly. 'You do feel well in yourself?'

'No,' she replied. 'I can't walk any more because naturally the leg has shrivelled. But I'm well organized. I have all my files here, and hot water to make tea. I don't mind putting up with just lying here. I only have this thing with the bones. The same bone was cracked six times, so you can imagine what situation I'm in. The right leg is fine, but not the other one. And I say to myself: "Why should I bother going out when the street is full of photographers?" And why should I keep moving from one room to the other? Why would I go into the living room? I have everything here – my files, my books, everything. I don't need to go and look at the kitchen! Why should I? There's nothing there! The secretary comes in three times a week. She types the letters and does the photocopying. I'm well organized. And now that Ramon is no longer here, there's another man called Manuel. Then there's a lady who's married to the man who works in the garage. She's very good. She brings me the mail in the morning. And I have a shop here that I call – they send warm food over, so I don't have to cook. I also have a very good American secretary who's married to a Frenchman, and she's very honest. She sees to all the business. Like I said, I'm well organized and I'm not inaccessible – and neither am I also miserable and morbid.'

Marlene was not miserable, though some would have regarded her as extremely morbid. My favourite French singer, and another very good friend, was Barbara, whom many claimed to have surpassed even Piaf. She was a dramatic performer to whom the subjects of death and love were a single entity. Marlene did not like her at first, though when she discovered that Barbara was known by the Germans as 'The Garbo of Song' on account of her intense aversion towards discussing her private life, she warmed to her. In January 1986 Barbara and the actor Gérard Depardieu had opened in the musical play, *Lily Passion*. This was a curious piece that tells the story of a Ripper-like young man who is so infatuated with the chanteuse Lily that he murders someone each time he hears her sing – and who eventually kills her because death is her one desire beyond love. Marlene adored the theme, and a few years later went to see Barbara at the Mogador Theatre in Paris. One of her big songs then was 'Sid'amour à mort', a harrowing pun on the AIDS theme, known in France as *le SIDA*. Then, at the end of her performance, after singing a number which translated as 'When I am dead, bury me inside my piano, like a crow', Barbara had flung herself over the back of her famous instrument in the most wonderful stage death I had ever seen.

Marlene asked me to send her a tape recording of Barbara's AIDS song, along with one of my own, and on 1 November 1989 she rang me:

'I called, dear, because I thought we should talk about death. You don't find that very encouraging? Well, if that's the case you're not as sensible as I thought you were. I talk about my death all the time. We all have to die, and when you have a family to consider, it's something you have to talk about. You've got to think about your loved ones. Tell me about your family.'

'There's nothing much to tell,' I said. 'And in any case, why should details of my private life go into a book about you?'

'Because, sweetheart, it would enable your readers to get to know the kind of man you are. They'll sympathize with you, like I do, for your lousy youth. So tell me about your parents.'

'I have no parents,' I confessed. 'None that I care to remember. I adored my mother – she died of a heart attack in 1971, but I've always held the man I was forced to call my father responsible. He was horrible to her – cheating her and always telling her how he wished she were dead. They adopted me as a baby, and he never stopped reminding me how lucky I was – you know, being taken in when so many others had been left in the home. He made it sound as though he'd bought me from a shop after the sell-by date, and that's how it was until I got married. I hated him for all the things he did to me, and for the way he treated my mother. Once or twice I tried to forgive him, but I only ended up tearing myself apart.'

Marlene spoke very quietly. 'No man is worth that, David. That's why you should take out some life assurance, to prevent your money from falling into the wrong hands.

'Now, let's talk about that friend of yours – the one who killed herself?'

'She was a very pretty blonde lady called Betty Mars, and I loved her very much,' I explained. 'Some people hailed her as the new Piaf.'

Suicides and suicide-attempts were not uncommon in the

high-pressure world of the music-hall. Edith Piaf, Johnny
Hallyday and Sylvie Vartan had all tried to take their own lives.
Mike Brandt, a big star in Europe during the early Seventies and
the idol of millions of women, had flung himself out of his
apartment window . . . aged just twenty-seven. During the early
Sixties, Luigi Tenko, a young Italian pop star with whom Dalida
had had a brief affair, had killed himself after failing to win a song
contest. Dalida herself had swallowed an overdose of barbiturates
in the spring of 1987, though few people in France had been
surprised, considering her acute neurosis. Betty's death, however,
had cut out a part of my heart.

Marlene's attitude towards what had happened to these two
very talented entertainers stunned even me:

'Dalida swallowed pills. She was always moaning about wanting to
die. Thank God she found the guts to do something about it and
put us all out of our misery. But who was the other one? Betty Mars
– as in Mars Bar? I never even heard of her. Did she take pills?'

'She flung herself out of her bedroom window,' I said.

'Oh, that one,' she chortled, 'well, jumping out of a bedroom
window wouldn't be my idea of ending it all, David. I mean, just
supposing there's somebody standing on the pavement? You might
end up killing them as well. When I do it, sweetheart, it will be
quick and painless. And don't sound so shocked. I know a lot of
people love me, but that wouldn't help me if I was suffering – if I
was in pain. I've already told you that I'm fine, right now. But that
doesn't mean to say that things won't get worse. That's often the
case when you reach my age. But if I was suffering, if I thought that
I was becoming a burden on my family, then of course I would do
it. It isn't that bad. I've had a good life and they would understand.
David, did you know Lilli Palmer? She was a very good friend of
mine, and she killed herself. She even told me when she was going
to do it – she came here to see me, and we talked about it. And what
right did I have to stop her? She was in terrible pain – she had
cancer. I loved her a lot, but I wasn't unhappy when she died. I felt
relieved because she'd put an end to all her suffering. If I get ill, and
if I know that I won't get better, then I'll do exactly the same thing.
I would be very upset if anyone tried to stop me. If only we all had
the right to choose the way we want to die. And to go back to what
we said, earlier – about taking out an insurance policy? Such a
thing is important. It prevents someone else being left with the

responsibility of paying for the funeral. When I die, my family will have to pay for nothing. I've given the matter a lot of thought, David. Everything's been arranged, down to the very last detail.'

Marlene had often told the story of how she would like her funeral to be. Rudolf Sieber, her husband, would be in charge of all the arrangements, and would be responsible for selecting the pallbearers. Douglas Fairbanks Junior would represent Queen Elizabeth of England and bring a 'production-line' wreath. Jean Gabin would be leaning against the porch, smoking a Gauloise and refusing to speak to anyone. Erich Maria Remarque would turn up after the ceremony, after going to the wrong church. Edith Piaf would be half-inebriated, sitting behind a screen with the rest of Marlene's female friends, no doubt singing a sad song. James Stewart would be asking everyone whose funeral it was, and Ernest Hemingway would turn up with the ears of a recently killed bull. Gary Cooper would be asleep. The service would be conducted within Notre-Dame, and would be followed by a quiet burial in a country churchyard, near to which would be a good restaurant where the faithful would be able to tuck in 'after seeing me off'.

By the end of 1989, of course, most of the figures from this entertaining, would-be vignette had themselves moved to greener pastures. Marlene would not tell me the names of the characters in the revamped final extravaganza, though I was assured that I had passed my audition:

'It will probably be the only time you ever get to see me – and I don't want any tears, dear! And you had better bring your notebook and pen. Everything will have to be written down so that you can tell the world what they said about me. And to get back to what I was telling you about Lilli Palmer – did I ever tell you about a very close rival of mine, the one who wants to commit suicide? Well, I won't tell you her name other than that she's very, very famous. When her doctor told her she was terminally ill, she looked at her insurance certificate. And you know, your family can't inherit your money if you kill yourself, so she took it to court – privately, of course – and she won her case. Now she can die with dignity.'

Over the next few months I studied every newspaper minutely searching for news, or even clues, to this mysterious 'suicide'. Then, on the evening of 15 April 1990 – it was Easter Day, and eighteen hours before the first newsflash went out – I received a call from Paris informing me that Greta Garbo had died, not of kidney failure, but 'as secretly and mysteriously as she had lived'. So was this the suicide Marlene had told me about? Two days later, whilst I was writing my own eulogy and reminiscing over our brief meeting – at a Barbara recital, no less – with the Divine One, one of my sources in Paris confirmed that it was. Even so, the best obituary of them all – loath as I am to admit this – appeared in the British tabloid newspaper the *Sun*, under the headline: GOD, SHE WAS GORGEOUS! And above the moving script was a cartoon of the great star, floating on a cloud outside the gates of heaven. The caption was: SHE STILL VANTS TO BE ALONE!

I rang Marlene at once, and even rebuked her for putting me through such a scare. In December she had posted me an empty envelope with the words ONLY HERE TILL NOËL scrawled on the back, and this had caused me so much anxiety that my agent and I had actually formulated a plan to travel to Paris on Christmas Eve to talk some sense into her. This had been called off at the last minute when a third party had telephoned to inform me that she was spending the festive season with friends in Versailles, though according to Ramon she never even left the apartment. And as usual, it was she who ticked me off:

'You can be very, very stupid at times, David. I told you not to worry. Didn't I tell you that? And didn't you tell me once that you were a realist? Well, if it makes you feel any better, you can stop worrying. I won't do it just yet. Who knows? I may not even do it at all.'

1

'Solang noch Untern Linden'

Making a film was just like getting on to a bus. You may not always appreciate the ride – but it's necessary, wouldn't you agree, if you want to get to your destination?

For more than half a century critics, reporters and biographers speculated over Marlene's age. She herself gave away few secrets in her two biographies and, though I myself often stuck my neck out during our conversations, this was one subject that I would never have broached. I got to know her intimately in 1989, sixty-seven years after she had made her first silent film and even then she had had several years of theatre work behind her. This pointed to the fact that she must have been around eighty-four, which many people assumed to be her age.

My friend Roger Normand, the ex-dancer who had worked with Mistinguett, and who many years later wrote a song for Marlene, told me an interesting anecdote which had concerned the French charm-singer Lucienne Boyer ... she of 'Parle-moi d'amour' fame. In 1962 Marlene had paid a visit to Pathé-Marconi's Boulogne-Bilancourt studios to record several songs for a new album and Lucienne had been rehearsing with her daughter Jacqueline in another studio. Marlene had some time before expressed her admiration for the song 'Tom Pilibi', with which Jacqueline Boyer had won the Eurovision Song Contest. She is also thought to have liked her mother, which from my point of view seems to have been unlikely. Marlene was not a great fan of the female voice. After the recording session, the two stars had been introduced by Roger, and they had chatted briefly about the war: Lucienne had worked for the Resistance, helping British parachutists to land in France. Then, for some reason Lucienne had remarked that they had much in common, including their age . . . at which stage in the conversation, 'Marlene went into her handbag and fished out her birth certificate, dated 27 December 1900'. I never mentioned this episode to her – nor did I ask her this most personal of questions. All was revealed when she rang to discuss the photographs for this book. It was the eve of *my* birthday, and when I told her how old I was, adding that I only had one to go before the big F, she chuckled:

'Thirty-nine? You're still a child, David! Did you know that I'm fifty years older than you?'

'Well, not quite fifty,' I responded. 'And in any case, it's none of my business how old you are. You're as old – or as young – as you feel.'

'Well, I'll tell you,' she said. 'I was born in December 1900. So that makes me as old as this century, right? But if you want to know anything else about that period of my life, you'll have to read my book. I've said all that I want to say about those years. It was all so long ago.'

'But you didn't write a great deal about your sister, did you?' I pressed, trying to remember if indeed she had written anything at all.

'Elizabeth was almost two years older than I,' Marlene said, almost wearily. 'We remained close until 1974, when she died. During the war she was arrested and interned by the Nazis. That was because of me, and because of our Jewish connections. The rest you will have to work out for yourself.'

Her father was Louis Erich Otto Dietrich, who at the time of her birth was a lieutenant of police. Prior to this he had fought in the Franco-Prussian war, and for his bravery had been awarded the Iron Cross. In 1883, probably against his family's wishes, he had married Wilhemina Elizabeth Joséphine, the seventeen-year-old daughter of the Conrad Felsing who had founded the watchmaker's shop on the Unter den Linden. This was Berlin's most fashionable street, linking the Brandenburg Gate with the Royal Palace, a beautiful thoroughfare that Marlene was still worshipping sixty-five years later when she recorded Walter Kollo's haunting song, 'Solang noch Untern Linden'. The 'Jewish connections' were distant relatives on her mother's side of the family. Then as now, much of the world's jewellery trade was handled by the Jewish community. This, and the fact that her father's family had accused him of marrying beneath himself were to alienate Marlene from them.

Sadly, Marlene never really got to know her father, who died of an undiagnosed illness (possibly influenza) in 1911. By this time the family were living in Weimar, one hundred and fifty or so miles from Berlin, having moved there on account of Otto's career. The girl, baptized Maria Magdalena and finding this too much of a mouthful, had shortened her name to Marlene. Then, to her horror, her mother married again.

Edouard von Losch was an officer in the Prussian Grenadiers who had fallen in love with Marlene's mother whilst she had been working as the family's housekeeper. Although he is reputed to have been very strict with his two stepdaughters, he did acknowledge Marlene's early musical development by arranging for her to study the violin at the respected Auguste-Victoria Academy in Berlin. Apparently she did well, though she did later confess that the school had been almost like a prison. Her nervousness and apprehension, however, did not prevent her from becoming the leader of the school orchestra, with which she made several semi-professional appearances before leaving in 1918. She then spent a brief period studying the violin under Paul Elgers at the state-run *Hochschule für Musik* in Berlin, so brief, in fact, that her name was never added to the register. Whilst there she ruptured a tendon in one of the fingers of her left hand, and was advised by Elgers to give up her studies. She refused to do this until she had seen a doctor, though when she did she was told that a ganglion had developed on her wrist. A few days later she sold her violin, an act which caused a rift between her and her family. Edouard von Losch had only recently been killed fighting at the Front, and now that Marlene's career prospects had been shattered the rest of the family wanted nothing to do with her.

I asked her if she had ever regretted giving up the violin:

'Oh, sure! Also, I would have loved to have taken up the piano. It's a beautiful instrument. I was reminded of that a few weeks ago. You know my very favourite pianist, the Russian, Ashkenazy? He played here at the Théâtre des Champs-Elysées. I went to see him, and he was terrific. He'd just played a tour of Germany, but now he lives in France. He's the best I ever heard. I heard all the great pianists, and every one of them was afraid of expressing too much sentiment and being called kitsch. You told me you'd written a song for that singer friend of yours to Chopin's music? When Vladimir plays Chopin you cry. And he's such a nice man. This man Vladimir is not afraid of sentiment. To me, he's the best pianist we have. He's the kind of musician I would have liked to be.'

Leaving the relative security but unfriendly atmosphere of the family home, Marlene moved into a *pension*, where she shared a modest room with the journalist, Gerda Huber. The pair had met in a Berlin café. From there she set about planning her future. She was given a substantial reduction in rent when she began helping the landlady to prepare meals for the other tenants, and to earn money for her ever-increasing wardrobe she accepted a part-time job, sewing together gloves at home on a commission-only basis.

Early in 1921, having accepted several undisclosed roles in amateur theatre productions, she successfully auditioned for a part in the chorus of Guido Thielscher's touring company and travelled with them to a number of venues before joining the Rudolf Nelson Girls, who put on often inconsequential revues aimed at titillating male members of the audience, though they were often attended by Berlin's notorious lesbian set. Very much dissatisfied with this, Marlene took Gerda Huber's advice and auditioned for Max Reinhardt's drama school, then located in the Schumannstrasse. In her memoirs she remembers reciting an extract from Hofmannsthal's classic *Der Tor und der Tod* (*Death and the Fool*) and part of 'Gretchen's Prayer' from *Faust*. Maybe she was astonished when Reinhardt turned her down, though she was taken under the wing of one of his assistants, Bertholt Helm, who agreed to give her private lessons at his house. One of the other pupils was Grete Mosheim, who later became one of the most respected figures of the German theatre.

More semi-professional productions followed until early in 1922 when Max Reinhardt finally recognized her talent and cast her as Mrs Shenstone in Somerset Maugham's *The Circle*, which was a big success at the Kammerspiele Theatre, an establishment for 'experimental' drama next door to his larger Deutsches Theatre in the heart of Berlin. This led to her being offered a film test by Stefan Lorant, later to become synonymous with the magazine *Picture Post*. She was filmed 'climbing on to a fence and jumping down again . . . fifteen times' whilst laughing, sobbing and pulling faces, though she was not engaged by the Tempelhof Studios, for whom Lorant worked at the time.

Undeterred, she returned to Max Reinhardt and played the part of the Widow in *The Taming of the Shrew* in the production at the vast Grosses Schauspielhaus, the lead role of Katharine being played by Elisabeth Bergner. The play went on tour and was extremely successful, largely due to Bergner's awesome stage presence, but it gave Marlene a taste for William Shakespeare. A little later she played Hippolyta in *A Midsummer Night's Dream*. At around this time she also starred in her first film, *Der kleine Napoleon* (*The Little Napoleon*). Directed by Georg Jacoby, the film had few artistic merits and probably would have been forgotten altogether had it not been for Marlene's later fame. She played Kathrin, the little maid who has helped her mistress, Charlotte (played by the unrelated, long-forgotten Antonia Dietrich), to evade the over-amorous advances of Jérome Bonaparte (Paul Heidemann), Napoleon's younger brother. Marlene refused to speak about him, or the film.

During the summer of 1922 the director Joe May signed the now legendary Emil Jannings to play the lead in *Tragödie der Liebe* (*Tragedy of Love*) and, as a matter of course, his Czech-born production assistant, a handsome young man named Rudolf Sieber, was given the pleasurable task of doing a round of the Berlin acting-schools, searching for an actress who might add glamour to an otherwise depressing storyline. Jannings played a French wrestler who has been arrested after throwing his mistress from the roof of an apartment building. A favourite with the film company was Marlene's friend, Grete Mosheim, but as soon as Sieber saw Marlene he decided that the part would be hers. Joe May was only too willing to rely upon his judgement and she was given the part of Lucie, the monocled mistress of the judge presiding over the case.

When I asked her, quite innocently, if she agreed with some film critics that her first venture with Jannings had been nothing short of a masterpiece, she soon put me in my place:

> 'I've been trying to forget that film for sixty years! I hated it! How dare you accuse me of wallowing in the so-called glories of my past! There weren't any.'
>
> 'Are you trying to tell me that you actually hated all of your films, then?' I asked.
>
> Marlene calmed down at once – she had a terrible habit of doing that, then exploding again when I was least expecting it. 'Not all of them, but more than a few,' she confessed. 'On the set I was compelled to follow those men that I called my dictators. I wanted to become my own boss – to reveal my true personality. And as you know, that only really happened when I began singing on stages around the world.'

During the filming of *Tragödie de Liebe*, Rudolf Sieber and Marlene fell head-over-heels in love and, shortly after the fourth and final reel had been completed – the film lasted over three hours – Rudolf asked her to marry him. She consented at once, well aware that this might cause any number of problems, for Rudolf was Catholic, and Marlene a Lutheran.

Meanwhile, she was offered her next stage role, in Bjørnson's *When the New Vine Blossoms*, which opened at the Königgrät-zerstrasse in June 1923. She and Hilda Hildebrandt played the sexually aware daughters of a sexually parched couple who experience their final passion when the vines are blooming in their vineyard. One leading critic of the day described them as 'hardly grown out of their short dresses, yet fluttering across the stage like bright blooms, alive with joy'. Marlene also sang in the chorus, which had been organized by one of the most controversial figures of her day, the actress *extraordinaire*, Erika Meingast, who at the time was the lover of the Franco-German chanteuse, Marianne Oswald.

This fascinating but horrendous woman had been given a chapter of her own in my book, *Les grandes dames de la chanson*, so I was naturally interested in what Marlene might have had to say about her. I had met her in Paris shortly before her death, when she had remembered how Meingast had put her on stage with 'this plump but promising girl called Dietrich'. The same age as Marlene, she had been born in Lorraine, then a part of Germany. She had been sexually abused by her father, raped at fourteen, and left with deformed vocal cords after a bungled tonsillectomy. After singing 'Sans me parler', the song she shared with Marlene, she made French hackles rise by declaring, 'I'm just a normal, child-loving, German Jewish lesbian.' In September 1945 she infuriated Marlene by singing 'Les feuilles mortes', regarded by many as a symbol of intense patriotism, in German.

The first time I mentioned Marianne's name to Marlene, she pretended to throw up. This amused me, for there was little doubt in my mind that Marlene had emulated her when singing in *The Blue Angel*.

> I told her, 'Albert Camus went to see her at the Boeuf sur le Toit. He called her songs "*chansons* of soot and flame". Cocteau adored her. And she couldn't help the way she looked!'
> 'Aye-aye-aye, but she could! She looked like something out of a nightmare. She had orange hair, and she couldn't sing. Her reputation was terrible!'

Marlene's next play, prior to which she played a cameo role in Wilhelm Dieterle's *Der Mensch am Wege* (*The Man at the Roadside*), was Wedekind's highly controversial *Spring Awakening*, at the Deutsches Theatre. It will probably go down in history as the very first stage play to depict scenes of masturbation and homosexuality. Marlene, who played the part of Ilse, is said to have loathed it. She also played the maid in Molière's *Le malade imaginaire* and had a small but important role in Guter's *Der Sprung ins Leben* (*Leap into Life*) – important in that it furnished her with the financial resources to marry Rudolf Sieber on 17 May 1924.

The ceremony took place in the Kaiser Wilhelm Gedächtniskirche in Berlin, and immediately afterwards the couple moved into an apartment at 54 Kaiserallee. A neighbour was Leni Riefenstahl, who some years later would direct a number of Nazi propaganda films. Frequent visitors were Grete Mosheim and Erika Meingast, occasionally accompanied by Marianne Oswald.

Marlene became pregnant at once, and her only daughter, Heidede, was born in January 1925 – she would never be known, however, by any name but Maria. For a few months Marlene enjoyed what she termed 'the joys of motherhood', until Pabst asked her to appear in *Die freudlose Gasse*, though for some inexplicable reason her name did not figure in the credits. This film, released in its English version as *Joyless Street*, was also the last film which Greta Garbo made in Europe before sailing for America and inevitable Hollywood immortality. In the movie, the two actresses acted out a scene which may have been typical of the time: whilst they are queuing for rations outside a butcher's shop, Garbo collapses with hunger and Marlene rushes to her aid. Later in the film she kills the butcher.

Marlene dismissed her only movie with Garbo in a few choice words: 'That one was pure kitsch. I don't even want to remember it, let alone talk about it.'

In her next film, Arthur Robison's *Manon Lescaut*, Marlene had second lead after Lya de Putti. There was even a fight scene between the two which some have compared with the one with Una Merkel in *Destry Rides Again*. Money was her incentive and would remain so during her film-making boom of the next two years. Berlin was gradually recovering from its economic crisis and of course it was imperative that her daughter should only have the very best in life. There were two films with the Hungarian-born Alexander Korda: in *Madame wünscht keine Kinder* (*Madame Doesn't Want Children*) she danced the Black Bottom and, in *Eine du Barry von heute* (*A modern du Barry*), she did a loose imitation of the black star, Joséphine Baker, whom she had seen in Berlin. In both films the star was Korda's wife, Maria. In Willi Wolff's *Kopf hoch, Charly!* (*Head up, Charly!*) she played another monocled demi-mondaine. This brought her to the attention of the horribly flamboyant Erick Charell, an extremely promiscuous homosexual who engaged her for his production of *Vond Mund zu Mund* (*From Mouth to Mouth*), which opened at the Grosses Schauspielhaus towards the end of 1926.

This high-camp extravaganza was something of a cross between a Mistinguett revue and what might have been playing at one of the numerous transvestite night clubs which at the time presented Berlin in all its decadent glory. Lasting more than four hours, it was divided into eighteen tableaux, set to the music of Offenbach, and it told the somewhat inane story of a group of children who fall asleep in the Garden of Desire. At various stages God descended from a pink cloud, and there were adventures involving an Indian war dance, Casanova, and a medieval knight rescuing a damsel in distress. Initially, the actress Erika Glassner was given the role of compère but, when she became ill three days before the première, Marlene was asked to stand in. Erik Charell decided that Marlene would look good emulating Gaby Deslys. She was made to wear a costume of buttercup yellow silk and tulle, a necklet of red silk roses, and the most ridiculous lampshade head dress imaginable and, as Gaby Deslys had done, she descended to the audience via a ramp. Topping the bill was the notorious lesbian chanteuse Claire Waldoff who had recently been in trouble with the authorities for singing a number called *Willy, Don't Talk So Much*, which poked fun at the Kaiser. Like Marianne Oswald, Waldoff had the tendency to drop her voice half an octave during certain songs, and Marlene began doing the same. Examples of the Waldoff 'truc' may be heard in her early French recordings, though of course by this time the major influence on her singing style was Damia, of whom more later.

Marlene certainly lived life though never without her husband. She, Rudolf and Claire Waldoff regularly visited the Eldorado, a notorious haunt of transvestites and homosexuals which stood on the Martin Lutherstrasse. And yet, astonishingly, she would later confess to me how much she had always disliked anything that strayed beyond the realms of 'normality'. Even so, when the director Wolff asked her if she would wear another monocle, a symbol of lesbianism, for a part in his 1927 film *Der Juxbaron*, she consented and the production was one of the most successful in Germany during the dying days of *cinéma-muet*. It was followed by a role as a whore in *Sein grösster Bluff* (*His Greatest Bluff*) co-starring and directed by the actor, Harry Piel.

Undoubtedly, Marlene's greatest stage success thus far in her career was *Broadway*, which opened at the *Komödienhaus* during February 1927 to stupendous reviews. Written by Philip Dunning and George Abbott, it had been given its première at New York's Broadhurst theatre in 1926 and had just ended a successful run in London at the Strand. The German-language version was produced by Viktor Barnowski and it was controversial even for pre-war Berlin. The action took place within the sleazy Nick

Verdis's Paradise Club in Times Square and dealt with the antics
of a gang of bootleggers, prostitutes, gangsters and jazz-band
musicians. Marlene played the part of Ruby, a dancing 'chorine'.
In order to prepare for the role she took lessons in tap and worked
out in a men's gymnasium. There was one scene in the play where
she had to lie flat on her back and pedal her legs in the air. This
turned her into an overnight sex symbol and, when the production
moved to Vienna during the first week of June 1927, she was given
the more substantial part of Pearl, who shoots the murderer of her
lover whilst speaking the plum line: 'Turn around, rat! I don't
want to give it to you like you gave it to him . . . in the back! The
last thing you'll see before you go to hell will be Joe Edward's
woman, who swore to hell she would get you!'

Needless to say, she was sensational in the part and
photographs of her appeared regularly in the press, particularly
when she struck up a friendship with the actor Willi Forst, who
had taken over the lead in the Viennese production of *Broadway*.

Willi Forst had been born in Vienna at the turn of the century,
and at the time of *Broadway* was perhaps the most popular actor
on the German-language stage. Contrary to the numerous press
'revelations', however, he and Marlene did not have an affair, for
she was still very much in love with Rudolf, who was now
self-appointed househusband and nanny to Maria. To prevent
tongues from wagging, she and Forst stayed in separate rooms at
the plushy Krantz-Ambassador Hotel, though the press were
alerted when the Austrian film director, Gustav Ucicky, asked Forst
to play the lead in *Café Electric* for the actor vowed he would only
sign his contract provided Marlene was offered a major role. She
was given the lead.

Café Electric was not without its share of drama. The head of
the film company, Count Sascha Kalowrat, had a crush on
Marlene. The fact that he was fifteen years older than her did not
worry her quite so much as the size of the man – all three hundred
and sixty pounds of him – and the fact that he was always looking
up her skirt. What she did not know was that he was terminally ill
with leukaemia. Half-way through the shoot he became so weak
that he stopped visiting the set. Eventually he had to be taken to a
nursing home outside Chevalier. Marlene should have returned to
Berlin, but the success of *Broadway* had earned her a

twice-extended season. When Kalowrat, whose weight had slumped to eighty pounds, announced on his deathbed that he would like to see his leading lady's legs for one last time she consented and, if one is to believe one source, she walked into the sick-room, raised her skirt, and walked out again.

'Where in God's name did you read that rubbish?' she barked, when I repeated the anecdote. 'Do you honestly think that I would have done a thing like that?'

On a lighter note, it was during the filming of *Café Electric* that Marlene became fascinated with an actor called Igo Sym and the interest was not in the man, as it may have been with Willi Forst, but in the fact that he was a renowned exponent of the musical saw. As the technique involved in the playing of this was not dissimilar to that of the violin, Marlene asked Sym to give her lessons. She was still playing the saw during World War Two, whilst entertaining troops in North Africa.

Returning to Berlin, Marlene enjoyed a brief sojourn with her husband and daughter before starring in *Prinzessin Olala* with Hans Albers and Hermann Böttcher. It was a resounding success and firmly established her as one of Germany's most promising young stars. Incredibly, she also found time to appear in two minor farces at the Staatstheater – *Duell am Lido* and *Die Schule von Uznach*. She was still on friendly terms with Claire Waldoff and it was probably through her that she was introduced to Marcellus Schiffer in January 1928. Schiffer had recently achieved fame, and perhaps notoriety, by publishing a volume of 'immoral and unsavoury' fairy tales and even Berlin had been offended by his portrait of two nuns ascending to heaven with crucifixes between their legs. Schiffer's wife, Margo Lion, was another mannish chanteuse who was very much in vogue at the time and with her in mind he had collaborated with Mischa Spoliansky on a sparkling revue called *Es liegt in der Luft* (*It's in the Air*), which had been scheduled to open at the Komödie Theater in May 1928. As a matter of course Marlene was invited to attend the auditions – a mere formality, for Schiffer and Lion signed her up at once, along with Kate Lenz and Hubert von Meyerinck.

The setting for *Es liegt in der Luft* was a posh Berlin department store. Whilst shopping there a young couple lose their twin children, who are adopted and raised by store clerks and age as the revue progresses. After many years, the couple return to the store to ask about their children who are now married with children of their own, but the old couple do not realize that their own offspring are in fact their grand-children. Taking the lead with Margo Lion and Marlene was Oscar Karlweiss. The three joined the rest of the cast to play every conceivable occupant of the store – shoplifters, cleaners, telephone operators and even the animals which had been deposited in the lost and found department. The most popular song of the revue, which the critics considered had more than a subtle hint of lesbianism, was 'Wenn die besten Freundin', for the two young ladies are buying lingerie not only to titillate their beaux, but to impress each other.

Another number, Marlene's duet with Hubert von Meyerinck, was about shoplifting and actually contained the line. 'We do it for sexual kicks!' This and the other songs were committed to disc in May 1928, Marlene's first visit to a recording studio. They did not, however, feature on her list of favourite songs which she forwarded to me whilst we were compiling our album, *The Essential Marlene Dietrich*.

Towards the end of the year Marlene portrayed Hypatia in George Bernard Shaw's *Misalliance*, an outspoken young woman who cannot prevent herself from telling her parents about the sexual potence and physical beauty of the men she would like to have as lovers. This was followed, still at the Komödie Theater, by the part of Eve in Shaw's *Back to Methuselah*. Her flesh-coloured costume for this raised a few eyebrows and made her appear naked, even from the orchestra stalls, and she may have been thinking of this moment when, twenty-five years later, she commissioned her very first cabaret gown from Jean-Louis.

If 1928 had been frenetic for Marlene, then the next year would be even more so. *Ich küsse ihre Hand, Madame (I Kiss your Hand, Madame)* was directed by Robert Land, who had done so well with *Prinzessin Olala*, and starred the devilishly handsome matinée idol, Harry Liedtke, as Marlene's leading man. It was shot in Paris and Berlin and featured a novelty gimmick – several songs dubbed on to a silent feature, performed by Marlene and, over Liedtke's voice, Richard Tauber. Immediately after this film she signed up for *Die Frau nach der Man sich sehnt (The Woman One*

Longs For), directed by Kurt Bernhardt, who a few years later would direct Maurice Chevalier and Jeannette MacDonald in *The Merry Widow*. In this she played a forerunner to the mysterious Shanghai Lily, the dangerously beautiful Stascha, who has caught the train to the Riviera to taunt her lovers, only to cast them aside once they have outlived their usefulness. At the end of the film one of these gets even with her by putting a bullet into her heart, and Marlene is said to have enjoyed the 'experience' of dying on the screen – something she would repeat several times, and always as the recipient of a bullet.

In April 1929, Marlene worked with the French director Maurice Tourneur on *Das Schiff der verlorenen Menschen* (*The Ship of Lost Men*). Her co-star was Fritz Kortner, whom she does not appear to have liked very much. Off set she was often seen in the company of the British actor, Robert Irvine, who was also in the film. Again it was a platonic relationship, though many critics did not think so and the content of the film did not enhance anyone's reputation. Marlene played an American aviatrix who crashes her plane near a pirate ship. Rescued, she is initially mistaken for a man on account of her flying suit, though as soon as the truth emerges she is almost subjected to gang rape. Her next film, again with Willi Forst, really got her into trouble with the critics. Scripted by Walter Wassermann and Walter Schlee and directed by Fred Sauer, it began as *One Night of Love*, changed to *From the Diary of a Seducer*, then again to *Love Letter* and was finally released as *Gefahren der Brautzeit* (*Dangers of the Engagement Period*). Forst played a bed-hopping baron who unwittingly seduces the fiancée of his best friend in a railway carriage and who, filled with remorse, later shoots himself. The film was an unmitigated flop throughout Europe, though surviving prints of the South American version show why it attracted a cult following in Brazil. In one scene, Marlene and Forst gave the impression that they were masturbating each other under the table. What most cinemagoers did not know, of course, was that the print had been 'doctored' and the hands of the two stars substituted for those of two other actors. Even so, a small portion of Marlene's audiences would remember the film twenty-five years later when she sang at the Copacabana.

A big disappointment at this stage in Marlene's career was her failure to obtain the part of Lulu in G.W. Pabst's definitive film of *Pandora's Box*. She told me, 'I actually passed the audition and filmed a brief test. My part as a silent observer was somewhere in the third reel, but Pabst cut it out.' Pabst had been impressed by her man-eating demi-mondaine role in *Die Fau nach der Man sicht sehnt*. In the meantime, of course, he had espied a young and exciting ex-Ziegfeld girl named Louise Brooks in *A Girl in Every Port*. He is alleged to have quipped, 'One sexy look from Dietrich and the film would have become a burlesque!'

In September 1929 Marlene opened at the Berliner Theater in the revue *Zwei Kravatten* (*Two Neckties*), with a score by her pal Mischa Spoliansky and lyrics by the 'Expressionist' playwright, Georg Kaiser. Her co-stars were Hans Albers and Rosa Valetti from *Broadway*. Like Brecht and Weill's *Der Dreigroschenoper*, which had only recently taken Berlin by storm, the revue was a scurrilous attack against society – in this instance, the 'filthy rich' of America who believed that money could buy everything, including love. It also accurately but inadvertently forecast the Wall Street Crash, which occurred just a few weeks after the première.

The plot was complicated. Mabel, a cynical American heiress to $30 million (Marlene), is guest of honour at a society ball. There is a lottery, and when this is drawn she breezes on to the stage and announces in English, 'Where is the man who won first prize in the raffle?' This has been won by a gangster who is on the run. Escaping from the room he offers the ticket and $1,000 to the wine-waiter, Jean (Albers), providing the two can exchange neckties. Jean collects his prize – a trip to America on a luxury liner. Mabel is booked on the same passage and, of course, she falls madly in love with him, unaware that they are watched by Jean's fiancée, Trude. In Chicago Mabel introduces Jean to her wily aunt, Mrs Robinson (Rosa Valetti) and they celebrate their engagement at the home of a wealthy senator. Jean then decides to return to his former sweetheart, learning that she has inherited a fortune greater than Mabel's. The most famous sketch in the revue, and the one which revealed Marlene at her most alluring, was so deceptively simple that her critics regarded it as 'an act of innocent provocation'. Leaning against the ship's rail with the wind-machine on full, twisting and blowing her long red skirt tightly about her legs, she created a vision of loveliness which no Berliner had ever seen before. Twenty-five years later, when she recorded her famous *Berlin-Berlin* album, she would rekindle the flame which had been lit in *Zwei Kravatten*:

> *Nach meine Beene ist ja ganz*
> *Berlin verrückt . . .*

Most important of all, the public no longer regarded Marlene as 'just another siren'. She had become androgynous, so much so that the film director, Josef von Sternberg, watching one of her performances, misinterpreted her translucent expression and dismissed it as 'one of cold disdain'. The great German actor, Emil Jannings, who seems to have been with him at the time, commented some time later, 'Dietrich had the habit of veiling her eyes – like a cow that's giving birth.'

Both men would help fashion her destiny – the one whilst seeking self-glorification, the other at the expense of his own career.

2

'That So-and-So Whore Called Lola-Lola'

Many people ... journalists in particular ... have too often associated me with the parts I played in my films. If I played a whore, then they assumed I must have been a whore.

Jonas Sternberg was born in Vienna in 1894 into an orthodox Jewish family, who lived in one of the poorer districts of the city. At the age of fourteen he had emigrated with his parents to New York though, already staunchly independent, he had refused to continue his schooling in a foreign country and had instead taken a number of menial jobs before becoming an assistant film-cutter and repairer. During World War One he had served in the Signal Corps, making army-training films, and afterwards he had been appointed assistant director, then director, to several Hollywood film companies.

Ebullient and impatient, he had not got along with the executives at MGM, nor with some of the stars. In 1925, two weeks into the shooting of *The Masked Bride* with Mae Murray, he had walked off the set and the picture had been completed by Christy Cabanne, who had earlier achieved recognition directing Ramon Navarro in *The Midshipman*. Prior to this Sternberg had finished *The Exquisite Sinner* with Conrad Nagel, only to see most of his work end up on the cutting-room floor. Disillusioned, but still proud enough to change his name to Josef von Sternberg, he had moved to Paramount and, in 1928, had scored an unprecedented triumph with *Underworld*, the first American film to have crooks and gangsters as its central theme. This has been followed by *The Docks of New York* and *The Last Command* with Emil Jannings, a man who was only slightly more temperamental than he himself was, but whom the Americans had taken to their hearts after seeing him in *The Last Laugh*.

Typically perhaps, Paramount had camouflaged Jannings's unsavoury characteristics by 'rewriting' his biographical details. Thus he was hailed as 'a pleasant, kindly guy from downtown Brooklyn', though nothing could have been further from the truth. Emil Jannings was a sheepish and unpleasant man who gleaned little pleasure out of being alive. He could barely read or write, he was prone to gluttonous binges, he trusted nobody – he is even known to have kept most of the money he earned from his films in a large locked box under his bed. He was also psychotic, demanding his way every time a scene was shot, and treating his fellow actors like dirt, so much so that many of those who had worked with him once inevitably refused to do so again. On screen he typified the 'dirty old man', and there were some who thought that this role must have extended into his private life.

In 1929 the largest of all the German studios was the Universum Film Aktiengesellschaft (UFA), and they were given the task of producing Jannings's first 'talkie'. On top of this, the actor personally informed Erich Pommer, the production chief, that only one director would be suitable. This was von Sternberg, who wrote in the preface to his book *The Blue Angel*, published in 1968:

> I received a flattering cable from Emil Jannings, asking me to guide him in his first sound film. This touched me deeply, as I had told him in plain language that I would not do another film with him were he the last remaining actor on earth. Jannings was impossible to handle . . .

All the same, von Sternberg left America as soon as he could and, in August 1929, he arrived at Berlin's Zoo Station to be met by Emil Jannings and a delegation from the UFA. Jannings's first choice for material – he declared that it would prove the perfect vehicle for his acting abilities – was *Rasputin*. Von Sternberg flatly refused to have anything to do with the proposition and suggested *Professor Unrat*, an immensely popular novel which had been written around 1905 by Heinrich Mann, whose brother Thomas had won that year's Nobel prize for literature. He knew, of course, that the subject matter of *Professor Unrat* was not an inspired choice – even the name translated as garbage – and he was settling an old score with Jannings. The proposed film was regarded as an attack on the German bourgeoisie, and even more so on the head of the UFA, Alfred Hugenberg, who was one of the key supporters of the National Socialist Party which would ultimately bring Hitler to power. The story itself, however, was relatively straightforward: the fatal attraction of a middle-aged English teacher for a beautiful cabaret singer, Rosa Fröhlich.

First of all, von Sternberg set about reshaping the script. He was assisted in this task by Heinrich Mann himself, now nearly sixty, and there were contributions from Carl Zuckmayer and Karl Volmöller. Some of the names were changed. Professor Unrat became the slightly more pleasant-sounding Professor Rath, and Rosa Fröhlich became Lola-Lola – this, claimed von Sternberg, was because his leading lady would be 'twice as sexy' as Pabst's Lulu. Most important of all the film was given the title *Der blaue Engel* (*The Blue Angel*). This was the name of the seedy night club where the heroine earned her dubious living entertaining her admirers.

Von Sternberg's major headache at this stage was who to cast as Lola-Lola. The main contender was Brigitte Helm, who had starred in Fritz Lang's *Metropolis* but at the crucial moment she became ill with appendicitis. Another suggestion was Trude Hesterberg, who had already worked with Marlene in three films. The most popular choice was Lucie Mannheim, an actress who had scored success after success at the Volksbühne Theater. For her von Sternberg and Karl Volmöller arranged a screen-test and asked her to supply a song that might be used in the film. She did this, and brought along a pianist named Friedrich Hollander. With typical flare von Sternberg dismissed the actress and kept the pianist. A few evenings later he, Jannings, Volmöller and Erich Pommer went to see Hans Albers in *Zwei Kravatten*, but as soon as they saw his pretty young co-star leaning against the ship's rail they all instinctively knew who would be given the part of Lola-Lola.

'Mr von Sternberg telephoned me one afternoon and asked me to bring one of my songs to an audition,' Marlene explained. 'I went to the audition, but I didn't take the song because I didn't think I would get the part. But I did sing something – a Peter Kreuder song called "Wer wird denn Weinen". I know that it didn't say the name Kreuder on the record label – that's because somebody else stole the song from him. People also said that Hollander played the piano for me, but it was somebody else, I can't remember who, but it wasn't Hollander. Then von Sternberg asked me what kind of songs were my favourites, so I told him, "I prefer songs which are American!" Then he asked me to choose one and I chose "You're the cream in my coffee". Would you believe, the pianist didn't even know the song. So I said, "This man is rubbish – get Hollander back".'

Der blaue Engel began shooting on 4 November 1929. It was not, as has often been stated, the first full-sound film to be made in Germany. This had been *Dich hab' ich geliebt*, made by the AFA, a rival to the UFA studio. What made *Der blaue Engel* unique, however, was the way in which it was filmed. Von Sternberg insisted that it should be shot in strict chronological order, which caused many problems for the crew because sets used only at the beginning and end of the film had to be left standing on the cramped lot, getting in everyone's way for weeks. The director's decision to film each scene simultaneously in German and English, based on his assumption that the finished product would do well in America, caused a mighty headache for the cast who were not only speaking on set for the very first time, but expected to do so in a foreign language. Even Marlene, whose English was passable, had trouble with her dialogue, particularly with the word 'moths' in the famous scene were she sang 'Falling in Love Again'. This kept coming out as 'moss', so much so that, after forcing her to go through the song 235 times in two days of shooting and still getting it wrong, he ordered one of the extras to yell, 'Bring me a beer!' as she came to the word. The film was a monstrous ordeal for her and it it took her a long time to recover from it. What is astonishing is that she would retain the song as her theme tune for so many years.

'I've read your first text about *The Blue Angel* and I think there is something which ought to be added,' she reprimanded, albeit gently. 'You say that I'm not keen on some of my songs – but sweetheart, I didn't like the songs from that film at all. All my film songs were written for the particular characters I played. That's why they were so completely different from the others. And you know yourself that the songs from *The Blue Angel* were written for that so-and-so whore called Lola-Lola. "I have a Pianola at Home . . . and I'm Alone!" Now, really! You know what that means? It was written for a whore to sing, and I've never been a whore, in spite of what some people have said. That is why I've never liked those songs.'

'Then why did you keep on singing them, for years and years?' I asked. 'You told me you hated "Falling in Love Again", yet you closed your show with it every time. Why didn't you drop it and choose something else for your theme tune? Anybody in their right mind would have ended up climbing the wall, singing songs they didn't like for years on end. Didn't you ever get fed up of the same old routine?'

'Not the other songs,' Marlene said, meaning the ones written by Colpet, Bob Dylan and Pete Seeger. 'The other songs I picked to my own taste. They were not written for old films. In one film, for instance, I had to sing a song called "Hot Voodoo". God in heaven, the things I had to do for my characters! I hated them! I hated every one of my film songs. And "Lola-Lola" was a song about a whore! As for "Falling in Love Again", that one was dreadful. I kept singing the same line over and over again. No, I never liked the songs from that film. "Kinde heut' abend", maybe – but only after I'd recorded it again. Mind you, I didn't mind the German words to "Falling in Love Again". They weren't bad at all. But I've never liked the English words . . . Every time the public expected me to sing that, I kept wishing I'd never heard of it.'

The score for *Der blaue Engel* contained four songs by Friedrich Hollander, Walter Rillo and Robert Liebmann, all of which were given excellent English adaptations by Jimmy Connelly. They were 'Nimm dich in acht vor blonden Frauen' ('Blonde Women'), 'Ich bin die fesche Lola' ('I Am the Naughty Lola'), 'Kinde heut' abend, da such ich mir was aus' ('This Evening Children') and 'Ich bin

von Kopf bis Fuss auf Liebe eingestellt' ('Falling in Love Again').
They were all recorded for the Electrola label between 28 January
and 5 February 1930, with Hollander's Jazz Symphoniker. In her
private appearances in night clubs, usually to entertain her friends,
she was also singing two more Hollander songs, 'Peter' and
'Jonny', the latter alleged to have been von Sternberg's favourite.

> Marlene said very little about her 'Svengali Joe'. 'I've said all I want
> to say about him in my book. He wrote a book called *Fun in a
> Chinese Laundry*. It's the vilest thing I ever read in my life. That's
> why I burned it . . .'
> And Emil Jannings – had she enjoyed working with him?
> 'How could anyone enjoy working with a man like that? . . . For
> God's sake, why do you insist in talking to me about my German
> films? That's a part of my life that I want to forget about. If you're
> going to write about *The Blue Angel*, just put what I wrote in my
> book, or what the critics of the day wrote in newspapers. And don't
> use biographies.'

Marlene's bitterness towards Jannings extended as far as her
autobiography *Marlene D*, published in France in 1984. For two
hours before every scene he would sit and sulk in his
dressing-room and he was prone to on-set tantrums. To a degree,
his neurotic behaviour was only to be expected – he had taken
great pains to launch himself into the world of sound, only to see
(in his opinion) a little-known starlet stealing the limelight which
he believed unquestionably ought to have been his.

There were fierce rows with von Sternberg, with Jannings
demanding that Marlene's part be cut and his own enlarged, all
falling on deaf ears, of course, for the wily director knew only too
well that he was on to a winner, a fact which was voiced
unanimously when the film had its world première on 31 March
1930 at Berlin's vast, castle-like Gloria Palast Theater. This was
the first of three gala screenings, and one at which neither Marlene
nor von Sternberg was present. She had been worried about the
film's reception and he had sailed for America to negotiate a
contract with Paramount. Under normal circumstances, this
would have waited but von Sternberg had a more solid reason for
being out of Berlin. Alfred Hugenberg of the UFA had tried to
postpone the première indefinitely, accusing the director of

caricaturing him with the Jannings' character – an accusation which was supported by Friedrich Hussong Neuland, one of Germany's most powerful journalists, in the newspaper *Der Montag Morgen.*

> Mann's hero is a repulsive bag of malice, but the film is the story of a man who has won our sympathy from the first moment ... a man lonely of spirit who is ruined by tragic consequences through his own weak character and, through inexperience he follows the false light which he takes to be a woman's love, but which is nothing but whoredom. The novel and the film have nothing in common.

This article incensed Heinrich Mann so much that he dispatched a telegram to the editor of the newspaper, asserting that *Der blaue Engel* had been made entirely with his co-operation and that Professor Rath had not been a caricature but a genuine character of his own invention.

Josef von Sternberg claimed in his memoirs that he only went back to the United States because of an executive decision by the UFA not to employ Marlene for any more films. In effect, they had expected her first film with them to flop. Another claim that he never wanted to work with her again may have been true, though where money was concerned the director would probably have worked with anyone, as had been the case with Jannings. Even so, he will always be regarded as her Svengali. In *Marlene Dietrich's ABC*, published in 1961, she summed him up in a simple phrase: 'The man I wanted to please most'. In an interview she once said that she had been the Eliza Doolittle to his Professor Higgins and she was not wrong. Even so, she was not let off lightly by the UFA. Alfred Hugenberg only agreed to release her from her German contract providing she was willing to sign another, to the effect that his company would be able to distribute in Germany whatever films she made if she followed her mentor to Hollywood. He was confident that once she left her native Berlin she would be very quickly forgotten.

There was little chance of this. Whilst Neuland and his cronies fought amongst themselves to blacken Marlene's name, his rivals sang her praises. Herbert Ihering wrote in the *Berliner*

Börsen-Courier, 'Marlene Dietrich sings and acts without any show of emotion, but her calculated phlegmatism is provocative . . . she is vulgar without seeming to act.' Hans Sahl, counteracting what Neuland had written in *Der Montag Morgen*, hailed her as being 'no longer a fake Garbo', and said she had 'an alluring and enticing walk, a dispassionate decadence, and a sensual aggressiveness in the way she speaks and moves'.

Lola-Lola has been described as 'a cold-hearted bitch', 'that brutal whore', and by Marlene herself as 'a stupid trollop who was out to humiliate a poor man' – obviously in this respect she was only being kind to Emil Jannings. What is remarkable is that Jannings appears to have gleaned great pleasure from accepting and playing self-abasing roles, and after one scene there was an unfortunate mix-up when the actor and the character became one. Having married her professor, Lola-Lola proceeds to humiliate him by getting him to give up his job so that he may work as a clown at the Blue Angel. From then on his path is a downward spiral towards despair and tragedy. On stage he is told to crow like a cockerel and, when he refrains, an egg is smashed over his head. In a howl of rage he rushes to the dressing room where he tries to strangle his wife, who in another touch of reality has taken a lover in the form of the handsome Hans Albers. In this particular scene, Emil Jannings really went over the top, squeezing Marlene so violently around the throat that Albers had to punch him whilst Josef von Sternberg and several set hands had to fight to drag Marlene free. She is said to have had bruises on her neck for a week after the incident, and Jannings is alleged to have evaded an attempted murder charge only because she later took pity on him.

No one of course will forget *The Blue Angel*'s exciting image of pre-war Berlin in its glorious decadence: the harbour back-cloth and smoky atmosphere of the tawdry night club and Lola-Lola, clad in silk stockings and suspenders, frilled knickers and silk top-hat, surrounded by backstreet doxies whilst perched on an upturned barrel, crooning almost nonchalantly

> From head to toe,
> I'm made for love . . .
> For that's my world,
> And nothing else at all!

The German lyrics to the song, which, impersonators still sing – even ones who know nothing of the language – are a far cry from the banal, but nevertheless better-known English words to 'Falling in Love Again'.

Marlene, along with the other stars from *Der blaue Engel*, was summoned to the second and third screenings at the Gloria Palast but, rather than sit in the actual auditorium, they were installed in a specially designed dressing room with a double-mirror-type window which overlooked the audience. Peter Kreuder, responsible for the film's musical arrangements, recorded the episode in his memoirs. Jannings complained about the fifteen metres of 'black' film which the cameraman had inserted after 'Ich bin von Kopf bis Fuss auf Liebe eingestellt'. This had created a false blackout intended to encourage applause in the cinema and Jannings knew that with such tricks of the trade any impetus would be on Marlene and not himself. Thus when Kreuder, who knew nothing of the blackout, refused to obey the actor's request to remove it (in the middle of the screening), he found himself on the receiving end of the surly man's fist. The news of this quickly spread to the audience and, needless to say, when the stars appeared on the stage after the screening the public did not scream for Jannings, or even Hans Albers. They yelled for Marlene.

The third screening of the film may be reminiscent of the penultimate scene in the film version of *The Sound of Music*. The entire cast appeared on stage to take their bows, then left one by one to gather outside the theatre's side entrance. Here a long line of Prussian police officers had been engaged to form a double arch towards a large army truck. Marlene and her friend, Willi Forst, her escort for the evening, were last to leave and were almost mobbed by the over-enthusiastic crowd. In the back of the vehicle, Peter Kreuder was sitting at an upright piano, surrounded by Marlene's thirty-six pieces of luggage, and playing 'Kinde, heut' abend'. Several cast members loaded crates of champagne into the truck, which then headed for the Lehrter station – the first leg of Marlene's long journey to America.

In spite of her spasmodic love–hate relationship with Josef von Sternberg, *The Blue Angel*, and everything that went with it, Marlene did emerge from her long solitude in later life, in the December of 1990, to appeal for the UFA studios at Babelsberg when informed that these were threatened with closure. Speaking on the telephone to a German newspaper she said, 'Those studios hold for me only the fondest of memories.' This statement was not, however, a true reflection of her feelings towards the German film industry.

'What did you think of that speech?' she asked. 'Do you think I was convincing?'

I could only be honest with her. 'I didn't actually hear the speech, but I read it in a newspaper – and I don't believe a word you said. I can't imagine those studios holding memories only of the fondest kind – not after what you said about the film.'

I was right, of course. She admitted, 'Well, you know I had to say that, because of all the other actors and actresses who began their careers there. But you know that I don't care about the studios in Berlin, or any others for that matter.'

In June 1991, I was 'warned' that *The Blue Angel* was about to surface again after sixty years (if one was prepared to ignore the dreadful remake of the film) courtesy of Trevor Nunn of the Royal Shakespeare Company. According to the publicity blurb which went out at the time of the announcement, the production was to be a new musical play by Pam Gems – who wrote the play about Edith Piaf from the novel *Professor Unrat* by Heinrich Mann. Marlene's name was not mentioned. And as for the actress who would play Lola-Lola? She was a thirty-one-year-old, called Catherine Neilson, who had appeared in the television series *Yellowthread Street* and the film *White Mischief*. Without seeing her in the actual part I was unsure whether she would have been capable of playing Marlene's most famous role adequately or not. The fact that Trevor Nunn had been unable to obtain who *he* had allegedly wanted for the part, however, brought a big sigh of relief from both Marlene and myself.

'First of all, the British wanted to make a film about your life,' I told her. 'Now, they're doing a play and they want to use the pop star, Madonna. I think that would be insulting – they also want to call the play *The Blue Angel*.'

I half-expected Marlene to lose her temper when I told her this, as she had when I had informed her of the play *Falling in Love Again*. In fact, she roared with laughter. 'Madonna, to play me!

That's funny! She gave an interview – she said she would like to sleep with me.'

'But that's disgusting,' I broke in. 'How can anybody with any decency say such a thing?'

Marlene laughed again. 'Well, if she said she had slept with me, that would be different. But no, she said she would like to. Oh, deary me! But you know, I can't stop the play if it's about *The Blue Angel*. I have no rights. But if it's about me . . .'

Marlene asked me to furnish her with the names and addresses of the playwright, the producer, and even the theatre manager. Then I was told that Madonna would not be playing her heroine after all. The 'official' reason was that she could not have coped with the mobs of fans when the production eventually went on to the road.

I read a few weeks later that Catherine Neilson had walked out on the production, one month into rehearsals, and that she had been replaced by a twenty-seven-year-old actress named Kelly Hunter. *The Blue Angel* opened at the end of September 1991, in a blaze of publicity, not in London but at The Other Place in Stratford-upon-Avon, as *Piaf* had, twelve years earlier. Newspaper arts' columns were headed 'Blue Angel Delight!' 'Sleaze outweighs sentiment!' 'Low-life Lola hits the high spots!' and the most original one of all, 'Falling in lust again!' This came from Irving Wardle of the *Independent*, who added that the new Lola-Lola was 'a talented tart who manages to turn the tables on her exploiters'. Kirsty Milne of the *Sunday Times* went a step further by describing Kelly Hunter as '. . . not voluptuously sexy but lean, toned and impudent'. *The Times* praised Professor Unrat (played by Philip Madoc) as 'the archetypal stuffed shirt, a squat tyrant bristling with rightmindedness and chauvinist arrogance'. The *Observer* enthused over Kelly Hunter's 'perfect flat stomach of sensational milky whiteness', a statement that made Marlene choke when I sent her the clippings and some of the pictures:

'Have you been to see the play, yet? Or should I say, is it worth going to see, considering the reviews? And the photographs you sent me – they weren't very flattering, were they?'

This then, was Marlene's attitude towards the film which many consider her greatest – and even though she cursed me black and blue when I told her so, without it she would never have become the legend we all loved for so many years.

3

'Just a Little on the Lonely Side'

You sometimes get impatient. You're nasty-tempered, but you're not afraid of expressing your opinion. In your past life you must have been a wild animal.

When Josef von Sternberg had left for the United States to sign a contract with B.P. Schulberg of Paramount Pictures, he had been seen off at the railway station by Marlene. Still very much the *Hausfrau*, she had given him a basket of fruit for the journey, in the bottom of which she had tucked a novel which she had read during the breaks in the shooting of *Der blaue Engel*. 'For the long sea voyage,' she is alleged to have said. The book was *Amy Jolly, a Woman of Marrakesh*, written by Benno Vigny, a young German journalist who is said to have based his story on his experiences whilst serving with the French Foreign Legion. The Amy Jolly character was actually based on an escapade in the life of Eugénie Buffet, the Tlemcen-born chanteuse who had been born in 1866. Still alive at the time, she died in abject poverty in 1934.

Like Marlene, Eugénie was the daughter of an army officer. She was also very much of a trouble-causer, especially when interpreting the *revanchard* songs written for her by the controversial anti-German and political activist, Paul Déroulède, who died early in 1914, on the eve of the outbreak of the war which he had desperately tried to prevent. Her great record success

40

in France was 'Sérénade du pavé', which Edith Piaf sang whilst portraying her in Jean Renoir's 1954 film, *French Can-Can*. Eugénie Buffet also sang 'Quand l'amour meurt', which was 'passed on' to Marlene, and both artists were awarded the *Légion d'Honneur*. By 1930, however, this hard-faced woman, who had begun her career as a camp-follower entertaining *légionnaires* and who had progressed as far as the screen to portray Letitia Bonaparte in Abel Gance's epic *Napoléon*, had been reduced to begging in the streets.

'I'd never even heard of this singer until I read the script for your book,' Marlene told me. 'Was she very famous – and was she a whore, like I was in the film?'

'I don't know,' I replied. 'Some people thought she resembled Helen Morgan, the actress who sang in the original show. And apart from the song I told you about, practically all of her records have disappeared. You remember how I told you about Gaby Deslys leaving most of her fortune to the poor of Marseilles? Eugénie wanted to do the same, only she drank most of it away as quickly as she earned it. She also caused riots wherever she sang because of her political beliefs.'

When von Sternberg called Marlene from the ship, explaining how he intended using *Amy Jolly* as the basis for her first Hollywood film, she is said to have been distressed over being invited to 'play the whore again'. What is remarkable is that someone else had sent a copy of the book to Adolph Zukor – probably Marlene herself – so that, when von Sternberg arrived at Paramount, he was told that the film company had already purchased the rights to the book from Benno Vigny himself. Not only this, they had hired a failed scriptwriter named Jules Furthman to 'rewrite' the story as they thought it should have been written in the first place. Thus, *Amy Jolly, a Woman of Marrakesh* became *Morocco*, the story of the sultry cabaret chanteuse who falls in love with the tough, couldn't-care-less *légionnaire*, and who eventually leaves her wealthy fiancé in order to join the 'rearguard' of *female* camp-followers (in Eugénie Buffet's day some of these were male), who are willing to risk all by trailing after their lovers across the burning sands of the desert. Equally remarkable is that none of the cast was ever shown a completed script. In order to keep everyone on their toes, von Sternberg turned up on the set each morning with the few sheets of paper which Jules Furthman had laboriously typed out the night before.

Marlene was very reluctant to go to America, and the reason for this should have been obvious even to a man as hard-headed as Josef von Sternberg: a doting but practical husband, and a five-year-old daughter. The director had negotiated a seven-year contract on her behalf, hoping that a promise of wealth might persuade her to accept a 'brief' separation from her family. He had not, however, estimated Marlene's independence which, even in those days was never less than staunch.

I asked Marlene if, in her opinion, she thought the Americans were searching for another Garbo.

'Sure – but I told them that they would have me for one film, and that after that I would decide what to do. I didn't want to take my daughter to a strange country that I might not like.'

'And you weren't too keen on playing Amy Jolly, were you?' I asked. 'Is that because the character in the film was completely different from the one in the book, or was there another reason? You wouldn't have looked good doubling for Eugénie Buffet – she was fat.'

'There were lots of reasons,' she confessed. 'None of my roles were ones which I would have accepted normally. What I am saying is that they didn't compare to some of the parts other Hollywood actresses were getting.'

'Then why accept them?' I asked.

'Because I needed the money, honey!' Marlene bellowed, placing tremendous emphasis on the word 'money'. 'And because I'd refused what some of the directors called the casting couch, that's why!'

'You mean that some actresses actually slept around, in order to get themselves launched?' I quizzed, pretending to be amazed.

Marlene chuckled. 'Not just some of them, David – most of them. I had a husband and a daughter, but they still went around saying that I was a whore.'

Garbo's first talkie, *Anna Christie*, had been given its world première in New York one month prior to Marlene's arrival there on 9 April 1930. Like *The Blue Angel*, the film version of Eugene O'Neill's famous play had been shot alternatively in English and

German and had proved a great success with the less-liberated American cinemagoers who were not used to seeing prostitutes on the screen. Even so, according to the writer Adela Rogers St Johns, who believed that the director Clarence Brown had chosen *Anna Christie* to compete with von Sternberg's film, Garbo never had to suffer the 'indignity' of becoming the character she is portraying, even if she had been seen taking a stroll around the grounds of her Hollywood home, stark naked.

On the face of it, some of the American journalists were unfair to Marlene, making comments she could hardly comprehend, yet she remained sufficiently aloof to ignore most of them and tried her best to continue with her career. She deeply regretted the fact that whilst she had struggled in Germany to prove her abilities as a serious actress, on the other side of the Atlantic she was still expected to play the *cocotte*. And, if her arrival in New York had not been heralded with the same fanfare of publicity that had been awarded Garbo, photographers did demand that she perch on top of her mountain of luggage to display her legs. She was then whisked off to a hastily set up press conference at the Ritz-Carlton Hotel. Von Sternberg had already briefed her on this, to the effect that she would be expected to take a leaf out of Garbo's book and discuss nothing whatsoever about her private life. Privately, Adolph Zukor had told her to ignore von Sternberg and give precise answers to whatever questions came her way. Marlene was also aware of some media suggestions that she was having an affair with 'Svengali Joe', as the Americans had dubbed him, and she refused to be manipulated. She made a point of telling everyone that she had a husband and daughter and explained how she had arranged to make gramophone recordings of her voice to be sent back to Germany. She also made it very clear that Rudolf was expected to join her as soon as he could get a visa.

Adolph Zukor probably started out disliking her, and one can hardly blame him when one remembers that no less than $500,000 had been set aside for her publicity campaign alone, but he did very soon come to admire and respect her and, if Marlene had reluctantly agreed to just the one film for Paramount, then there would be eleven more.

After a brief sojourn in New York, Marlene travelled by train to Hollywood, not complaining once during the five-day journey,

Paramount had agreed to distribute the English-language version of *The Blue Angel*, though not until *Morocco* had been completed. This did not worry her unduly, for she was already aware of the differing tastes of the two nations, and she was certain that any film directed by von Sternberg would be universally successful. Her insistence that she continue working with him and her constant praise of the man, made the rumour of a relationship seem more plausible of course, and when she told reporters that her husband would be sailing for American 'any day now', few of them believed her. There was also a considerable amount of anti-German feeling within the film capital with the advent of sound, and some of the established American stars who had failed to make the transition – one of these was John Gilbert – were against any foreign entertainer stealing their limelight. In order to draw attention away from herself and von Sternberg she persisted in telling reporters how much she was missing her daughter, whilst presenting them with a list of taboo subjects. After-dinner speeches, fish, evangelism, operatic sopranos, dieting, horse-racing and movie and theatre premières were, she declared, her most-hated topics of conversation.

The real thorn in Marlene's side at this time, however, was von Sternberg's wife, Riza, who had walked out on him half-way through the shooting of *Der blaue Engel*. The former actress had rented an apartment in New York and had contacted her husband regarding possible divorce proceedings. Von Sternberg seems to have still been fond of her, for he had sent her a telegram urging her to reconsider and in the meantime to join him in Hollywood – he had even taken an option on the apartment next to his own. Riza did one better than this. She moved in with him. Marlene is said to have been distressed over this. She herself was living in a smaller, but no less comfortably furnished apartment across the way and, if she did not wish for an actual relationship with her mentor, she certainly yearned for his company as a friend. Riza did her utmost to get in the way of this, inasmuch as she placed an inordinate strain on the director and the star. He is alleged to have snarled at a journalist, when asked why he should not just marry Marlene and end the speculation. 'Me, marry Marlene? I would rather share a telephone booth with a frightened cobra!'

Fortunately for all concerned, von Sternberg 'persuaded' his wife to return to New York without disrupting the filming of *Morocco*, but many years later Riza spoke to John Kobal. During Josef's pre-Dietrich days, she declared, her husband's films had borne the legend 'A Josef von Sternberg Production', since which time only Marlene's name had appeared in large letters. This was of course very true, although the same could have been said about most of the major Hollywood stars.

I only mentioned John Kobal's name once to Marlene, though it was a case of 'once is enough'. Born in Austria in 1940, he had moved to Ottawa with his family ten years later, and had first seen Marlene in concert in Toronto in 1958. According to one of the stories which circulated about him, he followed her to a restaurant, overwhelmed her with his charm and good looks, and was invited to sleep on the couch in her hotel suite with the proviso that he should be gone the next morning. From then on he had collected just about every photograph that had been taken of her, adding them to the Kobal Collection, said to have been the largest such collection in the world. Such was his reputation in the trade that many rare stills were given to him by MGM in the early Sixties, including colour shots of Charles Boyer and Greta Garbo in *Marie Walewska*. The Kobal photographs in Alexander Walker's book *Dietrich* were stunning, yet what Marlene said about this man was dreadfully insulting whether he deserved it or not.

Marlene had been introduced to the Hollywood glamour set at a party. This had been organized not especially on her behalf, but to announce the impending marriage of David O. Selznick and Louis B. Mayer's daughter at the Beverly Wilshire Hotel. Amongst those present were J. Robert Rubin, Harry Rapf, Irving Thalberg and, of course, the father of the bride-to-be – all top executives from MGM. B.P. Schulberg was warning the opposition, in a subtle way, that here was indeed a contender for the Garbo crown. She had had a number of pre-publicity photographs taken in New York by Irving Chidnoff, which had revealed an ability to smile as well as look sultry – something which some people considered Garbo incapable of – and the guests at the party had been a little surprised to find her naturally pleasant, and easy to get along with. Soon afterwards there was another photographic session, this time by E.R. Richee, and it produced a number of more dramatic yet nevertheless enchanting portraits, one of which would later cause her problems with at least one member of the French music-hall fraternity. By this time she had gone through the usual 'hollywoodization' by having her eyebrows shaved, by being forced on to a diet and, it was alleged at the time, by having her wisdom teeth removed to give her that famous hollow-cheeked look. In fact Marlene told me in 1989 that she still had her wisdom teeth.

An important precedent which Marlene set at the time, whilst preparing for her role as Amy Jolly in *Morocco*, was the trend among women for wearing trousers. In Berlin, for practical reasons she had always worn slacks around her apartment and at many of the night clubs she had frequented, particularly the Eldorado, where many of the female clientele had worn men's suits as a means of expressing their sexual preferences. There was, however, nothing sexual in Marlene's decision to wear trousers in Hollywood, indeed, her femininity seemed only to intensify when she was sporting tails and top-hat later in her career. If she was asked why she had preferred attending social functions in 'nonconformist' attire, her response would be that not only were men's clothes more comfortable to wear, they were also cheaper, and easier to buy off the peg.

Given Marlene's later fondness for wearing trousers, and in particular Levi denims, was she into women's lib in those far-off days, or was there something else – something that has recently been suggested by some muck-raking journalists?

'You know what I feel about this thing they call female liberation, David? I was asked the very same question a few years ago, in Schell's film. It's called penis-envy. Women want what a man has between his legs, but they don't want the man that goes with it. I hate those kind of people. No woman can go all through life without a man – unless she's a lesbian. And sweetheart, I was never one of those!'

Marlene's co-star for *Morocco* was Gary Cooper, then in his late twenties and fresh from his success as a swashbuckler in John Waters's *Beau Sabreur*. Tall, confident, and very good-looking, he was the perfect choice for the part of Tom Brown, the mysterious *légionnaire* who may be seen to care more for his regiment than for one woman alone. Von Sternberg did not like directing him, not because Cooper was a difficult man, far from it, but on account of the actor's great height, which only made the diminutive but otherwise self-assured 'Svengali Joe' feel painfully insignificant whenever they were standing side by side. It is also interesting to note that whenever Marlene played a scene with Cooper, she was almost always posed above him. According to contemporary reports, Cooper also found von Sternberg an 'interminable bore'. Lee Garmes, the cameraman who worked on *Morocco*, remarked that the director once became so irate with Cooper for yawning persistently that he threatened to walk off the set if it happened again . . . and that this was a cue for everyone to begin yawning, including Marlene. Cooper is also said to have been very impatient because of the time it took von Sternberg to go through each of Marlene's scenes. At this time she was about eighty per cent fluent in English and still had to learn long pieces of dialogue phonetically. True or not, the two stars soon became close friends, so much so that the gossip columnists read more into the situation. This was not true, although when Cooper's girlfriend, Lupe Velez, was told that something could have been going on between the two, matters almost got out of hand. Velez had recently completed the gory *Where East is East* with the master of horror, Lon Chaney, and in 1944 she would stage an even messier suicide. In between she would allow Hollywood to take advantage of her fiery nature and nickname by filming eight very successful comedies in the *Mexican Spitfire* series. For the time being she was content with threatening to scratch Marlene's eyes out in public. I would have loved to find out what had happened next but Gary Cooper, sadly, was another topic that Marlene refused to discuss.

Morocco contained many of the Dietrich hallmarks that would later become associated with her legend: her entrance, emerging from the mist-enshrouded ship, the interior daytime shots which were actually filmed at night so that the lighting brought out the best in her angular face, and the frequent use of slatted shutters and shady backstreets, influencing an entire generation and much emulated, though never with von Sternberg's precision and authority. The desert scenes were actually filmed on a strip of beach at a place called Guadalupe, but according to von Sternberg they were so realistic that when the Pasha of Marrakesh saw the film he commented that the film crew must have spent a lot of time in his city without his knowledge. Another feature of some interest was the pair of dolls – one Japanese and the other a golliwog – which were seen in Amy Jolly's room. Marlene had brought these with her from Berlin, they were her good-luck talismans and would appear in several more films.

Morocco, like *The Blue Angel*, was not without controversy. Although Gary Cooper was advertised as the main star of the film, like Emil Jannings before him, he was forced to accept the fact that he was dealing with a major force, particularly as some of the posters proclaimed, 'Marlene Dietrich, the Woman All Women Want to See!'

The maxim was, of course, a thinly disguised *double entendre*. Befriended by the fabulously rich Kennington (Adolphe Menjou), Amy Jolly is working as a *diseuse* in a night club whilst supplementing the manager's income by selling apples during her spot. Her first song is Georges Millandy and Octave Crémieux's turn-of-the-century hit, 'Quand l'amour meurt', a maudlin piece which she croons whilst immaculately dressed in top-hat and tails, not quite certain whether she is directing the words at the pretty young woman sitting amongst the rich clientele next to the stage or the handsome *légionnaire* sitting with his cronies in the smoke-filled auditorium. Finally, she takes a carnation from the girl's hair, kisses her fully and shockingly on the mouth, then tosses the flower to the soldiers. This kiss is made to appear even more scandalous when, later in the film, Amy and Tom kiss behind her fan.

I tried to interview Marlene about *Morocco* by mentioning the Eugénie Buffet song, but she clammed shut:

> 'I detested the song. And did you see the photograph of me, with Gary Cooper and Maurice Chevalier – the one in the man's suit and trilby hat? Josef von Sternberg wanted me to look like a lesbian – and I only sang that song because he asked me to.'

Morocco had the odd touch of ironic comedy, particularly the scene where Amy Jolly, Mistinguett-like in plumes and showing her legs, sings 'What Am I Bid for My Apples?' There was also a hint of *The Blue Angel* with the star wearing suspenders and humming 'Give Me the Man'. What had to be changed in the transition from novel to filmscript was the outcome of Amy and Tom's romance: he is court-martialled for brawling and, though she tries to put in a good word with his commanding officer, he is forced to spend the night in jail, from which he emerges with abject indifference. Amy therefore agrees to becoming Kennington's wife but whilst celebrating her engagement learns that Tom's regiment is about to leave for who knows where. The film ends with her offering Kennington a final, despairing look before kicking off her high heels and setting out across the desert with the camp-followers, and to an uncertain fate. The final scene was a masterpiece.

The film was premièred on 16 November 1930 and Marlene was nominated for an Oscar, though the award that year went to Marie Dressler for her role in *Min and Bill*. *The Blue Angel* was put on general release on 5 December, which meant that both films shared the same publicity budget, said to have been more than $600,000. Needless to say, the coup paid off handsomely. The American public, most of whom had never even heard of Marlene Dietrich, were without warning 'hit for six' by her portrayal of two vastly differing characters, something which thus far had not happened in Germany.

Riding high on the crest of a wave, von Sternberg at once began making preparations for Marlene's second American film. The script for this bore the somewhat bizarre title *X-27* but, when he told her that it narrated the story of a prostitute who becomes a spy and who later betrays her country for the love of a worthless man, she simply shrugged her shoulders and told him to get on with things. She had already contacted Rudolf to say that she would be back in Berlin for Christmas, come what might, which indicates that the house, car and servants provided by Paramount, not to mention the $125,000 she had allegedly been promised for each film she made, meant nothing in comparison to what she was going through, separated from her loved ones. Many years later when she sang 'Wenn der Sommer wieder einzieht', the German adaptation of 'A Little on the Lonely Side', she was probably thinking of her early days in Hollywood.

When von Sternberg presented the script of *X-27* to the executives at Paramount he was told that the title would have to be changed. It became *Dishonoured*, which neither he nor

Marlene liked. There was another argument when she asked Adolph Zukor to engage Gary Cooper as her co-star. Apparently, the actor had detested the director to such an extent that he had once come close to hitting him. Whatever the reason, Zukor and von Sternberg decided that the actor most suited to the role of Lieutenant Kranau would be Victor McLaglen, an ex-boxer and the son of an English clergyman, who had shot to fame in 1925, playing the strongman in Lon Chaney's *The Unholy Three*. The cameraman and musical arranger, however, were from *Morocco*, and Marlene did approve of at least two members of the supporting cast: Gustav von Seyffertitz had starred with Greta Garbo in *The Mysterious Lady*, and Lew Cody was famous for his partnership with Aileen Pringle. Warner Oland was contracted to play X-27's lover, General von Hindau.

Sixty years on, the plot of *Dishonoured* may seem a little trite and semi-fantastic, although the main character did have much in common with Marlene: she is a woman without roots, a patriot of love, as opposed to a supporter of any particular country or culture. This seemingly detached attitude towards the realism of life – one of her first lines in the film is, 'I am not afraid of life, though I'm not afraid of death, either' – would emerge time and time again during our conversations. Also, X-27 is the widow of a Captain Kalowrat – a sarcastic reference to the fat count who had produced *Café Electric* – who, in order to make ends meet after the death of her husband, had turned to prostitution. However, as a spy working for the Austrian Secret Service she may be said to excite more men than in her previous profession, wearing a succession of Travis Banton designs ranging from an aviator's leather all-in-one to a sparkling cape and tunic. McLaglen's uniform, it is said, was a copy of the one which had been worn by Marlene's father. X-27 is also a humane creature. Pushing one lover towards suicide after being made aware of his treason, she falls for the Russian aviator, Kranau, and it is only then that she allows her heart to rule her head, setting him free at the expense of her own life.

The final scene of *Dishonoured* was, although the term had not yet been invented, pure Hollywood soap. Within her cell, moments away from facing the firing squad, X-27 begs the priest to help her die in a uniform of her choosing. She selects the garb of a prostitute. Then she sits at her piano and plays Ivanovici's *Waves of the Danube* until a young lieutenant arrives to escort her to her death. The closing lines are classic: 'Is it time?' 'Are we going to walk together?' 'Do you have a looking-glass?' The young man draws his sabre and she checks her reflection in the blade. Outside he raises the same sabre to give the order to fire, then promptly flings it aside and delivers a speech of which Shakespeare would have been envious: 'I will not kill a woman! I will not kill any more men, either! You call this war – I call it butchery! You call this petulism – I call it murder!' During this brief interlude, X-27 puts on more lipstick and adjusts the seam in her stocking before the commanding officer gives the final instruction to the firing squad.

> 'I really admired the last few minutes of the film,' I told her, not that I expected her to agree with me. 'You were smiling blankly into space. If was as if you'd already seen heaven.'
> 'Von Sternberg asked me to act as naturally as possible, but how the hell could I? I'd never been shot before. And a woman like that whore – putting on her lipstick as though she was on her way to a party! It was terrible, terrible . . .'

Terrible or not, Marlene did manage to make the theme of the female spy more popular than her rival, Greta Garbo, who later that year made *Mata Hari* with Ramon Novarro. In this there was no death scene, though critics and public alike howled at one of Novarro's plum lines, 'What's the matter, Mata?' *Dishonoured* was also made to earn its popularity. It was released on 6 March 1931 in direct competition with major films starring Mary Pickford, Barbara Stanwyck and Constance Bennett, and at a time when many American cinemas were still showing *Morocco* and *The Blue Angel*. And it caused a sensation. Norbert Lusk, reviewing it for *Playbill*, wrote of the final scene: 'It is as if the Delphic Oracle has stepped down from her pedestal to give her opinion of the weather.'

Marlene had actually left Hollywood on the very day *Dishonoured* had finished filming. Not only did she refuse to give any interviews, she also refused to have anything to do with the cutting. Von Sternberg later claimed that because of her hasty departure several scenes remained in the picture which would otherwise have been re-shot. These include the piano scene, where very close scrutiny will reveal a slight change in the parting of Marlene's hair, which probably gives an insight into the director's manic obsession for detail. Some time later, when questioned about this, Marlene shrugged her shoulders and said, 'Who cares? I wear it differently, now!'

Marlene's first port of call, en route for Germany, was London. She was met there by her mother, and after attending the first night of *Morocco* at the Carlton Theatre the two travelled on to Berlin. They were met at the railway station by Rudolf Sieber and informed that Maria had been taken ill. Marlene's concern was such that she refused to acknowledge the crowd of reporters waiting in the forecourt. She climbed into her friend Gerda Huber's car and rushed straight to the apartment at 54 Kaiserallee. Fortunately, it was only a minor ailment and after just one night in Berlin she was able to continue her schedule. She attended the première of *Morocco* in Prague, at the Lucerna Theatre, and decided to stay in Czechoslovakia for a few days. Newspaper reports suggested that she was suffering from a guilt complex because had had to leave her daughter behind. This seems to have been the case, for when she returned to Berlin she told Rudolf that this would never happen again and that she had already arranged to take Maria to Hollywood when she returned there in the spring. She did not ask Rudolf if he wanted to go with her, although he did have his reasons for wishing to stay in Germany. Firstly, he was perfectly happy working for Paramount, dubbing films into German, including *Morocco*. Secondly, he had become involved with a pretty young singer named Tamara Matul.

Marlene never discussed her marriage with me and I can only assume that she had her reasons. The fact that her union with Rudolf never ended in divorce and the fact that both partners would go on saying for another forty-five years that they still loved each other must have counted for something. Tamara had danced with Marlene in the chorus of *From Mouth to Mouth* and she had first met Rudolf in 1927. She was a close friend and Marlene not only seems to have approved of her relationship with Rudolf, she also kept up the payments for the Berlin apartment until Hitler's rise to power in 1933, when the couple moved to the comparative safety of Paris.

Marlene and Maria arrived in New York in April 1931, accompanied by her friend, Gerda Huber, whom she had engaged as a nanny and general companion. In the harbour she walked into a real-life drama when she was accosted by two lawyers who served her with a writ from Riza von Sternberg. The charge was one of libel and 'alienation of a husband's love', and followed an alleged in-depth interview which Marlene had given to an Austrian newspaper, *Neues Wiener Journal*, in which she had accused Riza of being an undutiful wife, adding that von Sternberg had intended divorcing her before she divorced him. Marlene accused the newspaper of misinterpretation of facts. This was the first time that such a thing had happened to her but it would not be the last:

> 'Reporters are bigots who only draw attention to themselves at our expense,' she said scathingly. 'These bastards can always say what they want about me because they know that I'm not in a position to fight back. Sometimes I feel sorry for them because they don't realize how stupid, how pathetic they are. They never tried to understand me – and I was never interested in dictators. The public always came first. But I'm starting to fight back. People don't get away with things now, not like they used to.'

Marlene played Riza von Sternberg at her own game by refusing to settle out of court and, in order to prevent the gossips from having a field-day, she sent Rudolf a cable, urging him to join her in Hollywood. He arrived on 19 July, without Tamara, and was met at the Pasadena railway station by Marlene, Maria and von Sternberg. The four were mobbed by reporters and for once Marlene was perfectly happy to answer questions about her family life before scrambling into the gleaming white Rolls-Royce which Paramount had supplied to whisk them back to Marlene's home in Beverly Hills. Several weeks later, with the scandal still raging about her, she and Maria posed for a photograph by E.R. Richee, and when this was published in a newspaper she received hundreds of letters from her female admirers, most of them mothers in the same situation.

On 7 August 1931, Josef von Sternberg appeared in court on a charge of contempt after failing to pay his wife's alimony. He had in fact paid her a total of $22,000 in back payments and a property settlement but, when he stated this under oath, Riza took the stand and swore that he had furnished Marlene's apartment, besides opening several accounts in her name in a number of department stores. Judge Roth, presiding over the case, came out in Riza's favour and found von Sternberg guilty of contempt. She was awarded substantial damages, including $1,300 for her journey from New York. Marlene's lawyer had advised her to stay clear of adverse publicity, declaring that this would be bad for her career. When she and Rudolf took the stand the next day, however, she announced, 'I would prefer the publicity to the payment of a single penny on these absurd charges.' This statement in effect caused the executives at Paramount to persuade Riza to drop the case and, to compensate her for any 'inconvenience', they paid her a staggering $100,000. According to one report, Marlene was so pleased with the outcome of the case that she took Rudolf home and cooked him his favourite omelette. Von Sternberg, on the other hand, was seething. He told reporters that Marlene had made a fool of him and vowed, not for the first time, never to work with her again.

When not working with Marlene, however, the director was far from successful. Many of his early American films had failed and his new venture, *An American Tragedy*, did not enhance his reputation for coming up with what the critics called 'an old turkey'. Based on the novel by Theodore Dreiser, it was filmed on location at Lake Arrowhead. The two stars were Frances Dee and Phillips Holmes but the story was so 'hot', with Holmes drowning his pregnant girlfriend in graphic detail, that the film was banned by the censor in Britain. Marlene visited the set whenever she could, always taking Maria and Gerda Huber with her and always taking great care never to be condescending or sycophantic after their quarrel which, incredibly, she managed to patch up. Needless to say, von Sternberg soon agreed to make another film with her, and he began working on his new idea the moment Rudolf Sieber set sail for Europe.

Shanghai Express is generally regarded as the greatest of the von Sternberg–Dietrich ventures, aside from *The Blue Angel*, and it was her biggest box-office success to date. What made it so great was not just the high-camp acting, but the dialogue: this was so unbelievably bad that almost every one-liner remains an undisputed classic. Von Sternberg himself gave instructions that every spoken word on the train should sound like the train and the actors deliver their lines as though they are falling asleep. The story takes place on the Peking–Shanghai express and concerns an odd group of travellers who are taken hostage by Henry Chang, a Chinese revolutionary leader (Warner Oland). One of these is the notorious prostitute and breaker of men's hearts, Madeleine, alias Shanghai Lily, who tells him that she is on her way to Shanghai 'to buy a hat'. Another passenger is Captain Donald Harvey (Clive Brook), with whom Lily has once had an affair. He appears so utterly stuffy that one wonders instinctively how this could have happened. Lily's costumes, too, are way over the top. They range from a black outfit complete with feather boa and eye veil, to a fur coat with a collar so enormous that Marlene at times seems lost in it.

As the film progresses we do get to know a little more about Donald Harvey but Madeleine–Lily retains her mysterious allure right through to the end – almost a caricature of Marlene herself in later years – even when she gives herself to Chang to prevent him from blinding an elderly traveller (Gustav von Seyffertitz). In the end, the revolutionaries' cause is abandoned when Chang is stabbed to death by Hui Fei, Lily's sultry Chinese maid (Anna May Wong). When the train finally reaches its destination Lily, wearing her veil again and an abundance of black plumes, tells Harvey that she has always loved him.

And, did Marlene enjoy this experience? Not likely!

'Wasn't that film bad, David? I mean, wasn't it so unbelievably bad? You said yourself that everyone spoke as though they were falling asleep.'

'I thought *Shanghai Express* was a superb comedy,' I began.

'But it wasn't supposed to be funny,' she yelled.

'No,' I argued. 'It was more than funny. It was hilarious! The one-liners were magnificent! Marlene, would you mind if I copied them into the book?'

To which she said, drily, 'Honey, do with them as you like.'

The lines in the film which, according to most contemporary sources, had audiences howling from one side of America to the other were as follows:

'That woman is a coaster!' 'What in the name of Confucius is a coaster?' 'A coaster is a woman who lives by her wits along the China coast . . .'

DIETRICH: It took more than one man to change my name to Shanghai Lily, the notorious white flower of China . . .

MRS HAGGERTY *to Dietrich:* I have a boarding house in Shanghai. Yorkshire pudding is my speciality.

DIETRICH *to Mrs Haggerty:* What kind of house did you say?

CARMICHAEL *speaking about Dietrich and Anna May Wong:* One of them is yellow, the other is white, but both their souls are rotten . . .

BROOK *to Von Seyffertitz:* We're going to be in here for three days. Is there anything I can do for you?

BROOK *to Dietrich:* All I can suggest is that you get down on your knees . . . to pray.

DIETRICH *to Brook:* I think you are right . . . if God is still on speaking terms with me.

This last line, for me at least, led towards a moment of great intensity when the camera closed in on Lily's praying hands – a stroke of von Sternberg genius which convinced the observer that Shanghai Lily was not just another 'tart with a heart of stone', but a woman with a conscience.

The same may be said for Marlene's next film with von Sternberg, which delved even deeper into the psyche of the so-called hard-bitten whore. *Blonde Venus* told the 'sinfully moral' tale of a woman who only gives herself to a man in order to pay for her sick husband's treatment against radium poisoning. Marlene played Helen Faraday. Her co-stars were Herbert Marshall as the husband and a very young Cary Grant as her handsome lover, Nick Townsend. The film also had the advantage of a child as a central character – the Faradays' son, Johnny, was played by Dickie Moore. But it was one of von Sternberg's proposed scenes between the mother and her child – she hides him under a restaurant table whilst trying to pick up a man – that got the director into trouble with B.P. Schulberg of Paramount. Upon reading the script, he is alleged to have raved, 'This is the goddamnedest piece of shit I've ever read in my life!' Von Sternberg, of course, retaliated in the only way he knew how by walking off the set, and a few days later he was replaced by Richard Wallace, whom Marlene had met through Maurice Chevalier. The fact that this man, who in 1929 had directed Chevalier in his first Hollywood film, was a friend did not deter Marlene from flying into a rage. She would work with von Sternberg, or not at all.

What Marlene did not realize was that in Hollywood even the top stars were not considered irreplaceable and, when she failed to turn up for shooting on the morning of 27 April, Schulberg immediately suspended her, to which she is alleged to have said, tongue-in-cheek, 'Von for all, and all for Von.' More drama was to follow when Schulberg announced Marlene's replacement, the horrendously outspoken Tallulah Bankhead, who quipped, 'Well, I always did want to get into Marlene's pants.' She also told one journalist, when informed that Marlene had allegedly sprinkled gold dust in her hair to make it sparkle, 'So what? Now I'll have to start sprinkling gold dust in my pubic hair.' Von Sternberg was then threatened with a $100,000 suit for damages, though his reaction to this was to accuse Schulberg of 'undervaluing' his talent. The matter would have gone to court, had it not been for a macabre twist in events – an episode that would almost cost Marlene her sanity.

Smouldering with anger at her home on the junction of Sunset Boulevard and North Roxbury Road, Marlene was in all probability seriously considering her return to Berlin when, on Friday 13 May she received a letter threatening to kidnap Maria unless a $10,000 ransom was handed over. The letter, made up of words clipped from newspapers, ended:

HAVE THE MONEY BY 16 MAY. LEAVE YOUR CAR IN FRONT OF YOUR HOME AND PUT MONEY PACKAGE ABOUT SIX INCHES FROM REAR ON REAR BUMPER. KEEP SILENT. DON'T BE CRAZY. QUICK ACTION. WANT ONLY $5 AND $10 BILLS. LINDBERGH BUSINESS.

Marlene did not remain silent. She summoned the Beverly Hills Chief of Police and von Sternberg provided her with an armed bodyguard. According to one newspaper report, Marlene kept her cool by cooking for the police and supplying everyone with cups of coffee. The police drew the conclusion that the letter had been the work of an amateur, though it was taken seriously on account of the recent Lindbergh case, in which the son of the celebrated aviator Charles Lindbergh had been kidnapped and, after an agonizing search lasting several weeks during which the police had followed dozens of false trails, the boy had been found murdered. The kidnappers had never been caught but the case had led to a spate of would-be abductions all over America.

Besides involving the police, Marlene and von Sternberg hired several private detectives who masqueraded as house guests and household staff. Marlene herself made up a package of fake dollar bills and left it in the precise spot indicated by the letter. Even then the police failed to catch the criminals, who jumped out of a taxi, grabbed the packet and got away before they could give chase. The following morning Marlene received another letter, made up like the first one, again demanding money. With enormous willpower she ignored it altogether, though she never let Maria out of her sight for a moment. She had bars put up at every single window in her house, had the locks changed and installed an elaborate alarm system. What kept the criminals at bay, however, was the enormous media coverage she received. Though twenty men were interviewed by police, no one was ever arrested and charged. Surprisingly, the episode was mentioned in *Marlene D*:

The bars which I had put up at the windows are still there today. Their installation shattered our sunny dream, our freedom and our joy. We were prisoners. There was to be no more strolling around the streets of Beverly Hills to look at the moon, no more picnics on the beach. My fear never left me. Any other director would have allowed me to get over such an ordeal, but not von Sternberg. I had to be up at five every morning and ready to leave for the studio. Maria suffered from travel-sickness, but it was fear that tied my stomach in knots, and in order to fight against my urge to vomit I always carried lemons. Even so, I often had to stop the car to throw up at the roadside . . .

The ordeal had not frightened Maria because her mother had

sworn to protect her come what might. This protection, however, had far-reaching consequences. Maria was not allowed to attend school with the other Hollywood children. Instead, Marlene paid for a pair of tutors – one English and one German – and she set out a rigorous timetable. If contemporary sources are to be believed the child is said to have begun over-eating and became preoccupied with 'the darker aspects of life'.

B.P. Schulberg, meanwhile, had seen the error of his ways and a few weeks later, as if nothing untoward had happened, von Sternberg and Marlene continued working on *Blonde Venus*. A new scriptwriter, Sam Lauren, had been brought in to assist Jules Furthman, and a couple of songs added to pep up the rather banal storyline. For one of these Marlene ambled on to the stage wearing a gorilla costume, then proceeded to do a striptease, pulling off each arm to reveal a fortune in bracelets. Finally, jerking off the head and donning an immense Afro-styled wig she began crooning a sultry 'All night long I don't know right from wrong!' which was later hailed as her 'Hot Voodoo' sequence. For this one scene there were over one hundred takes. Later in the film, and in a scene reminiscent of the one in *Morocco*, she sang 'Qu'est ce que vous voudrez?' in a white tailcoat and top-hat. The song had been supplied by Paramount, of course, and Marlene hated it. She had wanted to do two songs by the turn-of-the-century English music-hall star Harry Fragson – 'Reviens' and 'Je sais que vous êtes jolie' (the 'e' on the word *jolie* signifying that the song was being sung to a woman). Unfortunately, these two songs would have to wait until her cabaret act. *Blonde Venus* also had a classic one-liner which would have been worthy of Marlene's last film. Backstage in the tawdry cabaret a fellow prostitute introduces herself as Taxi Belle, to which comes the quick retort, 'Do you charge for the first mile?' There was also plenty of assurance that Marlene's stay at Paramount would be a lengthy one, for von Sternberg forked out $300,000 to have her dressing room completely refurbished. The design was by Wiard Ihnen and the finished structure, comprising mirrored bathroom, dressing room and lounge, measured sixty by thirty feet. It was an unnecessary extravagance even for Hollywood and became known as 'Von's Revenge'.

Blonde Venus was not the success that von Sternberg had

anticipated and, after the première, he left Hollywood 'to go looking for a hurricane in the West Indies'. Hoping to drag Marlene away from the 'whore' image which he had been responsible for in the first place, he wanted to cast her as a lion-tamer in his circus film *The Lady of the Lions* and had deemed the hurricane to be an essential backdrop. Luck was not on his side. Feeling more than a little depressed over this, according to Marlene, because he had even wanted to control the elements, he returned to Hollywood only to find that she had left for New York.

4

'Look Me over Closely,
Tell Me What You See'

The public have always been tricked into believing I'm something I'm not. That was von Sternberg's fault.

It was at the Ruban Bleu in New York that Marlene began a series of bizarre, often unexplained friendships. She had met Tallulah Bankhead, though they were by no means on amicable terms, during her fight with B.P. Schulberg. When they crossed swords again in the summer of 1931, Tallulah had just made *The Devil and the Deep* with Charles Laughton and the success of this had made up for her disappointment at losing out on *Blonde Venus*. One evening at the famous club Tallulah sent a message to Marlene's table, wanting to know why she was wearing gloves. Marlene's response was to send her the gloves on a plate. This incident led to the pair becoming reasonably good friends, though neither would ever trust the other. Many years later Tallulah and Marlene's daughter appeared together in the play *Foolish Notion*. Considerably more interesting, from the point of view that a tape recording of the event turned up whilst we were working on this book, was the sketch which Marlene executed with Tallulah around 1955 on *The Ann Sothern Show*. It raised more than a few eyebrows at the time and, when listened to intently, it makes one

61

wonder exactly where the line was drawn between acting and reality.

MARLENE Tallulah, I'd appreciate it if you didn't keep referring to me as a grandmother. You're overdoing it . . .

TALLULAH Don't speak to me about overdoing it – speak to your daughter!

MARLENE By the way, Tallulah, I had a letter from what was once the beautiful city of Paris . . . before you got there!

TALLULAH Oh, Paris. What a time I had there, Marlene!

MARLENE Did you buy any new gowns?

TALLULAH Oh, and what gowns! And how expensive! Honestly, darling, the prices they charge you for just a little snip of a dress . . .

MARLENE I know. Five hundred dollars covers nothing.

TALLULAH What did you pay for the one you're wearing, darling . . . two hundred and fifty?

MARLENE That gown you have on now. What colour is it?

TALLULAH Well, it's a new colour . . . battleship grey.

MARLENE Battleship grey? It's lovely. But isn't it just a little tight around the boiler room?

TALLULAH Not at all, Marlene. I wore it to a dance last week . . . a sort of shaped-down cruise. I think it fits me perfectly. Just my size . . . twelve.

MARLENE What size?

TALLULAH Twelve . . .

MARLENE What size?

TALLULAH I told you twice . . . TWELVE!

MARLENE Oh, twice twelve . . . that's more your size!

TALLULAH Marlene, I'm going to make a statement that I want you to answer, true or false. Would you do that?

MARLENE Of course.

TALLULAH Well, here's the statement. That figure you have is not all yours . . .

MARLENE False!

TALLULAH Just what I thought. Now, don't make any more cracks about my gown. I paid a pretty penny for it . . .

MARLENE My goodness, that was a clearance sale!

TALLULAH What are you talking about? You should see the prices they soak you for dresses over there. I was soaked at every shop in Paris.

MARLENE Yes, I heard you were soaked in Paris . . .

TALLULAH Marlene, please let us drop this nonsense! We're too close to go on like this. One of us will only get bruised, and with the cast we've got this week I'm already cut up and bleeding. Now tell me, dah-ling, whatever happened to that divine chap you used to go out with? Geoffrey!

MARLENE Oh, we split up . . .

TALLULAH Really, darling? For good?

MARLENE No, only temporarily. He got married . . .

TALLULAH They do have a habit of doing that. Look, Marlene we might as well face it . . . the man problem gets a little tougher every year.

MARLENE You're so right, Tallulah. I wouldn't admit this to anyone else, but one day last week I had lunch alone.

TALLULAH NO-OH! Well, if you think that's something, as long as you've opened up to me, I'll tell you something. One day, about a month ago, I had breakfast alone!

MARLENE It's such a shame. Men seem to be disappearing.

TALLULAH They sure do . . .

Another friend was the female racing driver Jo Carstairs, a butch millionairess with crew-cut blonde hair, muscles, and a number of tattoos. In spite of the gossips, Marlene was only interested in her personality, which was said to have been electrifying. Carstairs, on the other hand, is thought to have hoped for more than a platonic relationship. A few years later, when she owned an island in the Bahamas, she boasted that she would one day build a dream house in which Marlene would be installed as her very own fairy-tale princess. Marlene took it all in with accustomed humour.

Even more off-beat was her friendship with the now-forgotten screenwriter and socialite, Mercedes de Acosta. Six years Marlene's senior, of Spanish descent, and proclaiming herself 'a religious cult and health-food fanatic', de Acosta would prove herself a dangerous and inglorious ally in 1960 with the publication of her autobiography *Here Lies the Heart*. Amongst its revelations were the author's reputed love affairs with Marlene, Greta Garbo, Alice B. Toklas, Malvina Hoffmann and the outrageous French artist, Marie Laurencin. Marlene is supposed to have turned up at de Acosta's penthouse suite armed with a huge bouquet of white roses, then cooked her a meal because she had seemed undernourished. De Acosta says she persuaded Marlene to allow her to wash the rouge from her cheeks, and that from then on their friendship had moved from strength to strength. These sexual confessions were pure invention.

Much more important, and very much more sincere, was Marlene's close friendship with the great French star Maurice Chevalier, a relationship she revealed purely by chance when we were discussing my next biography. My first choice, after Edith Piaf and Mistinguett, had been another legendary and controversial female, Joséphine Baker. But as there had been a recent spate of books about her I chose Maurice Chevalier . . . or should I say, Marlene chose him for me:

'Why don't you write a book about Judy Garland . . . or Chevalier? Now that would be really interesting. I can see it now . . .'

'I don't feel qualified to write about Judy Garland,' I told her. 'I liked her a lot, but the French music-hall's my particular territory. I suppose I could do Chevalier. I've got most of the information to hand. And, of course you would have to write something about him for me. You and he were very good friends.'

'I would be delighted to write the introduction to your book,' she enthused. 'It would be an honour. Maurice Chevalier was a very decent man.'

I began working on *Maurice Chevalier: Up on Top of a Rainbow* the moment I received Marlene's four-page handwritten *avant-propos*, as she called it, and the book was dedicated to her and my great friend, Jacqueline Danno. A nephew and niece of Chevalier's still lived in Paris, as did his secretary, François Vals and François's charming wife, Madeleine. These wonderful people have since become close friends and nothing was too much trouble for them whilst I was writing the book. I also spoke to the last love of Chevalier's life, Odette Meslier, the woman who had inherited his millions and La Louque, his mansion at Marnes-la-Coquette, just outside Paris.

For some reason, Marlene disapproved of Chevalier's family and when I told her that I had been in touch with them, she hit the roof.

'If you sent the Chevalier family the piece I wrote, then you're an idiot. It wasn't important to get their blessing for your book. Who's the other man you mentioned?'

'François Vals,' I explained. 'What is remarkable is that he started off as a fan, as I did with you. He saw Chevalier one evening in Bordeaux, and he asked him if he could become his secretary. They were close friends for twenty years. This morning he sent me a letter. It said. "Welcome to the family".'

'Then you must send me his address,' Marlene said. 'I knew the house of course. We used to drive out there on a weekend. Chevalier had a man to take care of him. He killed himself by jumping out of a window.'

'That was Félix Paquet. He was Chevalier's secretary.'

'You write what you feel in your heart about Maurice Chevalier. Like I say, he was a decent man. I first met him when I was doing *Morocco* with Gary Cooper. That was when he first came to America. Later on we became very close. Lovers, I guess. That's why you must write only the good things about him. People always write lies about famous people. You must write the truth.'

I decided to grasp the bull by the horns, considering Marlene had admitted that she and Chevalier had been lovers, and ask her the question which had been bugging me for some time. 'There's a book out in France at the moment – it suggests that you were responsible for Maurice Chevalier leaving his wife.'

There was a long pause. More than once, if I had 'pushed my luck', as she called it, Marlene had hung up on me, though she had usually called again to apologize or offer some excuse. I waited, then she said softly, 'It says what?'

I repeated the phrase, adding, 'Her name was Yvonne Vallée, and she went to America with him in 1929.'

'Do you want to know what really happened? We had an earthquake in Hollywood – I had a house in Santa Monica where I put my daughter and the maids whilst I was making a film. Maybe it was *Blonde Venus*, or the film I made after that. There was Mae West and Carole Lombard, both of them great friends of mine, and we were all in the same row of dressing rooms. We saw each other all the time and Chevalier also had a dressing room in the same row. And when we had the earthquake, we were all sent out of the building. We ran into the garden which separated the studios from the dressing rooms, and there stood Chevalier. He opened his arms and he said, "Now we can die together!" That's what started whatever there was between us – and I want you to make sure that you put that photograph of us on the cover of your book. Will you do that, for me?'

'The one with you sitting on his knee?' I asked.

'No,' she said. 'I don't care for that one. I don't look nice in that one! The photograph you want is where he's sitting with me on the steps of my dressing room. Underneath it he has written, "Marlinou . . . amie de toujours". And you must tell everyone that he loved me – and that I adored him.'

During and immediately after the Maria kidnapping scare, Chevalier had stayed at Marlene's home and this had incited great excitement amongst the Hollywood paparazzi. The couple were followed everywhere and were photographed dancing cheek-to-cheek at the Coconut Grove. In spite of von Sternberg's efforts to seize the pictures and destroy them – one may only assume that he must have been jealous – one appeared in *Photoplay*. Marlene again began talking about her return to Germany. In March 1932 she had given an interview for *Film Weekly* saying, 'I want to work in my own country and in my own language. I think I will go home for good next Christmas when my contract is up. Mr von Sternberg's contract expires at the same time.'

Von Sternberg had failed to locate his hurricane and he had travelled to Berlin to discuss the possibility of Marlene forming her own production company with the UFA, with himself at the helm, naturally. Such a move might have worked inordinately well on a temporary basis but, in January 1933, Hitler was elected Chancellor of Germany and the Jewish section of the German film industry disbanded rapidly, spreading its wings to France, England and America.

Whilst von Sternberg was in Germany, Paramount took advantage of his absence and announced Marlene's next film – *Song of Songs*, an adaptation of the well-known novel by Sudermann. His works had transferred well to the screen in the past but not without varying results. *The Undying Past* had become *Flesh and the Devil* for Garbo and Gilbert, one of the most successful silents of all time. *Wonder of Women* on the other hand, filmed in 1928, the year of Sudermann's death, and starring Peggy Wood and Lewis Stone, had been a costly flop. Marlene was given the novel to read, although she was not initially keen on working with Rouben Mamoulian, even though Paramount had hired him with von Sternberg's approval. Neither did she think the film would work – it had already been filmed twice, first with Elsie Ferguson and again with Pola Negri. In the end, it was Maurice Chevalier who swayed her opinion. Together Jeannette MacDonald and he had starred in Mamoulian's *Love me Tonight*, and this had earned him the title 'The Highest-Paid Star in the World'. Even so, Mamoulian would have to wait until the end of the year before knocking the world sideways with *Queen Christina*.

Song of Songs caused Marlene a great deal of trouble. When she read what the scriptwriters Samuel Hoffenstein and Leo Birinski had done to a perfectly good novel she told B.P. Schulberg that she would not do the film. This resulted in her being threatened with a lawsuit for $180,000, which was Paramount's expenditure so far. The company also took out an injunction preventing her from leaving America before the film's completion. Reluctantly, she signed the contract but only when Maurice Chevalier agreed to stay by her side until the end of shooting. The storyline was, of course, far-fetched. Marlene portrayed Lily Czepaneck, a poor girl who works in her aunt's library and who meets and falls in love with a young sculptor (the stage actor Brian Aherne in his first major film role). And this being Hollywood, the path towards lasting happiness cannot be straightforward. Taken in by a licentious baron (Lionel Atwell), she eventually rids herself of a life of drudgery by setting fire to the house. Then, after singing the newly arranged 'Jonny wenn du Geburtstag hast' in a cabaret, she marries her sculptor.

I asked Marlene if she had liked this film, and her response was pretty much the same as before.

'Not particularly. The film was too old-fashioned. But I did like the song, "Jonny". That's why I sang it for years – though never in English, as you wrote. So far as I know, no English words were ever written – I think maybe they were trying to tell me something, aye-aye-aye! And if you're going to ask about that stupid statue, you needn't bother. Work it out for yourself.'

Marlene had recorded 'Jonny' [this is the spelling on the record label] twice on 11 March 1931. Both versions were arranged by her friend, Peter Kreuder but, the 'jazzier' take was not issued until 1990 when a French company released it on an album. As for the nude statue of Lily Czepanek, this was the work of Scarpitta, an Italian sculptor living in Los Angeles who had achieved some recognition with his statuette of Mussolini mounted upon a horse. After the film's première Paramount was inundated with letters and calls demanding to know if Marlene had actually posed for the statue. She had, but in her clothes – the rest had been left to the artist's imagination.

Song of Songs was a good deal more successful than her previous film and this pushed Paramount into offering her an 'alternative' contract which, they promised, would make her the highest-paid actress in the world after Marion Davies. Marlene declined. She would never look further into the future than her next film and even here she presented B.P. Schulberg with a few conditions of her own. The film would tell the story of her heroine, Catherine the Great. It would be directed by Josef von Sternberg and, most important of all, she would be allowed to visit Europe before making it. B.P. Schulberg did not stand in her way, even though he was uncertain that she would ever return to Hollywood. The Motion Picture Production Code had recently been introduced – primarily because of such films as *Shanghai Express* and Garbo's *Susan Lennox, her Rise and Fall*, aimed at forbidding prostitutes from being depicted as on-screen heroines. This act had thrown von Sternberg into a fit of despair, for he had made a fortune and a name for himself doing exactly that.

With this probably on her mind, Marlene arrived in London at the end of May 1933 and at once expressed a desire to be taken to Soho, to see how real prostitutes went about earning their living. According to the friend who was with her, she gave him money to go into a café and told him to keep an eye on her just in case she went too far. Then, hitching up her skirt and showing a good inch of suspender and stocking-tip, she walked up and down the street for half an hour, stopping dozens of men, but failing to 'score' even once. She later said that as a whore she had been a complete failure and that von Sternberg should have realized this by expecting her to play the fallen angel every time.

In June 1933 Marlene arrived in Paris, as one reporter put it, 'like the Queen of Sheba'. Though she booked in at the expensive Hôtel Trianon, she spent much of her time at the Ansonia, a much smaller establishment favoured by emigrés. Here she was able to renew her friendship with Friedrich Hollander and she met many of the Parisian pre-Existentialist set. Some, like the chanteuse Marianne Oswald, she would detest from the word go. Others would remain lifelong friends, including the lyricist Max Kolpe. Some years later, when she had nominated him her favourite songwriter, he would Americanize his surname to Colpet.

Another important influence was a twenty-eight-year-old singer-songwriter named Jean Tranchant, who sometimes visited the Ansonia with Damia, at that time the greatest singer in France. One evening, Tranchant boasted that he could write a song about any subject and at the drop of a hat. Marlene told him to have something ready, in the style of Damia if at all possible, within twenty-four hours, and he did just that, writing 'Assez' with his friend, the orchestra leader Emil Stern. Not to be outdone by this show of bravado, Peter Kreuder, then living in Paris, wrote her two songs: 'Wo ist der Mann' with Max Colpet and 'Mein blondes Baby'. Colpet also gave her 'Allein in einer grossen Stadt' and Marlene herself chose 'Ja so bin ich', by Stolz and Reisch. These five songs constituted her very first repertoire of *chansons-parlées*, and were recorded in three sessions for Polydor on 12, 15 and 19 July 1933, with her friend Peter Kreuder directing Walberg's orchestra. At the last moment, however, Marlene decided to record 'Moi, je m'ennuie', a very popular song which she 'borrowed' from Damia and which caused everyone a great deal of trouble.

As a stranger in Paris, Marlene was unaware of the 'unofficial code of practice' exercised by the music-hall fraternity: the fact that any new song was the exclusive property of whoever had introduced it until six months after that artist had actually recorded it. Damia managed to keep most of her songs exclusive by not recording them at all. Marlene's excuse for recording 'Moi, je m'ennuie' was that when Jean Tranchant had introduced her to Damia, he had not bothered telling her that she was a singer. This was not true, according to Damia, who had performed in Berlin at the time of *Der blaue Engel* and whose recitals there had been described as 'brimming with *Weltschmerz*'. Marlene had turned up at one of the theatres with flowers. This German word had also appeared in her *ABC*, wedged between Orson Welles and Mae West: '*Weltschmerz:* the pain, the sorrow of the world that at moments grips the heart of the individual.' This had been Damia's unique art form. She had begun her career in 1909, dancing the *apache* with Max Dearly at London's Savoy Hotel, and had only become a singer when the manager had asked her to do something different. Incredibly, she had seen France through World War One with a song called 'Malédiction', a piece which would not have inspired hope in any soldier, which was why the French authorities had asked Damia not to sing it in her Montmartre night club.

Damia herself remembered clearly her *second* meeting with Marlene in July 1933 at Chez Kornilof. This was a Russian-styled restaurant in the heart of Paris, also favoured by emigrés and not always a good advertisement for one's character. Damia's lover at the time was the great Russian bass Fyodor Chaliapin, whose entourage often included the infamous Kiki de Montparnasse, arguably the most vulgar woman ever to set foot on the music-hall stage. Damia also said that her 'difficulties' with Marlene had nothing to do with any song, but because both had been photographed in similar poses by E.R. Richee.

When we discussed these songs, Marlene had forgotten all about 'Assez':

'Perhaps the title says it all – "Enough!' she quipped.

'Moi, je m'ennuie', however was one of her better songs, though it was not included on her list of favourites: 'Aye-aye-aye! That was a beautiful song, you know. *Et dans ma vie, une manie . . . toute ma détresse. . . . Partout je traîne, comme une châine . . . ma lourde peine comme autre bien. . .*'

And I finished, '*Et dans ma vie, tu es ma mie . . . moi j'm'ennuie.* Marlene, that was fabulous. It was almost as good as . . .'

'As the version by Damia?' she asked.

I explained that what I had meant was, Marlene's voice at the age of ninety – for those few bars at least – had sounded just as good as it had sixty years before. Then she actually agreed that Damia was quite possibly the best *chanteuse-réaliste* of her day.

'So, you did like her!' I exclaimed.

'And you're putting words into my mouth again,' she said, starting to get a little impatient. 'Damia was a good singer, but I never got very excited about her. She was too morbid for my taste. You keep talking about all these French entertainers. Why are all of them women? Are you a feminist? Are you into penis-envy?'

'Not at all,' I replied. 'I happen to think that the female voice is more suited to realist songs. Yours was! You'd never hear your friend Jean Sablon doing a song by Damia . . .'

'Jean Sablon was never my friend,' she said, in such a way that I knew I had touched a nerve. 'You'd never hear me doing a Damia song, either.'

'But you sang three!' I cried. ' "Moi, je m'ennuie" and "C'est mon gigolo" were two, then there was "On ne lutte pas contre l'amour". She was singing that in French before you recorded it in German.'

'Good for her,' Marlene replied, sarcastically. 'Did you also know that she stole "Ich weiss nicht zu wem ich gehore" from me?'

'That became "Qui j'aime",' I said. 'But it wasn't Damia. It was Lys Gauty. And what about "Mir ist so nacht dir"? That was written for you by Mischa Spoliansky but you refused to record it after hearing Mistinguett's version.'

Marlene was starting to get angry, but there was nothing like Mistinguett's name for making matters infinitely worse: 'God in heaven, can you wonder why? David, why don't you shut up about these women? Or are you losing your marbles, sweetheart? I do not like Damia or Mistinguett and I never did – okay?'

Though not a Jew, Rudolf Sieber had left Berlin in the spring of 1933, along with Erich Pommer and Max Reinhardt, to take up a new position with French Paramount. Naturally he had taken Tamara Matul with him and, during her stay in Paris, Marlene went to see them often. There was also a brief excursion into Germany where she was told that *Song of Songs* had been banned on account of its 'scenes of immorality'. Marlene knew only too well that the real reason behind the ban was her much-publicized statement that she would never work in a Nazi-controlled environment. But was there any substance to the rumour that whilst in Berlin she actually entered a recording studio?

'You said that you were looking for some of my more obscure songs to put on your album? Well, I recorded several songs in Berlin just after I did *The Blue Angel*, and I also did some in 1933 when I went back there. Don't ask me the titles – I cannot remember them any more. And I don't know what happened to them. Maybe they're still there, locked up in some cupboard, waiting to be discovered after I die. Or more likely they were destroyed by the Nazis. You know how much they hated me.

It is not known if Marlene saw her mother and sister Elizabeth whilst in Berlin, and if so why she did not persuade them to get out of the country while it was still relatively safe to do so. Quite simply, they may not have perceived how dangerous the near-future would become. Suffice to say when Marlene returned to the United States on 20 September 1933 she flatly refused to discuss Germany with the horde of reporters waiting for her in New York harbour. She said, politely, 'I am here because I'm going to make a film. That's all I have to say.'

I make no apology for the statement that *The Scarlet Empress* remains, after Garbo's *Queen Christina* and Edith Piaf's *Étoile sans lumière* my favourite film of all time. I do not even care what the critics said about it . . . its historical inaccuracy, its sinister neo-Gothic sets and its syrupy dialogue. I have to admit that Louise Dresser as the Empress Elizabeth was appalling with her way-over-the-top Yankee drawl, and neither can I deny that Gavin Gordon, a young actor of almost ethereal good looks who had played a virgin priest opposite Greta Garbo in *Romance*, was weighed down by a silly moustache and a 'ten-cent' wig. What made this film important for me was its imagery, very much like an expensive French music-hall revue, divided into tableaux by a series of high-camp dramatic captions. Even the opening credits remind the viewer that he is not to take seriously what follows: 'Based on a diary of Catherine II . . . arranged by Manuel Komroff.' This was, of course, von Sternberg's way of flaunting the too-harsh dictates of the Motion Picture Production Code – the fact that if anyone did regard Catherine the Great as a whore, then no one did so more than the lady herself. The director then contradicted himself by issuing a statement: 'The film is not necessarily authentic, but something beautiful to appeal to the eyes and the senses.'

The Scarlet Empress was a terrific test of Marlene's acting abilities and one which she passed with flying colours. She was able to portray a reckless young girl with comparative ease and not without a touch of irony. When introduced to the stiff-necked Russian court she kisses everyone's hands to the rhythm of the music and in a later scene reverts to the games of her childhood by playing Blind Man's Bluff with her handsome bodyguards whilst the rest of Russia prays for the dying Empress Elizabeth. There is also the element of sado-masochism following the scenes of torture depicting the reigns of previous tsars – the dashing Count Alexei (John Lodge) kisses Catherine most savagely before offering her his whip to punish him. Fear too is present in the perpetually sardonic grin of the half-wit Grand Duke Peter (a splendid characterization by Sam Jaffe) whom Catherine is forced to endure as husband and bed-mate, certainly until she has given birth to Russia's heir. The close-up of her face during the marriage ceremony is sheer poetry. Seen through a veil and illuminated by a solitary candle, a tear courses down her cheek. Suffice to explain that she is about to commit herself to a life of drudgery and humiliation, from which she will be spared total misery only by her love for Alexei. He is in fact two-timing her, or so she is led to believe, with the Empress Elizabeth. Thus in a fit of rage she stomps on the miniature he has given her and flings it through her window into the night. It is only then that she has second thoughts about him. Running outside to search for the medallion, she is seized by two guards who do not recognize her. She seduces one of them – and Russia gets its heir. At this stage in the film, a von Sternberg caption appears to announce, 'Whilst Peter terrorizes Russia, Catherine coolly adds his army to her list of conquests.'

The closing scenes of *The Scarlet Empress* were sublime, with Catherine becoming ruler of Russia, overthrowing her despotic husband and having him murdered by her lover, before riding pell-mell up the palace staircase with her soldiers to the strains of *The Ride of the Valkyries*, panting in a cavalry officer's white fur *shako* as the music changes swiftly to the *1812 Overture*, more than a century before it was written.

From my own point of view, the film did have a particular scene which, with a little forethought considering Josef von Sternberg's mania for detail, could have been improved upon. It is something which also occurred in *Queen Christina*: the fact that although the adult Catherine and Christina have sultry, sexy foreign accents, when portrayed as children they sounded as though they had stepped straight out of the Bronx. Marlene and I never discussed *The Scarlet Empress*, which may be just as well, for the part of the young Catherine had been played by her daughter, Maria. On the other hand, the fact that the film flopped at the box office did not necessarily mean that it was a bad film.

In England, Elisabeth Bergner had just completed *Catherine the Great* which, of course, was no better from a historical angle. For some reason known only to the bosses at Paramount, the première of Marlene's film was held back for eight months. Thus, when the British movie opened in New York in 1934 it received sensational revues. Not so *The Scarlet Empress*, which was hammered by critics on both sides of the Atlantic, one of whom boldly suggested that if this particular Catherine had had a fondness for selecting her soldiers for their physical and sadistic attributes, then this was merely Marlene Dietrich portraying an extension of herself. The film was further dismissed by the *Observer* as 'ill-mannered and lecherous', with C.A. Lejeune writing Marlene off as 'a good pair of legs, and few other resources'. This mistake of confusing the actress with the part would be brought up time and time again in our conversations.

Early in 1934 Marlene visited Paris again. This time she was able to renew her friendship with Billy Wilder, whom she had met in Berlin on the set of *Der blaue Engel* – at the time he had been a hard-up journalist. Since then he had moved up in the world and was directing his first French film, *Mauvaise graine*, with Danielle Darrieux. There were also more entertaining soirées at Chez Korniloff, still in the company of Chaliapin and Damia and Peter Kreuder. Since her last visit two of her best German songs, 'Allein in einer grossen Stadt' and Kreuder's composition 'Mein blondes Baby' had been released by Polydor, two numbers which would still be in her reportoire forty years later.

Peter Kreuder's memoirs, *Nur Puppen haben keine Tränen*, were published in 1974. Marlene despised most of the things he had written about her, although one incident was amusing enough. It had allegedly happened in Paris, when Kreuder had spent an evening on the town. On his way back to his hotel he had been picked up by a beautiful woman in a posh car. Scarcely able to believe his luck, Kreuder had allowed her to drive him to her house, where for several hours they had made love in an opulently furnished room, sipping champagne between performances. Afterwards, he had taken a taxi to Marlene's hotel. Several days later she had presented him with a gold wristwatch – her way of saying thank you for writing 'Mein blondes Baby', and for sorting out the Damia situation. She also informed him that a special celebration had been organized. Thus he, Marlene, Erich Maria Remarque and a number of others had made their way to the very house which Kreuder had visited with his woman-friend. And to his horror he was able to witness a live sex show between the same woman and a middle-aged man. That Marlene and her friends had watched him a few nights before would therefore appear to be an incontestable fact.

Upon her return to America, Marlene was asked to go through the script of her new film with von Sternberg. Based on Pierre Louÿs's *La femme et la pantin* (Marlene had confessed to liking his *Aphrodite* and *Les chansons de Bilitis* which she had read in the original French), von Sternberg had changed the name to *Capriccio Espagnole* after commissioning the Spanish-sounding American John Dos Passos to rewrite the script. Dos Passos had already worked on *42nd Parallel* and *Manhattan Transfer*, neither of which had been successful, and to test von Sternberg's already dangerously short fuse, when the director arrived in Hollywood the scriptwriter fell ill with rheumatic fever. Von Sternberg, in an unusually generous mood, installed him at the Plaza Hotel and told him to get on with things. He was not satisfied with the final script, however, and the text shown to Marlene had been practically rewritten by Sam Winston, the man who had edited both versions of *The Blue Angel*. The title had also changed again to *The Devil is a Woman*.

Von Sternberg had been particularly impressed by a young actor who had made his début in *Dynamite* in 1929 and who had since scored a big hit in *Bird of Paradise* with Dolores del Rio. His name was Joel McCrea and he was signed to play the romantic lead, Antonio. After five days on the set, McCrea quarrelled with von Sternberg over the inordinate number of takes he had been forced to do and there was a parting of the ways. He was replaced by

Cesar Romero, a then little-known actor who had that same year played a minor role in *The Thin Man*. Marlene portrayed Concha Perez, the superbitch who delighted in using and humiliating her men, a role which had first been played in 1920 by the opera singer Geraldine Farrar, and one which was far, far removed from anything she had ever done before. 'It is a final tribute to the woman I had seen leaning against the wings of a Berlin stage in 1929,' von Sternberg said, half-way through shooting, and he probably meant it too, even though Sam Winston's script could easily have been regarded as a spurious attack on the woman who, for the last six years, had persistently spurned the director's advances.

In casting Lionel Atwell as Don Pasqual, one of Concha's lovers, von Sternberg also created a clone of himself complete with off-beat clothes and drooping moustache. When Don Pasqual takes Concha flowers he finds her being entertained by a young gigolo. She submits him to extreme humiliation: his cigarette is taken from him and given to the younger man, who is also given a flower and paid off with the banknote which Concha snatches from Don Pasqual's wallet. Some critics, rightly or wrongly linking every scene played by Marlene to the military, suggested that this particular one represented a court-martial, with the maligned victim 'stripped naked of honour and dignity'. And if Don Pasqual was an extension of von Sternberg, this act of degradation was only reversed during the cutting of the film when the director told a journalist that he would be making no more films with Marlene Dietrich. Had he told her to her face, she might not have taken it quite so badly. And yet I had read somewhere that Marlene had always considered *The Devil Is a Woman* to be not just her best film but the only one she had retained a print of:

> 'I have all my films on video,' she told me. 'Every one – apart from the silents, of course. Those weren't my films. sometimes I was only on screen for a few minutes. No, I'm talking about the films I made after *The Blue Angel*. And what you wrote isn't right, David. *La femme et la pantin* isn't my favourite film. I don't have a favourite film any more.'

In spite of its superb photography and allegedly better-than-average script, *The Devil Is a Woman* was not a great success at the box office, primarily because the public found it very hard to cope with Marlene playing an evil woman. Neither were the two songs considered above mediocre ... Leo Robin and Ralph Rainger's 'Three Sweethearts Have I' and 'If It Isn't Pain, It Isn't Love' are unlikely ever to appear on any Dietrich album. Nor was the film widely seen in its day, unless a file copy was screened illegally in underground cinemas. Six months after its release the political situation in Spain deteriorated and the Spanish ambassador who saw the film accused it of insulting the Spanish Civil Guard by portraying one of its members drinking in a bar. This was an extremely ridiculous and spiteful excuse for banning a film and would not happen today, particularly as the scenario was set at a time thirty years prior to the then events in Spain, besides being highly fictionalized. The United States State Department were, however, so fearful of a rift in Spanish-American trade relations that the negative of the film was burned publicly in Washington.

Josef von Sternberg's professional decline after *The Devil Is a Woman* was, in retrospect, only to be expected. There had already been a shake-up at Paramount with the enforced departure of B.P. Schulberg and von Sternberg joined him at Columbia at the end of 1935. Their first venture was *Crime and Punishment*, starring Peter Lorre as Raskolnikov and featuring Marian Marsh in her first major role. Although the film was by no means a failure, most of the critics were accurate in pointing out that von Sternberg's 'Svengali treatment' had not worked on Miss Marsh and she was quickly forgotten. A few years later an optimistic Louis B. Mayer would entrust his latest discovery, Hedy Lamarr, to the ebullient little director hoping that she might receive what he termed 'the Dietrich glamour treatment'. The film was *I Take This Woman*, and the title would soon become an in-joke in Hollywood. Referred to as *I Re-take This woman* or *Mayer's Folly*, it was in and out of production for almost two years – firstly by von Sternberg, then by Frank Borzage and finally by W.S. Van Dyke, by which time most of the stars had also been replaced. Von Sternberg then went on to direct Wallace Beery in *Sergeant Madden*, an achievement which brought the acidic-but-true comment from the filmologist John Douglas Eames, 'He actually finished this one!' For von Sternberg, there would be no more good films.

5

'I Don't Know Who I Belong To'

You have to be sure of yourself, otherwise people are going to walk all over you.

Although there is a great deal of truth in Josef von Sternberg's claim that he made Marlene a star, she alone nurtured and perpetuated her legend. It was also a legend which might easily have faded, had she stayed too long with her mentor. Von Sternberg's Dietrich was, one critic said, 'little more than an automaton . . . a mythical creature of the night, and a goddess of the silver screen which might not have existed in real life'. The costumes, the songs, the settings and even the dialogue were all either far-fetched or too far-removed from Marlene's fans. The critics and the journalists did not count.

'The time had come for me to return to earth, as they say. And there's one thing we ought to get straight about that part of the book that comes after von Sternberg. It was because of those films that I was so often misinterpreted. Listen to this . . . I wrote it down. "Many people, journalists in particular, have too often associated her with the parts she has played in her early films. If she played a whore, they assume she must have been a whore." '

'I can't write that!' I gasped. 'Your fans would never forgive me if I repeated that!'

A few minutes later I called her back. 'Marlene, how about this?

"She has been too often associated with the parts she sometimes played in her films, and this is an unforgivable error. Marlene's unique artistry and profound courage of conviction means that she will go down in history as considerably more than a movie legend, considerably more than just another chanteuse." Does that sound like bullshit?'

'Sweetheart, you've taken my breath away. Of course it isn't bullshit. It shows you're honest, and different from the other biographers. They only told lies or made mistakes. I admire the way you talk to me. You're not afraid of expressing your opinion. And that's why I tried to get away from that kind of film. I didn't want people to keep getting the same idea about me.'

'So, what about the films you made *after* leaving von Sternberg? Did you feel they were any better?'

'Sure the films were a little better, but none of them were as good as they could have been. I was forced to accept lousy parts because I needed the mo-ney!'

After the première of *The Devil Is a Woman*, Marlene paid another brief visit to Europe, taking in Paris, Switzerland and Vienna. Here she rather hoped that Willi Forst, now directing his own productions, would offer her a part in her own language. No such thing happened because Forst's ardour had cooled somewhat since their last meeting. She was, however, seen often in the company of the actor Hans Jaray, then at his peak and pulling in the crowds with his perhaps appropriately named play, *Cissy*. Once more, journalists hinted at romance. Then, at the end of the year, she returned to Hollywood.

B.P. Schulberg had been replaced at Paramount by the equally artistic but somewhat less arrogant Ernst Lubitsch who, in 1933, had directed Gary Cooper and Helen Hayes in Ernest Hemingway's classic *A Farewell to Arms*. For Marlene this was something of an omen. She had always been fond of Gary Cooper and she had recently met Hemingway on her last voyage back from Europe. also, Lubitsch was the favourite producer of Maurice Chevalier: he had been responsible for five of his films, including a sparkling new version of *The Merry Widow* with Jeannette MacDonald. Thus she was absolutely delighted when he approached her with the idea of playing the upper-crust jewel thief Madeleine de Beaupré in *Desire*, for which Frank Borzage had been engaged as director. Lubitsch is alleged to have wanted Gary Cooper to play opposite Marlene again because the actor had confessed to still having an amorous interest in her. Marlene, however, had specifically asked for John Gilbert and Borzage had already arranged a test, well aware that the actor was past his best.

Marlene had met Gilbert in 1934 and even then he had been well into his physical decline. The reason for this, everyone knew, was chronic alcoholism brought on by Greta Garbo's rejection of him in 1926 when she had failed to turn up at their double-wedding ceremony with King Vidor and Eleanor Boardman. At this ceremony Gilbert had argued fiercely with Louis B. Mayer and had tried to strangle him. Mayer had fired him on the spot but soon afterwards Gilbert had edged back into MGM's good books. In 1929 he had made his first talkie, *His Glorious Night* but this had been greeted by giggles and hoots of derision when the hitherto macho star was heard to speak 'like a faggot'. It was reported at the time that the film soundtrack had been sabotaged by Mayer himself. In 1935, Gilbert's contract with MGM expired and the company did not renew it. He moved to Columbia and made *The Captain Hates the Sea*. This told of an ex-Hollywood writer's attempts to kick the bottle and was a dismal flop.

Marlene was quietly confident that Gilbert would be given the part of Tom Bradley in *Desire* and her coup almost paid off when Frank Borzage announced that shooting would begin in February 1936. She herself took great care in preparing him for the role, giving precise instructions to the cameraman Charles Lang and the lighting crew whose job it would be to iron out the heavy lines on Gilbert's face. She almost succeeded in weaning him off the bottle. Each day she visited his house on Tower Grove Road and even advised him to change his will. Gilbert knew that he would soon be dead and, although he had left his ex-wife Virginia Bruce two $50,000 annuities, the bulk of his estate had been bequeathed to his eleven-year-old daughter, Leatrice, from his marriage to the actress Leatrice Joy. Marlene was with him one day when he suffered a heart seizure whilst swimming in his pool. She gave him emergency treatment whilst waiting for the ambulance to arrive and no doubt saved his life.

Ernst Lubitsch, however, did not wish to risk Gilbert dying on him half-way through the film and, on 9 January 1936, he announced that he had been replaced by Gary Cooper. The very next day Gilbert died of a heart attack, aged just thirty-eight. Marlene attended the funeral, accompanied by Cooper and Dolores del Rio, and actually collapsed in the church. She later opposed the will, claiming that the original document which she had witnessed being written had been suppressed. In the new will, Virginia Bruce acquired the house and the bulk of his estate, with his daughter ending up with just $10,000. The mystery of the will has never been solved. Soon afterwards the house was burgled and ransacked by Gilbert's fans and most of the items not stolen were auctioned. Marlene bought a pair of bed sheets for $700.

Desire was a contemporary light comedy which many critics welcomed as a change from the 'somnambulic trips' which Marlene had made with Josef von Sternberg. Neither Lubitsch nor Frank Borzage was interested in her sex-symbol image, and for this reason they gave instructions to Travis Banton that she should be dressed in simple clothes which would appeal to the average woman in the street. Thus she was seen in a variety of jackets, skirts and blouses, and in particular a double-breasted jacket worn over a plain white dress. It is true that this made her look considerably more attractive than some of the elaborate costumes dreamed up by Banton for her earlier films and gone too were the sultry songs: sitting at a piano she sang Friedrich Hollander's 'Awake in a Dream' in a voice positively dripping with honey. Needless to day, *Desire* was her biggest box-office success since *Shanghai Express*.

It was disclosed a few weeks after John Gilbert's death that Marlene had wanted him as her co-star in *The Garden of Allah* but that she had disliked David O. Selznick so much that she had asked her close friend, the Russian-born actor Gregory Ratoff, to act as a go-between. Selznick, it appears, had a great deal of admiration for Marlene, though his feet were firmly fixed on the ground when it came to discussing her salary, as he indicated in one of his letters to Ratoff:

As far as Marlene goes, I am very pleased that she is interested in joining me, but you will have to get over to her some facts which I doubt she at present appreciates. Any

important theatre man will tell her, if he is honest, that she is
no longer even a fairly important box-office star . . . there is
no personality so important that he or she can survive the
perfectly dreadful line-up of pictures that Marlene has had,
and she is in no position to command any fabulous salary. I
am perfectly willing to give her a percentage deal whereby, if
she thinks that she is bigger than I think she is at the moment,
she will get what perhaps she thinks she is entitled to, and she
will get all the money she can possibly want if, and when, she
again becomes the star that she was after *Morocco* and before
the long line-up of *Dishonoured, Song of Songs, Blonde
Venus*, etc. I frankly want her on the right terms. I think she is
one of the most magnificent personalities that the screen has
had in many years, and I think that it is a crying shame that
she has been dragged down as she has been.

Marlene had also discussed making *Knight Without Armour* for
Alexander Korda in England and for an alleged fee of 'not less
than $450,000' – an astonishing amount for that time and double
the fee which Selznick would offer for *The Garden of Allah*. Even
so, the negotiations for both films took a while and, in the
meantime, Marlene signed to play opposite Charles Boyer in *I
Loved a Soldier*, a remake of Pola Negri's 1927 film *Hotel
Imperial*. For this production Ernst Lubitsch brought in Henry
Hathaway, who had just completed *Peter Ibbetson* with Gary
Cooper, who incidentally was still occasionally seen in Marlene's
company. She is said to have been fascinated by the script, which
told of a fugitive soldier who is sheltered in a hotel by a girl who
works there. The opening shot depicted Marlene on her hands and
knees scrubbing the floor and wearing scruffy clothes. Lubitsch's
idea was that as the film progressed and the girl's love for the
soldier grew stronger, so did her appearance become more
beautiful until during the final scene she married him in a
cathedral. Just what went wrong with the film may now never be
known. Most of the people involved with the production are dead
and Marlene refused to say anything about it. What is known is
that Ernst Lubitsch was fired and that Marlene herself walked off
the set during the filming of the fourth reel, when $900,000 had
been spent. Hoping to set matters right, Henry Hathaway then

brought in Margaret Sullavan, at the time courting Henry Fonda, who always made a point of accompanying her to the studio. One afternoon they were loafing around and Sullavan tripped over a cable, breaking her arm in two places. By this time the expenditure had risen to well over $1 million and the film company decided that enough was enough. After just twenty-eight days of shooting the film was cancelled.

The Garden of Allah was Marlene's first film as a loan-out star from Paramount and by the time shooting began she had already signed the contract for *Knight without Armour*. This is said to have pleased David O. Selznick who, unaware of Marlene's inherited mania for detail, had been terrified of his film over-reaching its budget by taking too long to make. Even so, the mogul kept out of her way whenever possible and assigned its direction to Richard Boleslawski. An ex-Russian lancer, he is said to have fulfilled Marlene's 'military requirements' for a film she despised.

> 'There's a brilliant line in *The Garden of Allah*,' I said to her. 'It says "Cursed is the man with relatives – do you have them in Europe?" And the photography was wonderful. Why did you hate the film so much?'
> 'Of all the films I ever made, that was the worst,' she replied.

Marlene had purchased a Filmo 16mm camera in Paris with a good supply of colour film, ostensibly to provide herself and Rudolf with a lasting memento of Maria's childhood. She never took lessons in photography. What she knew about cameracraft she had picked up from von Sternberg, who had personally filmed many of the famous scenes from *Der blaue Engel* and *Desire* without mentioning this in the credits. Marlene is also said to have taken her camera along to the film sets, filming the other actors or getting them to film her – she had even made her own Technicolor test for Paramount in 1935. A few months after this, whilst von Sternberg was making his ill-fated *I, Claudius* in England and pining for his Hollywood home, Marlene took her camera there – putting paid to any rumours that they were not on speaking terms – and she filmed every room, with close-ups of his personal effects. The director is reported to have wept when seeing it in his London hotel room.

Initially, Marlene was not interested in making *The Garden of Allah* in Technicolor because, she claimed, most of the colours turned out wishy-washy or gaudy, and never anywhere between. The costume designer Ernst Dryden had been instructed by Selznick not to dress Marlene in white because this would glare too much. Her response was that if this was the case, then the camera would not be allowed to move in on the whites of her eyes. Then, having made her point, she invited Charles Lang on to the set, and together they demonstrated to Selznick 'how to film a shot correctly' using the lighting techniques that Marlene had taught herself.

Still worried about leaving Maria at home, Marlene took her with her on location: she played one of the convent children, but was sent back to Hollywood when the temperature at Yuma rocketed to 136 degrees and most of the crew became affected by the heat. The film told the story of Domini Enfilden, the former convent girl who falls for an absconding Trappist monk. The role of Boris Androvsky was played by Charles Boyer, a 'leftover' from *I Loved a Soldier*. The couple marry but are forced to separate when Domini discovers the truth about her husband from a French soldier who is lost in the desert and who just happens to have been dining at the monastery when Boris was reported missing.

Thus the monk returns to his life of silent seclusion, giving the film a good ending, and a moving one. But though popular with cinemagoers, which was all that really mattered, *The Garden of Allah* was practically slaughtered not just by the critics, but by two of the world's foremost writers. Graham Greene, in the Christmas 1936 issue of the *Spectator*, described the setting as 'a cratered desert, like Gruyère cheese' and Marlene's speaking voice as 'a stylized, weary and monotonous whisper'. The French novelist and former music-hall starlet Colette, famed for her waspish comments about the women she found sexually attractive but could not have for herself said, 'Faced with the sugared rose of Dietrich's cynical mouth, the anaemic gold of her coiffure, and the hesitant azure of her gaze, we hung fire!' Other critics dismissed the film as a travesty of the 1927 original with Alice Terry and Ivan Petrovich, and Richard Boleslawski was accused of ruining a perfectly good story by engaging a bad scriptwriter and an equally

'I said to Billy Wilder, "You'd better get me Hollander, *then* I'll do the songs".' Rehearsing 'Within the Ruins of Berlin' with Friedrich Hollander on the set of *A Foreign Affair*, 1948.

Blowing a kiss to Spishek. A self-portrait taken in Warsaw in 1966. Spishek was the name Marlene gave to the Polish actor Zbigniew Cybulsky, one of the great loves of her life, who died tragically young.

Look me over closely, tell me what you see. 'I had this dress made for an appearance at a stage-door canteen, but I decided to wear something dowdy in the end, so that I could blend in better with the boys.'

'This reminds me of that time in the Riban Bleu in New York. Tallulah sent
a message to my table asking why I was wearing gloves. I sent her the
gloves... on a plate.'

Move over, Damia! A photograph of Marlene taken in Paris at the time of Michel Guyarmathy's request for her to appear in a Folies Bergère revue. Damia was the great French singer whom Marlene admitted to emulating at around this time.

(*below left*) 'The album cover I adored, naturally! And the one that I loathed!' *The Essential Marlene Dietrich*, which Marlene compiled and for which David Bret wrote the sleeve essay, was the only one of her albums since *Berlin-Berlin* that she had any say in. (*By courtesy of EMI*)

The Essential
MARLENE
DIETRICH

IMPERIAL
Marlene
Dietri

DIE ANTWORT WEISS
GANZ ALLEIN DER WIND
*Wenn die Soldaten
Sag mir wo die Blumen sind
Der Trommelmann*

'I had Joe Pasternak to thank for salvaging my career after I'd been branded box-office poison. The only problem was that after *Destry* they kept putting me in goddamned cowboy films!' A self-portrait from the set of *Pittsburgh*, 1942.

'I felt happy when Judy died. For the first time in her life she was doing what *she* wanted to do.' With Judy Garland in 1961, after the première of *Judgment at Nuremberg*.

'This is the dress that I would have worn had I made the film with Chevalier.' The film was *A New Kind of Love*, to be directed by Billy Wilder in 1951. It was shelved when the French star was prevented from entering the United States after being wrongly accused of being a Communist.

'Journalists have always assumed that just because I played a whore on the screen I was like that in real life. And is there any wonder, looking like that?' An unused publicity still from *Morocco*, 1930. Marlene refused to say why she had had her co-star, Gary Cooper, removed from the shot. In the original he stands behind her.

bad cast. Sadly, the director was unable to stand up to his critics, for he had been taken ill with an infection after drinking poisoned water from a desert spring. Although he went on to direct *The Last of Mrs Cheyney* with Joan Crawford and Robert Montgomery, he was unable to finish it and he died in the autumn of 1936.

Five days after completing *The Garden of Allah* Marlene and her daughter sailed for England on the *Normandie*. She had made all the necessary arrangements to enrol Maria at a school in Switzerland but in the meantime she wanted her to speak English properly, without the New York accent which had marred the first scenes of *The Scarlet Empress*. The voyage was an extension of their Hollywood way of life, with the pair spending much of the time in the four-roomed Deauville suite with its pale blue satin furnishings and baby grand piano.

Upon her arrival in London Marlene moved into the Dorchester, where supervising the unloading of her thirty-six pieces of luggage she caused a ripple of excitement, though not quite so much as she would during her many outings, wearing the latest Travis Banton designs and clinging to the arm of Douglas Fairbanks, who had a penthouse in Grosvenor Square. It was he who persuaded her, once Maria had left for Switzerland, to rent a flat in the very same block. Their friendship, like a great many of her others, was much misinterpreted by the media. Fairbanks had been offered the very difficult role of Rupert of Hentzau in David O. Selznick's new production of *The Prisoner of Zenda* but he had been unsure of accepting it lest it jeopardize his career. Marlene helped him to decide and the rest is cinema history. She was also visited by Josef von Sternberg, still trying to battle through *I, Claudius* and every now and then Rudolf Sieber came over from Paris, but without Tamara. Other friends who occasionally dropped in were the writer Walter Reisch, and Richard Tauber.

Marlene also caused a great controversy when she attended the première of Irving Thalberg's *Romeo and Juliet*, starring Norma Shearer, Leslie Howard and two of the cast from *The Garden of Allah* (C. Aubrey Smith and Basil Rathbone). Outside the Haymarket Theatre, a crowd of five thousand had to be held back by seventy policemen and theatre staff whilst Marlene was rushed to her car on the shoulders of two security men. On another occasion, after she had attended a screening of *Under Two Flags*, she was accosted in the Strand by a group of angry prostitutes, who unceremoniously relieved her of her gloves and blouse. Later, the women claimed that they had been only hunting for souvenirs, but the incident amused Marlene, who by way of her films with von Sternberg had become the self-confessed 'queen of all whores'. It was not a term which I liked to hear her or anyone else use, but I can understand why she used it.

Alexander Korda had hired Jacques Feyder to direct *Knight Without Armour*. He was an eccentric and enigmatic Belgian, whose habit of waving his handkerchief in front of the lens as opposed to shouting 'Cut!' had made even Garbo smile when he had directed her in *The Kiss* in 1929. With haunting music by Miklos Rosza and a script by Arthur Wimperis, who had first achieved recognition as far back as 1914 by writing a revue, *The Rajah's Ruby*, for Gaby Deslys and Harry Pilcer, it should have been a good film. It was not. Based on a novel by James Hilton, it told the story of a brave Englishman and a Russian countess who get caught up in the 1917 Revolution, but the dialogue was stilted and much of the continuity askew. One unavoidable problem was the ill-health that dogged Robert Donat, Marlene's co-star, throughout the production. A chronic asthmatic, in the days when cures and preventatives were not easily come by, he had to stay away from the set for eight weeks, and Korda became so concerned that he allegedly thought of replacing Donat with Laurence Olivier. Marlene refused even to consider the idea and helped to nurse him until he was well enough to complete the picture.

As Robert Donat had never been one of my favourite actors, I had not been aware of his asthma problem until, in May 1990, my wife Jeanne was diagnosed asthmatic and, during the next couple of months, was hospitalized three times. Marlene asked Ramon to call the hospital and when he could not get through she tried herself: one of the nurses told me that she had answered the telephone to a 'Marlene', and that when she had asked 'Marlene who?' the caller had hung up. That night she managed to get me at home. She was very upset. Ramon later told me that she had wept when first hearing the news:

'I was so very, very worried. You know that Robert Donat was a very good friend of mine and that when he and I were making a film he was taken ill with asthma? And then you wrote to say that your wife was very ill and that she'd been rushed into a hospital. Telling me something like that, don't you expect me to worry? I love you both so very much. You're very close – and I couldn't phone yesterday because someone was listening in.'

I explained what had happened and this seemed to calm her a little. Ironically, just over a year later Jeanne had another serious attack in Paris, shortly after we had been to Marlene's apartment, and she called our hotel. What is astonishing is that though she sounded deeply upset, and insisted that I should give my wife a big, big kiss from her, she declined to speak to her even though she was sitting right next to me.

Marlene's attention to detail, during the filming of *Knight Without Armour*, impressed Alexander Korda so much that he told her she could quite easily direct her own film in England. This statement came after the scene which called for Marlene to take a bath. Jacques Feyder had organized a flesh-coloured all-over body stocking but Marlene rejected this, claiming the wrinkles would show. Thus, when the scene was filmed orders were given to clear the adjoining sets. Marlene would enter clad in a white bath-robe, divest herself of this, and step into the tub. Without the body stocking, the camera would see her stark naked for a maximum of three seconds. This, of course, would be edited out by the man in the cutting-room. Unfortunately, things did not go according to plan. The first five takes were not considered good enough by the cameraman. By this time dozens of pairs of eyes had become fixed upon Marlene from a number of clandestine vantage points around the studio. Then she slipped upon a pile of soapy bubbles.

The relations between Marlene and the film crew had been better than anyone could have expected: right from the very first day when she had asked them, jokingly, for a token one penny for every original idea she came up with. She told a reporter, a few days into filming, that she had already collected three shillings and sixpence and these coins were in her handbag when she returned to Hollywood during the spring of 1937.

Then one afternoon, whilst relaxing in her dressing room at the

Denham studios, she received a visit from Mady Sojka, the German actress who had appeared with her in *Zwei Kravaten*, and a relation of von Sternberg's friend Johnny Sojka, the champagne-bottler who had been the inspiration behind her song 'Jonny'. She informed an astonished Marlene that she had been sent to London by Josef Goebbels with a lucrative offer for her to return to Germany, not just to augment the prestige of the Nazi party, but to revive her flagging film career. She was offered the opportunity to choose her own director, material, script, photographer and leading man, for which she would receive £50,000 tax-free in the currency of her choice and a three-year contract on identical terms. Marlene told Mady Sojka in no uncertain terms exactly what to tell Goebbels to do with his offer, though this did not prevent further visits from Hitler's ambassador, Joachim von Ribbentrop, who was in London at the time. It was the last straw when he tried to give her a gift of a Christmas tree from Hitler himself. Marlene showed him the door and the ambassador is alleged to have been physically threatened by her companion at that time, the German novelist, Erich Maria Remarque, whom she had met in Venice during the summer of 1935, a man who is said to have held so much inside information about the Nazi party that Hitler himself had added his name to their hit list.

Two years or so older than Marlene, this handsome, muscular Aryan had served in World War One, since which time he had enjoyed such diverse employment as making gravestones, flying an auto-gyro, and test-driving racing cars, before completing his first book, *Im westen Nichts neues*. This had been translated as *All Quiet on the Western Front* and filmed in 1930 with Lew Ayres and Louis Wolheim. Its success had been phenomenal and would never be eclipsed even though Remarque later wrote *Three Comrades* and *Arch of Triumph*, both of which were turned into successful films. The fact that he was able to write anything at all was, however, astonishing in itself for Remarque's biographers have all stated that when not suffering from self-inflicted anxiety and depression, usually brought on by excessive drinking, he would often sit staring at his typewriter for hours then close its lid without having written a single word. It would often take him an entire evening to construct a single sentence. It has been suggested that once Marlene had recovered from the shock of seeing his splendid naked body one morning on the Venetian beach, she quickly became interested in the darker, more morose side of his character. This, coupled with his great fragility, urged one French critic to say, 'Remarque's innermost sanctum is the reflection of a Damia song'. Remarque is also reputed to have told a friend that he would have been more than willing to give up his second wife in order to marry Marlene. And yet, during the mid-Thirties when their friendship was at its strongest, Remarque would often excuse himself from her company and spend the whole evening at the notorious Jockey Club, renowned for housing the Kiki de Montparnasse clique. Marlene did not approve of his binges and would never have gone with him to such an establishment, but neither did she try to discourage him because she was well aware that these soirées afforded him temporary release from a world he professed to despise.

Remarque spent a few days in London with Marlene in February 1937, and it was here that he poured out his heart, telling her how much he loved her, how he would rather die than be away from her for more than a day, and how dangerous it would be to stay in Europe. He, more than anyone, urged her to denounce her German nationality and apply for an American passport. He then promised to join her in Hollywood as soon as possible. His own passport was Panamanian and a few years later it would cause him a great deal of trouble.

Knight Without Armour lost its producer so much money that when Marlene arrived in America she was greeted with the news that she had been labelled box-office poison: her name appeared on a red-bordered advertisement alongside those of Joan Crawford, Greta Garbo, Fred Astaire and Katharine Hepburn.

'Everybody thought that I didn't care what they'd said about me,' Marlene confessed. 'That wasn't true. And you know what I did, David? I rang Chevalier right away. He was in Paris and when he found out what had happened he said, "That's it! I will never make another film in America until they apologize to you!" and he was good to his word, wasn't he? Chevalier never even tried to get a contract with Hollywood until 1950. And do you know what they started saying about Katharine Hepburn? They said she was a lesbian! Now, what I find really important is that her book has come out, telling the truth. She's a wonderful woman. The book, it's called *Me* . . . Anyway, that's what they said about Katharine Hepburn, and it wasn't true. And you know, within a couple of years we were both successful again, weren't we?'

A few days after arriving in Hollywood, Marlene paid a visit to the Los Angeles Federal Building to fill in her nationalization forms. The event was covered extensively by the media, and the clerk responsible for making out her application was reported to have dropped his pen several times and upturned his inkwell on account of his nerves. Marlene was told at the end of her interview that it would take another two years before she officially became an American. Satisfied with this, she posed for photographs and walked away. One of these was printed in *Der Stürmer*, the anti-Jewish newspaper much favoured by the Nazis, along with a spurious article by the editor, Julius Streicher, which said, 'Marlene Dietrich, the German-born actress, has spent so many years amongst the film Jews of Hollywood that she has now become an American citizen.' As for the photograph, Streicher scathed, 'What the Jewish judge thinks of the formula may be seen from his attitude as he stands in his shirtsleeves. He is taking from Dietrich the oath with which she betrayed her Fatherland.'

The article was ignored, although many of Marlene's friends did begin to wonder why her husband, Rudolf, had elected to remain a German. Marlene and I never discussed the topic – there was no need to – although there was an amusing incident which took place in Paris on 13 June 1991 when she tried to contact me at my hotel. The receptionist, a very charming lady named Charlotte Becker, assumed that her reluctance to say too much must have had something to do with Marlene's marked accent, and the fact that she probably could not speak French very well. Charlotte said, 'Miss Dietrich, I too am German. Would you find it any easier speaking in your own language?' To which Marlene yelled, 'I am not a German – I am an American.'

Working abroad had given Marlene a taste for adventure; this, and the fact that she had begun to tire of Hollywood because most of her friends were in Europe, caused her to announce that her next film, *Angel*, would be her last for Paramount. After this, she added, she would make films in France. Produced and directed by

Ernst Lubitsch, *Angel* was a subtle, high-society comedy not readily accepted by American audiences at a time when most of their comedies were either bland or too silly to laugh at. This time Marlene had two male co-stars, Melvyn Douglas and Herbert Marshall. She played the wife of an English diplomat (Marshall) who loved nothing more than to fly off to Paris for the odd week-end in her private plane. Here she is introduced to a dashing American (Douglas) who, because of her passion for flying, decides to baptize her Angel. Later in the film, the American turns out to be an old friend of her husband and their affair, of course, has to end. The film was a good one, but a flop, and may be best remembered today for Marlene's ridiculously long eyelashes, if nothing else. Even the scriptwriter, Sam Raphaelson, did not like it, and the *New York Times* reported, 'Dietrich hoists them [her eyelashes] up and down at one-minute intervals, like a Strong Man handling a one-thousand pound weight in a sideshow . . .'

Although Marlene had already announced her decision to leave Paramount, this did not prevent them from attempting to get one over on her by cancelling her contract with the brief statement, 'Marlene Dietrich will be permitted to work elsewhere'. There was also an alleged disagreement over her new project, a film version of Terence Rattigan's *French Without Tears*. It has since been revealed that Marlene did agree to stay on in Hollywood to make the film but that because of her 'box-office poison' tag, Paramount paid her $200,000 not to do it. There is little wonder, therefore, that when she left Hollywood at the end of 1937, she vowed that she would never make another American film.

In France, Marlene spent most of her time during the next few months commuting between the houses of her friends; the most important of these were Peter Kreuder, Noël Coward, Cecil Beaton and, of course, Erich Maria Remarque, who had at the last moment decided not to follow her to Hollywood, where MGM had been about to film his *Three Comrades* with Margaret Sullavan and Robert Taylor. In Paris, Marlene also caught up with the latest revues at the Casino and the Moulin Rouge and she was introduced to Michel Guyarmathy, who had recently taken over as costume designer at the Folies-Bergère.

Michel and I had first met when I had been researching *The Mistinguett Legend* and knowing him enabled me to question

Marlene about one subject no one knew about . . . the possibility, in 1938, of her stepping into Mistinguett's shoes, or rather her feathers!

'Marlene, did you ever regret not taking up Michel Guyarmathy on the offer to star in your own revue at the Folies-Bergère?'

The question was so direct and unexpected that she could not have denied the possibility of such a proposition. She also knew that, with my connections within the French music hall, I could not have made a mistake.

She said, in her serious-cum-hilariously-comical tone: 'But Mistinguett's been dead donkey's years – and I thought he was dead, too. What was he like?'

'He mistook me for a journalist, at first,' I explained. 'And I wasn't too impressed with him. His office looked as though it had been hit by a bomb and he was a dead-ringer for Hitchcock. Then he asked me for an honest opinion about a new star. I told him she didn't have a great deal of talent. Michel was grateful for my comments and bought me a drink – we're now the best of friends.'

Marlene chuckled at this. 'Aye-aye-aye! You asked me about the revue that man wanted me to do at the Folies-Bergère. Well you know, I never signed anything and I wouldn't have worked with him in any case. He was known all over Paris for being stingy – just like your friend Mistinguett. And you also wrote in one of your letters that he'd made a dress especially for me?'

'It was made of crimson velvet,' I began.

'No, David,' came the argument. 'I never wore anything made for me by that man. I told him that I didn't want it, so he gave it to your friend.'

'Mistinguett wasn't my friend,' I countered. 'I was only a child when she died.'

'Well, maybe so,' Marlene said. 'But you wrote about her, and you also wrote about that horrible woman who used to run the gay bar just around the corner from where I live. God in heaven, you do know how to pick 'em.'

[This was Manouche, the celebrated gangster's moll, who in her day had known many famous stars. Marlene had often visited her club, Les Chambiges, near the avenue Montaigne. Manouche's lover, Paul Carbone, had been killed when the Resistance had blown up the Nice–Paris express, and Mistinguett had become godmother to his posthumous child. Manouche had also organized the only ever recorded meeting between Marlene and Mistinguett. The ensuing scene, attended by members of the press had been described as 'harrowing'.]

> 'Did you know Manouche, Marlene?' I asked. 'She was Mistinguett's best friend in those days.'
>
> 'Any friend of Mistinguett can't have been all that nice to know,' she said. 'But I had heard of her – who hadn't? And why in God's name did you want to meet anyone like that?'
>
> 'We met her in 1974,' I enlarged. 'At around the same time we met Damia. She was fat and dirty looking, and foul mouthed. One evening she served us with a plate of runny eggs. Jeanne waited until she'd gone back into the kitchen, then she emptied them into a plastic bag, and shoved it into her handbag. But she did tell me all about your meeting with Mistinguett.'

Marlene refused to discuss this meeting, when according to one of Roger Normand's friends, it was 'handbags at fifty paces, and enough filthy language to shame a docker'. The photographs taken of the pair are truly horrendous and not at all flattering to either star. Even Mistinguett insisted that they should be burned before her eyes and issued a statement: 'Does Paris really want to see its beloved Miss smoking a clay pipe?' The negatives, however, were saved and still exist.

As for the fabled Guyarmathy gown, which Marlene was to have had made for her entrance down the famous staircase at the Folies-Bergère – this was given to Mistinguett a few years later. Mistinguett wore it during her last appearance in New York in 1951 when she was seventy-six. It was a sumptuous creation of crimson velvet trimmed with ermine and split to the hip to reveal the once-fabulous legs, which Lloyd's of London had insured for $1 million. What I omitted to tell Marlene, when I took her a copy of *The Mistinguett Legend*, was that it included a photograph of the dress!

> 'I saw the picture of Mistinguett wearing the dress,' she told me the next day. 'She looked a mess – flaunting herself at her age. I know her legs were famous but there was no need for her to make an idiot of herself. I guess she did her bit for France, like I did. And your book surprised me. I skipped through it last night, and I like what I've read so far.'

'I don't think the French liked me writing about Mistinguett's love life, though I kept it all very respectable,' I said.

'But what you wrote was beautiful, David, as well as respectable. You're a decent writer, in an age when decent writers seem to be disappearing. I get books and magazines sent to me here, and they are getting dirtier by the minute. Only today I got a copy of a magazine which used to be respectable, and on the cover are two men who are embracing each other. It says, "The world is full of homosexuals". They wouldn't have done this, years ago. In my day people had to be discreet. The world's changed dear, and not for the better.'

As the political situation in Europe worsened in the late 1930s, so did Erich Maria Remarque's moods. He became so depressed that early in 1939 Marlene decided to take him to Hollywood. The director, Frank Capra, had asked her to play the novelist Georges Sand in an as yet unscripted film about the life of Chopin. Considering her passion for the composer's music, this would have been the perfect vehicle for her talents. In order to avoid a scandal she and Remarque travelled on different ships and, to add to the confusion which must have baffled only the media, soon after the couple met up again in Los Angeles they were joined by Rudolf Sieber and Josef von Sternberg.

A few weeks later the film was cancelled. A certain Mr Brandt, who ran a cinema chain, placed an advertisement in several newspapers condemning Marlene as 'a box-office undesirable'. On top of this, Remarque had taken an instant dislike to Hollywood. Marlene therefore arranged for their return to Europe, though her send-off was different from the kind she was used to. Only a few days before she had become an American citizen but her attitude towards Hollywood had been well publicized and, as she boarded the *Normandie* on 14 June 1939, she was accosted by several agents from the Inland Revenue Service, who demanded that she pay her tax bill before leaving. Marlene claimed that for the year 1936-7 she had paid well over $100,000 in taxes, since which time she had not so much as set foot in an American studio. The agents then impounded her baggage – as usual there were thirty-six pieces – and threatened to keep them and Rudolf unless Marlene paid at once the $284,000 they said was outstanding for her film with Alexander Korda. She did not have much money on her and, as the ship's captain informed her that he would not permit any further delay, she acted on impulse, handing over as security her jewellery, including her priceless collection of cabochon emeralds.

Returning to Paris and working from her base, the Plaza Athénée Hotel, during the summer of 1939, Marlene made repeated attempts to get her mother and sister out of Germany. She was not successful but if Hitler hoped that she might 'see sense', if only to ensure the safety of her loved ones, then the events of 14 July only convinced everyone whose side she would be on if war broke out. Standing in the back of a truck in the Place de l'Opéra she gave an impromptu recital to the Bastille Day crowds, performing the songs from *The Blue Angel*, and several *chansons* including 'Je sais que vous êtes jolie' and 'Reviens veux-tu?' This time the song was directed to a young *légionnaire* who later achieved fame for a single moment by dancing with her whilst an *accordéoniste* played 'La plus bath des javas'.

A few days later, Marlene and Rudolf were reunited with their daughter and left for Antibes, where they were joined by Remarque and von Sternberg. Although the director was no longer interested in making films with Marlene, he was only too willing to offer her advice – a sporting gesture when one considers that she was in the company of her husband, her lover, and the actor, Jean Gabin, whom many would soon regard as more important than either.

Gabin, who had recently caused a sensation in Renoir's *La grande illusion* had begun his illustrious career not in films but on the revue stage, partnering Mistinguett. They had even recorded several hit songs but, worse than this, Gabin had also been the great star's lover for a time, which no doubt explains why Marlene gave him a suitably wide berth when they first met.

One man who impressed Marlene a great deal was the burly French comedian, Jules Raimu, almost always referred to by just his surname. Whilst in Paris, Remarque had taken her to see Marcel Pagnol's *La femme du boulanger*, starring Raimu, and, ten years later, she still hailed this as the best film she had ever seen. Now, Raimu was invited to join her in Antibes and her company was further augmented by the arrival of Jo Carstairs and her secretary, Violla Rubber, and Joseph Kennedy and his son, Jack. Marlene and Raimu were preoccupied with the prospect of making a film with Gabin and the actress Florence Marly, who was married to the director Pierre Chénal. Chénal had just acquired the script of *Dédée d'Anvers*, which was not too far removed from some of the roles Marlene had played for von Sternberg, and it seems almost certain that she would have agreed to make the film had she not received the totally unexpected telephone call from Hollywood which would in effect transform her life. It came from the producer Joe Pasternak, who had met her whilst she had been working in Berlin on *Der blaue Engel*.

Pasternak had been born in Szilagy-Somlyo, Hungary, in 1901, but in his teens he had moved to Philadelphia, where he had worked in a belt factory before taking up acting lessons in New York. Soon afterwards he was hired by Paramount, washing dishes, though by 1923 he had become fourth assistant director and, in 1926, he had joined Universal. They had sent him to Europe, to work in their Berlin studios, but with the rise of Nazism he had returned to Hollywood. His first film had been *Three Smart Girls*, featuring a fifteen-year-old Deanna Durbin, and it had made her an overnight sensation. He had also adapted a German film, *Kleine Mutter*, into *Bachelor Mother* for Ginger Rogers. Pasternak's big scriptwriter was the German-born Félix Joachimsohn who, like Friedrich Hollander, would soon Americanize his name and become Felix Jackson. Between them they had decided upon a remake of the western *Destry Rides Again*. The 1932 version starring the legendary Tom Mix had presented the public with a Tom Destry who had avenged the death of his lawman father with a combination of fists and bullets. The new version, however, would be worked around the talents of James Stewart, an actor not used to playing heavy roles. When Marlene was told of this, she refused to do the film.

'Can you imagine that, David? A man like Jimmy Stewart as a gunslinger, and me as his little trollop? That's why I said to Joe Pasternak, "No thank you, it'll make us both a laughing stock all over Hollywood." '

'So what made you change your mind?' I asked. 'You never saw a script until you got to America.'

'They told me that they'd changed the whole idea of the film,' she said. 'Then I reconsidered. I needed the money to get my family out of Germany.'

'But you are glad that you made the film?' I pressed.

'The film was great fun,' Marlene stressed. 'I learned how to roll my own cigarettes, and I loved what they called in America shooting crap – and that isn't what you think it means, either!'

'And the fight scene?'

'Oh, that was tremendous,' she exclaimed. 'Tre-men-dous.'

Joe Pasternak had elected to make James Stewart's on-screen performance comparable to the actor's character. The new Destry drank only milk, was mild-mannered and polite and, until the end of the film, did not even appear to know how to use a gun. Thus, the production's masculine element remained with Marlene's Frenchy (Felix Jackson had chosen this name because of her very close attachment to France) until the final scene, when Destry becomes tough and she expires in his arms, having flung herself heroically between him and his assailant's bullet. It was, of course, a typical exercise in Hollywood chauvinism: the public were not allowed to believe in Destry's apparent weakness, made even more so by Frenchy's great fortitude. It also has to be said that Marlene 'died' wonderfully, even better than she had in *Dishonoured*, because this time there was no kitsch. The other highlight of the film was the famous cat fight with Una Merkel, for which there was no rehearsal, and for which both actresses refused stand-ins. James Stewart is alleged to have been 'thrilled to little pieces' when asked to break up the scratching, spitting pair by dousing them with a bucket of cold water, which suggests that for one moment at least mere acting became reality. The ensuing scene, with a yelling, irate Frenchy evicting Destry from the saloon by hurling an assortment of bottles before finally drawing a gun, is equally memorable. Some years later Una Merkel admitted that after filming the scene she had been compelled to spend two days in hospital, whereas Marlene had emerged from the scrap without so much as a scratch. But what about the songs from the film? 'Little Joe the Wrangler' was never recorded commercially but the other two – 'You Got That Look' and 'The Boys in the Backroom' – who would ever forget those?

'Marlene,' I said. 'Tell me about the songs from *Destry*.'

'More whore songs, you mean?' she gruffed. 'They were even more dreadful than the songs from the German films. "See what the boys in the backroom will have . . . and tell them I died of the same." It doesn't make any sense at all, does it?'

'You sang it for nearly forty years,' I pointed out. 'You must have liked it at least a little bit.'

'And I keep telling you – I sang what the audience wanted to hear me sing.'

Destry Rides Again, for which Marlene was paid $75,000, rescued her from a temporary slump in her career which might or might not have been put right had she made *Dédée d'Anvers* with Jean Gabin. It was a remendous success all over the world and, according to most critics, was George Marshall's best-ever film as director. Only one film, *How the West was Won*, which he co-directed with Henry Hathaway and John Ford in 1962, had the same effect on cinema audiences as the one he made with Marlene and James Stewart.

But was there any truth in the statement made some years later by Joe Pasternak, about a romance between Marlene and her co-star? He said, 'Jimmy was a simple guy, but she wanted him at once . . . she took one look at him, and fell overboard.' One theory is that Marlene's interest in Stewart was stimulated by his fascination for reading Flash Gordon comics and this is not as ridiculous as it seems. In 1949 Edith Piaf confided in her that one of the more attractive traits of the boxing champion Marcel Cerdan was that he too liked reading comics and juvenile adventure books, 'pointing towards the fact that under all those muscles, he was a big soft kid'. During the filming of *Destry Rides Again*, Marlene presented James Stewart with a life-sized Flash Gordon doll, according to Pasternak 'life-sized down to the very last detail', and this is supposed to have started a passionate relationship.

'Has the book *Double Exposure* been released yet in England? No? Then you should try and get a copy from America. It's very, very beautiful. It's a book all about famous people, written by other famous people. Roddy McDowell put it together. The chapter about me was written by Jimmy Stewart. It was short, but Jimmy said a lot in a few words. Do you like Baryshnikov, David? Have you ever seen him dance?'

'Not on the stage. In some ways he reminds me of Harry Pilcer, the American dancer I wrote about who sang "Roses of Picardy". Apart from his obvious dancing abilities, Baryshnikov sings rather well, so in some ways he could be Pilcer's successor. And talking of dancers, I read in your book what you said about Nureyev . . .'

'Baryshnikov's a beautiful person to know, because he's so normal. He admires and loves women and he isn't a big-head like the other one. He wrote a very beautiful tribute to Astaire, and Jimmy and Roddy came to see me about the photographs. They wanted to have us in the book looking as we do now. I had to tell Jimmy that he looked a mess – he had a beer-belly and a beard, for God's sake! Eventually, I thought it might be a good idea. People always see us as we were forty years ago – they wouldn't even recognize us if they saw us now. You asked me some time ago, who was my favourite leading man and you said that I didn't have to answer that question if I didn't want to. Well, sweetheart, now you know the answer! And Jimmy and I are still very close. I told you about him coming to see me with his beer-belly and beard? That changes nothing – we all have to grow old. And we still care for each other – well, you know what I mean by that. We respect each other, David, and our first film together was one of the best things I ever did.'

According to Ramon, James Stewart was one of the stars who flew over from America especially to see Marlene (another was the pop star Michael Jackson), only to be told that they would have to make do with the walkie-talkie connecting the foyer to her bedroom.

In spite of the tremendous success of *Destry Rides Again*, its two stars did not seem particularly interested in teaming up again for another film. This would have to wait eleven years. Neither did Marlene wish to become typecast, as she had with Josef von Sternberg, although Hollywood did not work this way. Over the next few years she would play several adaptations of Frenchy but never with the same success as the original.

Marlene's next film for Universal, produced by Joe Pasternak and directed by Tay Garnett, was *Seven Sinners*. Again the film was made for money. The war had broken out two weeks before *Destry*'s release and Marlene was still anxious about her family and friends in Europe. Intensely superstitious, even if she did occasionally wear the dreaded green, she was very close at the time to the astrologer Carroll Richter, a Californian who upon their very first meeting had identified her as a Capricorn. Marlene set great store by such things. Once when I repeated what Jeanne had said about one of her employees having 'dirty shirt cuffs', the employee was given a severe ticking off.

> 'Your wife must be a good judge of character. She's a Capricorn. If I had to guess about you, I would say that you are Scorpio. You sometimes get impatient, you're short-tempered, and you're always expressing your opinion. In your past life you must have been a wild animal.'
> 'I can't remember,' I quipped. 'And in any case, I thought you no longer believed in life after death?'
> 'I don't. At least I don't believe that everybody's up there, floating around on clouds. But I do believe that we come back as something.' Then she chuckled. 'God in heaven, when I come back I'll haunt a lot of people.'

Richter told her, during the rehearsals for *Seven Sinners*, that by the end of the year, Paris would be occupied by the Nazis. She believed him, and sent a cable to Erich Maria Remarque, which was just as well, for he was able to leave France merely days before the Germans moved in. Within weeks, he had installed himself at Marlene's Hollywood home, no longer a lover but one of several refugees. Rudolf Sieber, Tamara, Hans Jaray, and the novelist Thomas Mann all arrived in America at around the same time . . . and all had been rescued by Marlene's money.

In *Seven Sinners* Marlene played Bijou Blanche, a brash but adorable chanteuse who entertains *matelots* in a rough and ready South Seas dive, and who is never happier than when they are fighting over her. Tay Garnett, who had recently directed Jean Harlow in *China Seas*, had already picked Broderick Crawford to play one of the leads but he was looking for a suitable 'tough guy' for the other. Ostensibly, he assigned this task to Marlene and she selected John Wayne, who was then contracted to another company. *Seven Sinners* was a hit at the box office, though nowhere near as successful as *Destry*. Wedged in between the bar-room brawls, the *double entendres* and John Wayne's already inimitable drawl were three songs by Frank Loesser and Friedrich Hollander. One was the catchy 'You Can Bet Your Life the Man's in the Navy' which Marlene never recorded commercially, more's the pity. Another was 'I Fall Overboard'. The third song, the unbelievably dreary 'I've Been in Love Before', rated Number 14 in Marlene's list of favourite songs. The press too were enthusiastic about the film. The *New York Herald Tribune* reported, 'If anything, Dietrich is better than she was in *The Blue Angel*.' Bosley Crowther, writing for the *New York Times*, a publication not always favourable to Marlene in the past, said:

Miss Dietrich's Frenchy in *Destry* was an Arno sketch of countless sultry bar-room belles. Her Bijou Blanche in *Seven Sinners* is a delightful subtle spoof of all the Sadie Thompsons and Singapore Sals that have stirred the hot blood of cool customers south and east of Manila Bay. If Miss Dietrich and her comedies were both just a little broader, Mae West would be in the shade . . .

Marlene's next few films, unfortunately, were not quite so memorable. *The Flame of New Orleans*, produced by Joe Pasternak and the first American film directed by the French exile, René Clair, had Marlene playing an adventuress posing as an aristocrat. She later accused Clair of being bad-tempered and autocratic and she despised her co-star, Bruce Cabot. The only enjoyable moment, she said, had come when she had sung 'Sweet as the Blush of May', accompanying herself at the piano. *Manpower*, directed by Raoul Walsh, was slightly better because she acted opposite Edward G. Robinson and George Raft, although when she turned up at the studio to film a test she tripped over a cable and cracked a bone in her left leg. Incredibly, she did not go to hospital. Her friend Herbert Marshall, who had lost a leg during World War One, gave her therapeutic advice and demonstrated how not to limp. Marlene finished the film but it was not a success. There was also the inevitable distraction early in 1941 when Jean Gabin arrived in Hollywood to fulfil a contract with Darryl F. Zanuck.

Gabin's recollections of his wartime activities were sufficient to move Marlene to tears. Since their last meeting he had been working on minesweepers. Once, whilst he had been returning from leave to rejoin his regiment at Cherbourg, he had narrowly missed being blown up with his car. Prior to this he had put his life at risk by smuggling a contingent of Jewish children out of Paris and across the Maginot Line. The biographer Charles Higham had described Gabin and Remarque as 'the two men who, in one case physically and the other intellectually, penetrated her psyche most deeply'. My friend Roger Normand, who knew all three, verified this. Marlene herself was more to the point when discussing Gabin with the journalist Carlos Clarens: 'Gabin had the most beautiful loins I have ever seen in a man . . . that final point in male beauty where the torso joins the hips.' She also credited herself with teaching him English, even if most of her time was taken up with cooking and playing the role of housekeeper. She wrote in *Marlene D.*

> My circle comprised all the uprooted French people who had lost hope. I was mother, cook, translator and adviser to them all. Cooking for them brought me great joy. My mother-in-law sent me an Austrian recipe book. Prior to this we ate hamburgers, sitting in drugstores surrounded by boxes of Tampax and deodorant. I was happier cooking than I was maintaining my so-called 'legendary' image. For me, cooking was a therapy. My greatest goal in life was perfection, patience my greatest virtue! My speciality was boiled beef with vegetables. I didn't like pot-roasts. That needs to be carved by a man, and I hated asking my guests to work! As for Gabin, he was out of his depth, clinging to me like an orphan to his adoptive mother. Mind you, I have to say that mothering him night and day delighted me so much . . .

Jean Gabin was revered by the French not just for his considerable acting talents, but because he had never pretended to be anything but 'a man's man and a man of the people'. Like his former mistress, Mistinguett, and like Erich Maria Remarque, he was mean, moody and unpredictable. Unlike Remarque, he was earthy and uneducated, but not illiterate. He hated snobs, bigots, and Hollywood in particular because he thought it combined the two, and he was overtly fond of what the French referred to as 'an artist's desire to play to the gallery'. These traits made him more sexually potent to his female fans than every one of his contemporaries and many men admired him who would not normally have done so. He had also inherited more than a little of Mistinguett's jealousy: one source reported that he only left Marlene after seeing her flirting with John Wayne on the set of their film *The Spoilers*. This is untrue. Patriotism, not jealousy, separated her from the man who is reputed to have been one of the four most important men in her life:

> One day, Gabin decided to join up with the Free French. I understood why he wanted to fight. After all, I was his mother, his sister, his friend ... and much, much more. I accompanied him to the port in New York, and we swore we would remain friends for ever. Gabin left on a destroyer bound for Morocco, and after I joined the American Army we lost track of each other for several years. I was so terribly worried about him ...

The Spoilers, Marlene's second film with John Wayne, saw her cast as Cherry Mallotte, the owner of an Alaskan gin-palace. Again, there were hints of *Destry* with the rough-and-tumble bar-room scraps, and in the hard-bitten saloon singer. The film also starred Randolph Scott, who later that year teamed up with her and Wayne again for *Pittsburgh*.

'The scripts were terrible, and some of the people who acted with me were even more terrible.'

'Even John Wayne?' I posed.

'No, not John Wayne,' she said. 'He and I had a lot of fun. I also got to like George Raft – we became quite good friends. But the others! It wouldn't be fair for me to mention names ... Well, I suppose I could say Bruce Cabot. That man was so vain, and he couldn't even read his lines, let alone remember them. And I didn't like René Clair either. He was a big-head.'

'Is that why you wanted to leave Hollywood, then, to return to Europe?' I asked. 'Because the films were so bad?'

'No,' she said. 'We were at war! Well, Europe was. It didn't mean a thing to the people in Hollywood that young men were fighting and getting killed. Everybody seemed to be living on a cloud. Nobody cared.'

Marlene enjoyed making *The Lady is Willing* in 1941 with Fred MacMurray and Aline MacMahon. It was a sparkling comedy directed by Mitchell Leisen, with whom she got on well.

'It was a well known fact all over Hollywood that Mitch was gay, but he was very respectable with it, if you know what I mean. Mind you, that never stopped us from pulling his leg by kidding him about the boys in the darkroom! Whilst I was making the film, I had a nasty fall and had to have my leg in plaster for a while, and whilst I was recovering I wrote some special words to "The Boys in the Backroom". One day, Mitch was feeling down in the dumps because somebody had written something bad about him in a newspaper. We cheered him up by arranging a surprise party. When he came into the room it was all in darkness. Then somebody switched the light on, and I did the song. You must include it in the book because I think the words are more interesting than the original!'

Marlene sent me the cassette a few days later, and listening to it makes me regret that I never got round to hearing some of the other 'alternative' lyrics she wrote.

See what the boys in the darkroom have done
To save us from having to spell!
See what the boys in the classroom have done,
To tell you we're wishing you well!
Perhaps we should have brought a present,
Or baked a cake with candles all aflame!
But me and the boys in the cloakroom resist
To say, 'Though we'd kill,
We'll work for you still!
The lady is willing . . . though lame!'
And we all know no diamond garters,
With rubies, and the drawing of a dame,
Could say what the boys in the backroom all said:
'That squip was our pup! His beer was our hop!
The boss-man was tops in the game!'
And now we eat, so come on over,
We're drinking to your glory and your fame,
For us and the boys in the backroom are done!
That's all of the pitch! In honour of Mitch!
Best son-of-a-bitch in the game!

Marlene's maxim at the time was, 'If the director's humane, I react accordingly!' She portrayed Elizabeth Madden, a Broadway sensation who raises an abandoned baby girl – until she realizes that it is a boy! – and one scene in the film required her to cry. If Mitchell Leisen's later claims that Marlene could 'weep hysterically on cue' were true, the ruse did not work in this instance. Marlene sprayed a special fluid into her eyes, did the scene, and spent several days with a violent headache.

Within a few months, however, the tears would be very real, for she had asked Universal's permission to leave Hollywood for a while to sing to the troops overseas.

For Marlene, life would never be the same again.

6

'When We Are Marching Through the Mud and Cold'

Lili Marlene grows out of my ears – I can't hear it any more.

Towards the end of 1942 Marlene was invited to work for the OSS (Office of Strategic Services), singing American songs with German lyrics on a number of shortwave broadcasts to the Third Reich. These performances were different from anything she had ever done before. Each song was chosen meticulously and delivered so intensely that she often broke down on air.

Eleven of these numbers were recorded the following year, though they remained elusive until the late Fifties when they were released on an album with the German version of 'Lili Marlene'. Two of them – 'Miss Otis Regrets' and 'Annie Doesn't Live Here Any More' were included on Marlene's list of favourite songs. Not every song, however, was a *chanson-réaliste*. 'Must I Go?' was a lullaby which she had first performed in 1930 and it had also appeared in some prints of *Blonde Venus*. Some years later Elvis Presley would sing it as 'Wooden Heart'. And 'The Surrey with the Fringe on Top' had been simply vibrant with joie-de-vivre.

I told her, 'What surprised me was the fact that all the songs had English titles.'

'I know,' she cut in. 'And I sang them in German. I know what you're going to say. Did they contain anything which would upset Hitler? Of course they did, though nobody would be able to tell, today. And we couldn't be bothered to give them German titles.'

Performing on the radio was however not enough for a woman who had given up her country on account of the Nazis. For two years she had pleaded with Abe Lastfogel of the American Entertainments Organisation (the United States equivalent of ENSA) to be allowed to sing to the troops overseas and, in March 1943, her request was granted, though she was prevented from leaving the United States for a whole year because of film commitments. *Follow the Boys* was a star-studded extravaganza meant to boost the morale of the American soldiers. Vera Zorina and George Raft played the leads and Maria Montez, Dinah Shore, Andy Devine, the Andrews Sisters, Sophie Tucker, Lon Chaney Junior and even the pianist, Artur Rubinstein, appeared as themselves. In her sketch Marlene was sawn in half by two GIs, supervised by magician Orson Welles. The second film was one of her most popular – *Kismet*.

It has been alleged that when Marlene signed the contract for *Kismet*, the comparatively low fee of $100,000 was for this and another film, one which she never made. It has been further suggested that she used the $50,000 to help finance her wartime tours. If so, it was money well spent. *Kismet* was an extremely colourful fantasy adventure, set in the days of Old Baghdad. Marlene portrayed Jamilla, the queen of the Grand Vizier's harem. The Hays Office actually prohibited the use of the word 'harem' in the film, though it did crop up from time to time amongst the publicity handouts. Playing opposite her was the British actor, Ronald Colman. One of the production's highlights was Marlene's 'exotic' dancing ... little more, in fact, than a series of merged-together shots, as Garbo had done in *Mata Hari*. Even so, the ploy worked remarkably well. Her legs were given four coats of golden paint, her fingernails were painted pink, and she wore a top-knot wig which made her several inches taller than her co-star. The Hays Office also prevented her from showing her navel and even ordered a pantie line to be seen under her flimsy silk costumes so that she did not appear naked. The two songs from *Kismet*, though suited to the oriental locations, seemed so wrong to her

that she refused to sing them. From now on, there would be no
more 'factory' songs for Marlene. Her repertoire would be chosen
with the same precision as a connoisseur selecting fine wines. She
had already performed the Jean Sablon creation, 'Je tire ma
révérence', on the radio several times.

> 'Je tire ma révérence, et m'en vais au hasard par les routes de France
> . . . de France et de Navarre . . . Whenever I sang that song, I
> always sang it as my salute to France, the country I have loved more
> than any other. Did you like the original song by Sablon?'
>   'Your version was more sincere,' I told her. 'You did so much for
> France during the war. You put your own life on the line, like
> Joséphine Baker and Edith Piaf. That's why General de Gaulle
> awarded you the *Légion d'Honneur*.'

Marlene knew that it was useless arguing with me on that score,
for I loved France as much as she did. The entertainer Marie
Dubas spent the early part of the war in South America, for no
other reason than that she had been born a Jew. Mistinguett's
ship, half-way across the Atlantic when war was declared,
narrowly missed being hit by a torpedo. From then on, the great
star, worked behind the scenes helping the Resistance. Joséphine
Baker, in poor health, kept up her work for British Intelligence.
Edith Piaf had sung for her boys from Belleville in Stalag III in
Germany. By posing for photographs with the boys and later
having the shots enlarged and mounted on to false identity papers
she had enabled more than two hundred men of her friends to
escape. Another chanteuse, Lucienne Boyer, had helped large
numbers of British parachutists to land in France. In 1965 when
Marlene had played a 'farewell' concert at the Théâtre des
Champs-Elysées she had paid tribute to these entertainers, and all
the other unsung French heroes by tearfully announcing, 'You
have made me cry. I admired you for your courage during the war,
and I love you very much.'
   Before leaving for Europe, however, to sing to the troops,
Marlene had to contend with two personal matters. Rudolf
Sieber had decided to settle in California with Tamara Matul.
Marlene bought them a chicken farm in the San Fernando Valley,
where Rudolf would live happily for another thirty years, but

always declining to give interviews. Maria also moved out of Marlene's Hollywood home, now that she had aspirations of a career on the legitimate stage, not however as Dietrich's daughter but as an actress in her own right. Max Reinhardt had established an acting school in Hollywood and she enrolled under the name of Maria Marlowe. Reinhardt, it appears, had completely forgotten that her mother had once turned up at his Berlin studio for an audition. After several weeks of tough rehearsals she appeared in Keith Winter's *The Shining Hour*, not as Maria Marlowe, on account of there already being a Julia Marlowe, but as Maria Manton. The critics were far kinder to her than they had been to her mother of late. The Reinhardt philosophy was that talent made a star, and not good looks and sex-appeal, which probably explains why his distinguished acting school had great trouble adapting to the artificialities of the film capital. Maria, like her mother, was a survivor, and when the Reinhardt School became the Geller Workshop she stayed on to appear with some success in Lillian Hellman's *The Little Foxes* and Sidney Howard's *The Silver Chord*.

Marlene is said to have been against Maria's marriage to Dean Goodman, a young actor-director who was also the secretary of Maria Ouspenskaya, the oldest actress in Hollywood at that time, and hailed by many critics as the ugliest. Goodman was also alleged to be gay, and if he and Marlene shared a few stilted telephone conversations they are not thought to have met. She did not attend the wedding, and afterwards only visited Maria when Goodman was away from home, usually in a furniture van. The marriage ended in divorce soon afterwards.

Early in February 1944 when Marlene was in Europe, she was made aware of a confidential list published by BBC's Dance Music Committee, upon which were printed seven names under the heading 'Collaboration Artistes and their Material'. In effect, this meant that the recordings of Charles Trenet, Mistinguett, Maurice Chevalier, Alfred Cortot and Lucienne Boyer could not be played over the British airwaves. [The other two names were Sacha Guitry and Doctor Mengelberg]. Marlene could not vouch for the rest of these people but she was very upset that Maurice Chevalier had been branded a traitor.

I sent Marlene a photocopy of the BBC list, though it seems she had a copy already:

'Chevalier was a decent man. I mean, he might have done things out of stupidity, but never because he was a traitor – and I know what it's like to have people spreading rumours . . .'

'He was arrested by the Perigueux maquis in 1944, because of what Pierre Dac said,' I explained. 'And Joséphine Baker caused him a lot of trouble. Whilst she was ill in hospital he went to see her. She accused him of being a traitor. A lot of people said that he paid money to get himself off the hook, but that wasn't true at all. You'll see that when you read my book.'

'I tried desperately to get in touch with him,' Marlene said, and the sadness in her voice was only too obvious. 'I tried and I tried, but it was impossible. Nobody knew where he was.'

'He was hiding with friends in the Dordogne,' I replied. 'One of them was Félix Paquet, the man we spoke about.'

'The man who jumped out of the window and killed himself?' she sighed. 'I didn't know that. But they cleared Chevalier, didn't they – and isn't that all that matters?'

In April 1944 the USO assigned Marlene to head a hastily put together entertainments package which included Jack Snyder, Lynn Mayberry and a young comedian named Danny Thomas. A devout Roman Catholic of Lebanese parentage, in spite of his real name, Amos Jacobs, Thomas had begun his career as a radio actor in Chicago and had quickly progressed to Broadway. Although most of his success would come after the war, with roles in the remake of *The Jazz Singer* and *I'll See You in My Dreams* and in his own television series, Thomas once said that the happiest moments were when he was touring with Marlene. They developed a close friendship that endured by way of the telephone until the comedian's death in 1991, when he was almost eighty. Danny Thomas had been the California contact mentioned several times by Marlene in our conversations. She is also said to have been fond of his family: of his three children Marlo was a well-known actress and his son Tony was partly responsible for a number of cult American comedy series, including *The Golden Girls* and *Soap*. In *Marlene Dietrich's ABC* she wrote:

Danny Thomas is my friend. He is my teacher in the art of making people laugh . . . people who not only don't want to laugh, but who would prefer not being there watching you. He can drum better on two dirty helmets than many can on the best pair of bongo drums. . . .

During the USO tour, Danny Thomas acted as Master of Ceremonies. Marlene, in case of capture, wore the uniform of honorary colonel. After brief stop-offs in Greenland and the Azores – and a hair-raising flight in a dilapidated C-54 which made everyone but Marlene airsick – the party touched down at Casablanca, then moved on to their first engagement, the Algiers Opera House. Joséphine Baker's, Damia's and Tino Rossi's earlier attempts to entertain the rowdy soldiers had been greeted with orange peel and had failed dismally. Not so Marlene's, which was greeted with cheers and screams – there were even reports of young men swooning.

One evening a bomb was dropped in a suburb of Algiers, causing a power failure. Marlene was half-way through 'Symphonie', the song written for her by Georges Tabet, and instinctively the two thousand or so GIs took out their flashlights and directed them on the stage. At the end of her spot, by which time the power had been returned, she played them a few classical airs on the musical saw. To do this correctly, of course, she had to sit on a stool, hoist up her skirts, and place the instrument between her knees. According to Danny Thomas, 'Everyone got down on all fours to look up into paradise!' The next night Marlene's hotel was hit by a bomb, but she carried on as though nothing untoward had happened.

The next stage of the tour took the party to Italy. On the journey, in order to get away from her sick friends, Marlene went into the cockpit and asked the pilot if she could land the plane. Later she insisted upon visiting those areas worst hit by the shelling and gave impromptu performances from the back of army trucks, oblivious to the danger. Danny Thomas commented that she was greeted each time with 'an orgasmic cry of humans on heat', and that her most requested song was 'The Boys in the Backroom'. In September 1944 there was a brief visit to London, where she stayed at the Savoy and disappointed the media by refusing to wear anything except her uniform.

In London, she was told of the exploits of the French singer Léo Marjane, a pretty blonde who had introduced a famous song called 'La chapelle au clair de lune' ('The chapel in the moonlight'). shortly before the outbreak of war, Marjane had sung 'J'ai donné mon âme au diable' ('I Gave My Soul to the Devil'), a theory she was now putting into practice during the German Occupation of Paris by flaunting herself as the mistress of von Stuchnabel.

> 'That woman disgusted me,' Marlene said. 'She should have been shot. She used to ride around the streets of Paris with that man in an open-topped carriage . . .'
>
> 'Her big song at the time was "Je suis seule ce soir". It was regarded as an open invitation to her Nazi lover when she sang it on the German-controlled radio,' I explained.
>
> Marlene bellowed down the phone. 'But if you like Léo Marjane, you need to have your head examined . . .'
>
> 'She also sang "Lili Marlene" in French,' I furthered. 'Which reminds me – I checked your list of favourite songs and I was surprised to find that "Lili Marlene" wasn't there.'
>
> 'And shall I tell you why?' she shouted. 'It's been on every record that's been out. In every country they always have "Lili Marlene" and "Where Have All the Flowers Gone?" in German. "Sag mir wo die Blumen sind?" I don't like the German words at all – and "Lili Marlene" grows out of my ears! I can't hear it any more, for God's sake!'

The German lyrics to 'Lili Marlene' had been written by Hans Leip during World War One, at a time when he had been on guard-duty outside the barracks of Berlin. He had been hopelessly in love with two local girls – one named Lili, the other Marleen – hence the title. The poem had been rediscovered, set to music by Norbert Schulze and given to his lover – the Swedish singer, Lale Anderson, who had recorded it in 1941. In Germany, Goebbels had attempted to have the song banned, but he had been thwarted by the Wehrmacht radio station in Belgrade, who had played it several times each day for the benefit of the German troops. In England the song had been recorded by Vera Lynn and Anne Shelton. In France it had become a big hit for Suzy Solidor, known in Europe as 'The girl with the flaxen hair', and another bone of contention as far as Marlene was concerned.

Born in St Malo in 1901, Suzy Solidor had arrived in Paris thirty years later intent only on opening an antique shop. When business had proved bad she had been encouraged by the painter Domergue to take up singing as a profession, and she had turned her shop into a night club, La Vie Parisienne – an establishment which some had considered an extension of the Third Reich. Many famous artists had painted her portrait – two hundred or more – and she had often appeared on stage surrounded by them, dressed like a sailor. Her rich baritone voice, coupled with the fact that she was unashamed of telling everyone she was a lesbian, quickly earned her a cult homosexual following, and she is said to have inadvertently swollen the pink-triangle ranks in concentration camps due to the large number of Nazi agents-provocateurs alleged to have frequented her club. Manouche, my link between Suzy, Mistinguett and a number of others, told me, 'When Suzy belted out a song, there were so many of her pictures around her that half the audience got seasick! She also did an imitation of Dietrich which was ten times better than the one Dietrich did of herself!'

The song in question was the superb 'La légende des étoiles', which Camille François and the orchestra leader Walberg had written for Marlene in 1934, hot on the heels of her success with their 'Moi, je m'ennuie'.

> Il s'embarqua sur un bateau,
> Avec les autres matelots,
> C'était un marin qu'avait vu d'la peine,
> Qu'avait d'la déveine,
> Vogue les voiles . . .

Marlene often sang 'La légende des étoiles' but her recording of the song may be one of those allegedly lost or destroyed by the Germans during the Occupation. Alas, we may never know. Her introduction to 'Lili Marlene' during her concert tours, however, was almost as famous as the song itself:

Here is a song that is very close to my heart. I sang it during the war. I sang it for three long years – through Africa, Sicily and Italy. Through Alaska, Greenland and Iceland. Through

England and France, through Belgium and Holland, all through Germany to Czechoslovakia . . .

'I'll never believe that you actually hated "Lili Marlene",' I told her, more astonished by this particular revelation than I had been by most of the others. 'Never in a million years!'

'Well,' she confessed, at length, 'maybe I did like the song at first. Then, when I returned to France after the war, I heard it being sung by Suzy Solidor . . .'

'I know she's said to have collaborated with the Germans during the Occupation,' I said, 'but nothing was ever proved.'

'Well,' she grunted. 'I suppose everybody's entitled to their opinion. I didn't like her and I didn't like "Lili Marlene" after she'd ruined it – okay? And I don't particularly like the German text to the song – it doesn't have the last verse, because it was not translatable. Don't you agree?'

I told Marlene that I preferred the English lyrics which she had sung to the song to the ones that began 'Underneath the lamplight . . .' and she gently rebuked me.

' "Underneath the lamplight . . ." ' she repeated. 'That's exact! At the end of the German version it says, "If I should die, who will stand with you underneath the lantern?" That is the whole idea of the song because it's a war song. And seeing as you don't understand any German, I'll explain. The song begins, *"Für der Kaserne . . .* in front of the *Kaserne . . ."* What does that mean, in English?'

'Barracks,' I replied.

Marlene continued, 'Okay, barracks. The men in the song, they are going to war – the bastards! They are going to be soldiers, so they are sent to the barracks where they train to fight, where they wait for the call to the Front. The soldier says, "Who will stand with you under the lantern?" Then he adds, "If I should die . . . if something bad should happen to me?" Well, when I recorded the song in English, they didn't want me to sing that last verse, so I sang something else. Shall we sing the last verse, you and I?'

'You want me to sing with you?' I gasped.

'Sure – why not?'

> Give me a rose to show how much you care,
> Tie to its stem a lock of golden hair,
> Maybe tomorrow, you'll feel blue,
> And then will come a love that's new,
> My love for you will ease my might,
> I'm warm again, my heart is light . . .
> It's you, Lili Marlene!

'Well,' Marlene chortled. 'We didn't get it exactly right – but you get my point? There's nothing there about him dying. When I received your script, I checked with a friend who lives in California. He explained that the soldier never said the bit about the lantern in the original translation of the song. And I never liked the German text either. That's why I didn't put the song on the list.'

'And what about the beautiful costumes you wore, whilst you were singing to the soldiers?' I asked. 'Was that against your wishes, too?'

'Most of the time I wore my soldier's uniform,' she returned. 'But you have to remember, David, that some of those young men hadn't seen a woman for months – and I don't mean that there was more on offer than my songs, either. Everybody expected to see me looking as I had in my films, wearing jewels and furs – and most of those I only borrowed, you know. They had to be handed back afterwards. I would rather have performed in a simple black dress, like Piaf, or like that other singer of yours – you know, the one who put everybody in pain with the God-awful song about the woman who wanted to kill herself. Who in their right mind wanted to listen to that when we were at war?'

Marlene was referring to Damia, who had recorded 'Sombre dimanche' in 1936. Translated into English during the war it had become known as 'The Budapest Suicide Song'. The version by Artie Shaw had been banned by many radio stations during the war as too morbid.

To the strains of 'Lili Marlene' and 'The Boys in the Backroom', Marlene's jeep followed the American Fifth Army all the way up the Italian peninsula. After the Liberation of Paris she became the protégé of General George Patton, the stern-faced commander who recognized a fearlessness on a par with his own. He presented her with a rare, pearl-handled pistol with which to defend herself, or with which to commit suicide, should she be captured, and promptly packed her off to entertain the front-line troops. Many of these were hard, unprincipled individuals who had a pretty good idea that they would not come out of the war alive and few knew how to behave in front of a lady – not that this ever bothered Marlene. 'I'm just one of the boys,' she said. 'Don't give me any special privileges.'

Whilst in Bari she contracted a severe bout of pneumonia. This was so bad that one of her appointed bodyguards summoned a priest. For several days she was despaired of, but her life was saved by Sir Alexander Fleming, who had recently discovered penicillin and Marlene agreed to be one of his guinea pigs. Up until his death in 1955 she would never forget his kindness. In 1944 she arranged for his wartime rations to be augmented by a regular supply of eggs, always sent by the basket, and this would continue for ten years. She also asked Carroll Richter to supply him with his horoscope, which is not as ridiculous as it seems, for Fleming, like Marlene, believed in such things.

On 6 June 1944, it was Marlene who broke the news of the D-Day landings to some five thousand American troops stationed in southern Italy, the following day leading them into Rome to scenes of mass hysteria in which her jeep disappeared under a blanket of flowers and she was almost mobbed. Her military escort, Lieutenant-Colonel Robert Armstrong described her as 'an incredibly brave lady, just like one of the boys in her Eisenhower jacket, boots and helmet'. And, of course, she gave them 'Lili Marlene'.

Ten days later, she was back in New York, weak, but raring to go as she attended a Ladies' Day war-bond rally in Wall Street. Soon afterwards she returned to Hollywood, appearing at the Hollywood Canteen, the famous institution founded by John Garfield and Bette Davis, which raised millions of dollars towards the war effort. One could be greeted at the door by Dietrich and Betty Grable, and served lunch by Hedy Lamarr. Alternatively, one could sit next to the Andrews Sisters for a weekly game of bingo, or sip soup whilst watching Orson Welles perform his magic act. Johnny Carson revealed, a few years ago, 'I was just a skinny serviceman from Nebraska, and here I was surrounded by all these beautiful movie-stars. Suddenly, I was holding Marlene Dietrich in my arms, and we were dancing. It was unreal. Today, I can't recall a single word she said, but I've never forgotten that moment.'

Later on, in spite of her obvious ill-health, Marlene danced an incredibly frenzied jitterbug with a GI, something I would never have believed, had I not been sent the scrap of newsreel, which also included a slightly risqué sketch between Marlene, Jimmy Durante, and a host who was referred to as 'Mister Moore':

MARLENE: Reach for the sky, you coyotes! It's me, Deadeye Dietrich, the sheriff.

MOORE: Jeepers, it's the arm of the law.

DURANTE: The legs ain't bad, either. . . .

MARLENE: Say, where do you boys hail from?

MOORE: I hail from the pan-handle. . . .

MARLENE: I believe that. Your pan does look as though it's been handled! And you, Two-Gun Durante, tell me the truth. Did you ever shoot a man?

DURANTE: Did I ever shoot a man? Just take a look at my nose.

MARLENE [*screams*]: You're supposed to put the notches in the gun!

Early in September 1944, Marlene returned to Europe. Her first engagement was in Iceland, where she sang twenty songs, before playing Schubert on the musical saw. A few weeks later, she flew to Paris for a brief reunion with Maurice Chevalier, who had been vindicated of 'nefarious activities' during the Occupation. The singer was deeply moved, writing in his journal, 'Marlene should be ever-blessed for what she has done for me.' She then travelled by jeep across Holland and Germany, but when Patton's convoy headed back towards Belgium, the going became tougher than anyone had anticipated. As she she wrote:

We encountered no problems crossing Germany, but when we reached Aix-la-Chapelle we went down with crabs, which I thought was something you could only get from each other. They also said crabs didn't walk, but mine did. Then one day we were told that the ladies amongst us would be given permission to bathe 'in return for certain favours' . . . In other words, if we allowed the men to watch us. We didn't mind that because the prospect of soap and water enabled us to forget our shyness. It didn't make any difference to the crabs, they didn't mind moving house, and we eventually got used to them. In Aix-la-Chapelle there were also rats, indefatigable rats with frozen feet which scuttled over your face. That Christmas of 1944 was a lousy one. I kept asking myself how Christian men could adopt their term 'turn the other cheek', when we were at war. The Jews were more convincing, for the Old Testament said, 'An eye for an eye, and a tooth for a tooth'. Since that time I have renounced the existence of a God, or of any 'guiding light'. Goethe said, 'If God did make this world, then he should take another look at his formula.'

By far the most harrowing ordeal of Marlene's life took place during the harsh winter of 1944-5 when she was caught up in the Battle of the Bulge. Several days before Christmas the Germans, under the direction of von Rundstedt, unexpectedly launched a full-scale offensive against the United States First Army in the Ardennes. This was their biggest attack since Normandy, von Rundstedt's plan being to capture the Liège communications centre, thereby driving the Allies back to the coast. Within a few days the enemy drove a twenty-five-mile wedge into the American positions, though not without severe loss of life. The atrocious weather conditions had only helped von Rundstedt, but a few days before Christmas the skies cleared, giving four thousand Allied aircraft the opportunity to attack. On 27 December, Marlene's forty-fourth birthday, the 4th Armoured Division of Patton's Third Army made contact with the defenders of Bastogne, ending one of the most heroic episodes of the entire war. For eight days the American 101st Airborne Division, supported by a unit from the 10th Armoured Division, held out against the Germans who encircled them. Under the command of Brigadier-General McAuliffe, they successfully dissipated several attacks from the enemy, destroying 144 tanks and taking 800 prisoners. Marlene, stuck in the midst of this mêlée, was told by a German prisoner of war that a German general, ironically named Sepp Dietrich, had put a price on her head. She took this in her stride and, when the area in which she was stationed suddenly found itself almost totally surrounded by Dietrich's army, she insisted that there would be no star treatment.

In 1990 a book entitled *Millergate* was published in Britain. In his attempts to prove that the orchestra leader Glenn Miller had not died in the plane-crash of 1944, the author Wilbur Wright, had suggested that Marlene was rescued from her plight in the Ardennes by David Niven and an unnamed companion who could have been Miller himself. I sent Marlene the publicity printout that preceded the book's publication, and she called to discuss it:

'What's all this about Glenn Miller, all this rubbish about him still being alive after all these years? It says here, "Why did David Niven go with Marlene Dietrich to the Ardennes?" '

'The author was on the television the other day, and he claims that a lot of people think he's still alive. One suggestion is that David Niven went to the Ardennes when you were there during the war, and that Miller was with him – in other words, he wasn't killed in the plane crash. Apparently, Miller was still with him when he rescued you.'

'But that's not true!' Marlene cried. 'I didn't know Glenn Miller. David Niven, yes. And why the title?'

'Millergate's a pun on Watergate. The author says there's been a cover-up. His research points to the fact that Miller probably wasn't a passenger on the plane. There are suggestions that the airfield was closed, and some documents were even forged.'

'And who the hell is interested in reading all that? David Niven wasn't the one who saved me in the Ardennes. It was the other young man, on the field that was full of mines. He came to pick me up. He was with the French troops and there was a big discussion who should go first. So I said to him, "I'll go first. You're young – you don't want to die." And to answer your next question – no, it wasn't James Gavin. This man was with the French troops. His name was Jean-Pierre Aumont. He was the man who saved my life.'

Jean-Pierre Aumont, now a famous actor, certainly did escort Marlene across the minefield, after General Gavin personally commandeered a Flying Fortress to parachute him and his men into the danger zone. The story is supported by Max Colpet who, in his memoirs, remembered how Gavin strode up to Marlene and knelt humbly at her feet before whisking her off to Paris in his jeep.

In spite of her ordeal, in April 1945 she took another calculated risk when she visited Belsen in an attempt to locate her sister Elizabeth. One may only imagine how dreadful this must have been: she was forced to sift through some of the remains in the burial trenches and many of the bodies could only be identified by the tattooed registration numbers on their arms. This took many hours, but after her ordeal Marlene found Elizabeth alive and reasonably well, if not a little under-nourished. Because of her Aryan looks, she had not been regarded as a prisoner, but as a hostage. Marlene at once took her back to Berlin, supervised a medical examination, and personally nursed her for several weeks.

Seemingly none the worse for her experience, Marlene spent several weeks visiting friends in Paris then, early in July 1945, she returned to New York. She was suffering from an infection of the jaw for which she had to undergo an operation. She was back on her feet, however, on 21 July to welcome home the Seventy-First Infantry. She was then told that General Gavin was in Paris and said to be missing her, so a few weeks later she rejoined him. It is not known for certain whether the pair actually became lovers, for as soon as Marlene reached Paris there was a reunion with Jean Gabin. This gave way to a cruel but probably accurate joke which drifted around the English-speaking section of the Parisian show-business circle. 'Why does Dietrich sing about Johnny? It's because the only real difference between her two men is a French letter.'

In September 1945, Marlene made what would be her last visit to Germany for fifteen years. She was met at Tempelhof Airport by her mother who, though she looked well, was anything but. Few people were interested in making Marlene's visit a joyous one, particularly when, after seeing the ruins of Berlin, she said, 'Germany deserves everything that's coming to her.' In another statement she said that the ordinary men and women of Germany were as much to blame for the Nazi atrocities as anyone, for they had, after all, elected their leaders. She also said, and probably meant it at the time, that after all the things she had seen and experienced in Europe, she would not be in any hurry to return to her Hollywood film career.

Leaving Berlin, Marlene travelled to Biarritz where she gave a lecture about her films to the students at the GI university. It was here that she received a telephone call, informing her that her mother had died, aged seventy-eight. Marlene made all the arrangements for the funeral, afterwards visiting some of Rudolf Sieber's relatives behind the Iron Curtain. If the photographs taken at the time show her smiling radiantly, then she was only putting on a brave face. She had adored her mother and her greatest regret was that she had been unable to get her out of Germany.

In Los Angeles, two years after the war, Marlene attended a

ceremony where she was awarded the Congress Medal of Freedom, the highest award any American civilian may receive. With it came a long, but meaningful citation:

> Miss Marlene Dietrich, civilian volunteer with the USO Camp Shows, performed meritorious service in support of military operations in North Africa, in Sicily and Italy from April 14 to June 16 1944, and in the North Atlantic Bases in Europe from 30 August 1944 to 13 July 1945, meeting a gruelling schedule of performances under battle conditions, during adverse weather and despite risk to her life. Though her health was failing, Miss Dietrich continued to bring pleasure and cheer to more than 500,000 American soldiers. With commendable energy and sincerity she immeasurably contributed to the welfare of troops in these theatres.

Perhaps the most important tribute of all, however, came from Marlene's beloved France. In New York, at a less public ceremony, the French ambassador, Henri Bonnet, presented her with the highly prestigious *Légion d'Honneur*. She was well on her way towards becoming an ambassador herself – for world peace – though she would never really shrug off the androgynous image formulated by Josef von Sternberg.

When I told Marlene *why* she was considered a great legend by her millions of admirers, she started to cry.

> 'The word superstar' is used too generally, these days,' I told her. 'If a man's got muscles and a hairy chest, he's got it made. If a woman's got nice tits and long legs, it doesn't matter if she can't act or sing. You weren't just an actress and a singer, Marlene. You were impeccably brave during the war, and you eased a lot of suffering by just being there. I saw a photograph once, taken during the war. You were signing your name in lipstick across this young soldier's chest, right over his heart. Can you remember that? And I'm sorry if I made you cry.'
>
> Marlene sniffled loudly. 'And you know, a few minutes later that young man died in my arms. God, I've never forgotten that. But those boys weren't just fans, David. They were comrades – and some of them knew that they were going to die. They knew it, and so did I. That's why I later sang 'Where Have All the Flowers Gone?' – for the ones who didn't come back.'

7

'Within the Ruins of Berlin'

I never watch any of my old films, and if I want to hear one of my
old songs . . . if it's really necessary . . . then I wait until I'm alone
and try to sing it to myself.

Marlene had met the writer Ernest Hemingway during one of her
frequent sea voyages from Europe to New York. Invited to dine at
the Captain's table, she had declined after observing that she
would be occupying the thirteenth place. Hemingway then
insisted upon making the number up to fourteen and she had
taken no persuading to change her mind. For some years she had
admired this man tremendously and, as with several others who
were as great in their respective fields as she was, she initially felt
very humble to be in his presence. This soon changed, of course,
and some time later she wrote, with tears in her eyes:

He was my Rock of Gibraltar. I fell in love with him at once –
I never stopped loving him. It was, however, only a platonic
love. I say that, for the love that Hemingway and I
experienced was pure and absolute – a love unencumbered by
doubt, and one which would last beyond the grave . . . if such
things were possible.

As the war drew to a close, Marlene spent a great deal of time with Hemingway and his wife, Mary, at the Ritz in Paris. These meetings gave rise to much gossip, of course, particularly when the tabloid press got hold of the story that Hemingway's most profound luxury was his evening bath, during which Marlene sat on a stool next to him 'crooning' his favourite songs. Nor did she object to him addressing her as 'my Kraut': her pet name for him was 'Papa'.

In her autobiography, Marlene had borrowed a term from her friend to describe her biographers:

'Biographers, biographers!' she told me. 'Everybody wrote about me – trying to work out what I was doing in bed, what I was eating, what I was thinking.'

'And did you write back to any of these people, after they'd sent you their books?' I asked.

'It would have been a waste of time!' she cried. 'The books were already written – and in any case, you can't tell these goddamned people anything. I just burned them. Hemingway had a word for them. He called them parasites. All they wanted to do was make money out of my name.'

She told me how upset she had been to receive Leslie Frewin's *Dietrich: The Story of a Star*, particularly as she had contacted him whilst he had been writing it and begged him not to proceed.

'I don't know if the book was good or bad because I never bothered reading it. But as to some of the other things that have been written about me, poor Hemingway would turn in his grave.'

I said, cautiously, 'You keep mentioning Hemingway. Is there anything special that you'd like to tell me about him?'

Marlene was adamant about one thing – whatever she and he had written in their years' long exchange of letters would remain locked in a bank vault for a long, long time and it was nobody's business but theirs what the hundreds of missives contained.

One evening, Marlene and Hemingway went to the cinema to see *Pays sans étoiles*, Georges Lacombe's most recent film starring that dashing young actor, Gérard Philipe. Her friend, Margo Lion, tagged along and all were stupefied not just by Philipe's acting talents, but by his intense physical beauty. Marlene insisted to Margo Lion that she would simply have to see him 'in the flesh', though no one was exactly sure what she meant by this. Her wish was granted a few weeks later, more or less, when the well known producer Jacques Hébertot invited her to a party where the actor was guest of honour. According to Roger Normand, it was love at first sight, although it is doubtful that there was any physical relationship between the two. Soon afterwards Philipe opened at the Théâtre Hébertot in a highly acclaimed production of Albert Camus's *Caligula*. Margo Lion played Caesonia and said in an interview, 'Gérard's beauty and youth knocked me sideways!' Marlene's fascination for the young man was, however, regarded as unhealthy by some of his friends, notably Raymond Radiguet, who many years before had been Jean Cocteau's under-age lover. He now showed a great deal of interest in Philipe himself, vying with Marlene, who over the next month sent him a seemingly endless supply of red roses and saw rather a lot of him backstage. She was also fascinated by Cocteau's new lover, the brilliant actor Jean Marais, probably the handsomest Frenchman aside from Gérard Philipe to have ever appeared on the screen. Then aged thirty-one, Marais escorted Marlene around Paris whenever Jean Gabin was unavailable. Within a year he would achieve world fame by playing the lead in Cocteau's *La belle et la bête* and Marlene would turn down the part of Death in *Orphée*. Even so Cocteau, whom she had met some years before in Hollywood, would remain a close friend for the rest of her life.

Another valuable friend, at least for the time being, was the film director Marcel Carné, whom Marlene met through Gabin. Carné had directed several of Gabin's pre-war films, though his most famous work had been *Les enfants du paradis*, starring Arletty and Jean-Louis Barrault. The film, it was alleged, had been made with some German backing, although if this was so, one wonders why Marlene would have shown any interest in its director. The second script for *Les enfants du paradis* had been supplied by the poet Jacques Prévert and the music by Joseph Kosma. What is not generally known is that by far their greatest collaboration, 'Les feuilles mortes' (translated into English as 'Autumn Leaves' and immortalized by Juliette Gréco, Yves Montand and Edith Piaf), was not written for any of these artists, but for Marlene. Prévert and Kosma offered it to her early in 1946, after she and Gabin had attended a performance of their ballet, *Le rendezvous*. Marlene took to the song at once because she believed that it suited her style at the time and she promised Prévert that she would record it.

She also told him that *Le rendezvous* had the makings of a good film – her first in the French language – and Gabin agreed to star opposite her, providing someone could furnish a suitable script.

Marlene began writing the script herself, aided by Prévert and supervised by Marcel Carné. Negotiations continued for several weeks and it was agreed that the project should be financed and co-produced by Pathé in France and RKO in Hollywood. Throughout these discussions, Marlene had held back from recording 'Les feuilles mortes' and quite suddenly relations between her and her co-scriptwriters became strained. Despite the fact that no one more so than herself had criticized directors for casting her as a whore, she asked Prévert to write her a scene where, upon getting out of a taxi cab, she paid the driver with a banknote that she extracted from her stocking top. Prévert refused to be responsible for presenting her in such an undignified manner, Gabin lost his temper and, because she only had eyes for him at the time, Marlene took his advice and cancelled the entire film. Needless to say, she also refused to record or even sing 'Les feuilles mortes', which is a great pity.

It has been suggested that after failing to bring Marlene and Gabin together in *Le rendezvous*, Marcel Carné offered them first refusal on *Les portes de la nuit* and that they chose to make *Martin Roumagnac* for Georges Lacombe instead. Undeterred, Carné had signed up an unknown actress, Nathalie Nattier, and the talents of two up-and-coming singer actors, Yves Montand and Serge Reggiani, both of whom had been launched by someone who would very soon become her best woman-friend, Edith Piaf.

'Marlene,' I asked. 'Did you enjoy making *Martin Roumagnac* with Jean Gabin?'

She spoke with extreme caution. 'Is it really the film that you're interested in, or the man?'

'Neither. I was just wondering why you only made one film in the French language.'

'The film was a big flop. Please don't ask me about it, or Gabin.'

Georges Lacombe's only claim to fame prior to working with Marlene was *Montmartre-sur-Seine*, Edith Piaf's first important feature film which he had directed in 1941. In *Martin Roumagnac* Marlene played an Australian pet-shop owner called

Blanche Ferrand. This explained her curious accent, which was reviled by the critics and, in time, by Gabin's legion of French admirers who flocked to see the film, only to come away disappointed. In spite of a strong supporting cast, including Daniel Gélin and Margo Lion, *Martin Roumagnac* was a flop, something which the ever-superstititious Marlene had anticipated, according to Manouche: 'There was this joke going around the set at the time, only it wasn't a joke, if you get my drift – those weren't pearls in Marlene's hair, but lumps of bird shit. She reckoned that working with all those damned birds only brought her bad luck, and that's the reason she lost Gabin.' Jean Marais told a completely different story, claiming that her obsession for Gabin was so intense that years after their split she would get him to stand with her in a doorway opposite Gabin's home, just to catch a fleeting glimpse of her *bel amour*. Knowing something of Marlene's character, I did not believe either tale.

Shortly after completing *Martin Roumagnac*, Marlene received a telephone call from Hollywood. Mitchell Leisen, the director of *The Lady is Willing*, offered her the role of Lydia, a rough and ready gypsy who comes to the aid of a crashed aviator and then joins British Intelligence as a secret agent in *Golden Earrings*. Marlene had vowed never to return to Hollywood and would have kept her word had it not been for the failure of the French film. She accepted Leisen's offer, partly because she was interested in starring opposite Ray Milland, but most of all because she needed the money.

She immediately set about 'designing' her own costumes for the film. Insisting upon authenticity, she visited several gypsy camps in and around Paris, including the one at Pantin, and even accepted their offer to spend several days living in a caravan so that she would get the feel of her new role. A few weeks later, she arrived in Hollywood and was horrified to learn that Leisen had already had the costumes made for the actress who was to play her double in the film. Marlene refused to have anything to do with them, so that one of the many faults of *Golden Earrings* is the fact that in some scenes, the costume in close up is not the same as the one being worn by her double in the long shots.

Marlene did not like working with Ray Milland and he is said to have hated her. According to the director's memoirs, during their first scene together when Marlene is eating stew, she swallowed the eye from a fish head, then made herself sick in front of him. The property department also provided dry ice so that the cooking pot she used appeared to be bubbling. But when the scene had to be re-shot the property man forgot to add the dry ice, and Marlene received second-degree burns to her hand. The production was further hampered by the major strike that hit Hollywood in 1947. Because no one was allowed to leave the film lot and cross the picket lines, Marlene had a bed set up in her dressing room and the rest of the crew and cast of *Golden Earrings* followed suit. On top of all this, Mitchell Leisen suffered a mild heart attack.

Some of Marlene's fans did not like her portrayal of Lydia, described by Charles Higham as 'a dirty, disgusting woman with thick, matted hair who underneath, is so terrifically glamorous that this dull, dreary English guy has to fall in love with her'. Even so, the film was a great success, so much so that there was some talk of Marlene and Milland doing another film together.

'That man was a pain to work with,' she admitted. 'The film was a big hit, but nothing in it was any good. "Golden Earrings" was never my song, either. Peggy Lee did it and it was a tremendous success. She's wonderful – not like some of the other American entertainers who think the world owes them a living. Did you know that she suffered from asthma, like your wife?'

'We met her once,' I said. 'After a concert. We had to help her up a long flight of steps from her dressing room to her car. There was an oxygen cylinder in the boot. In your book, you wrote that she was, "Honey-dripping singing, timing, phrasing, awakening no memories of other voices, but awakening all senses to a unique feast." '

'Well,' she said, 'that was exact. Did you know that she gave me the idea for "Go 'Way from My Window?" When she sang it, it was called "I'm Looking out the Window". But she sang it so beautifully that I could never sing the same words without feeling terribly, terribly guilty.'

For Marlene, 1947 was a year filled with perplexities and changes. With the events of the war forever embedded in her psyche and, at forty-six, a little too old to keep on playing the *femme-fatale*, or so some producers thought, though she was in fact more glamorous than ever, she was clearly at a crossroads in her career.

Perhaps the biggest changes were being effected in her personal life. Rudolf Sieber had been ensconced in his chicken farm with Tamara and though Marlene visited him often, she must have felt slightly uncomfortable in the other woman's presence. Tamara is said to have been extremely neurotic, and prone to fits of depression and rage. Also, there was no man in Marlene's life. Gabin had married and Remarque was in France, though still burning a candle for her. The neurotic writer had made up for not being with her by writing what many claim to be his best work, *Arch of Triumph*, which was a thinly disguised account of their close friendship. The book was made into a film in 1948, with Ingrid Bergman interpreting the role of Joan Madou. There was a somewhat mediocre re-hash of the plot several years later which the Americans turned into a television mini-series. It has also been suggested that Marlene was approached to play herself in the original film but that Remarque objected so strongly that she very quickly shelved the idea. Of her face, he had written, 'It is like a beautiful empty house waiting for the carpets and pictures. It had every possibility of becoming a palace or a brothel, depending upon whoever filled it . . .'

On Independence Day 1947, Maria married for the second time. Her husband was the twenty-five-year-old Italian-American stage designer, William Riva, whom she had met the previous year whilst tutoring acting and direction at New York's Fordham University. Marlene approved of the marriage this time but the couple politely declined any financial help from her, apart from a refrigerator, and set up home in an apartment on Third Avenue whilst saving for something better. Marlene was a frequent visitor, organizing everything as usual without being too pushy, and never too proud to put on a pair of overalls and pick up a paintbrush. The Rivas' first son, John Michael, was born during the summer of 1948, and headlines around the world immediately hailed Marlene as 'the world's most glamorous grandmother', a title which she would retain for many years before 'donating' it to Elizabeth Taylor. She also declared that a tawdry house constantly shaken by the passing elevated trains was no fit place to bring up a baby and shelled out more than $40,000 to buy them a four-storey house on the exclusive East Ninety-Fifth Street. Again, she organized the décor and even helped design the nursery.

According to some reports, Marlene was also said to be 'pining' to have an affair with Gérard Philipe, who had just scored an enormous hit playing what would today be described as a 'toy-boy' in Raymond Radiguet's superb *Le diable au corps*. On the strength of this, early in 1947 Ernst Lubitsch asked her advice about a proposed film based on *Der Rosenkavalier*, and she suggested Philipe for the role of Octavian, the Cavalier of the Silver Rose. She had purchased a copy of *Le diable au corps* and screened it constantly for her friends. Ernst Lubitsch was apparently unimpressed with Philipe's acting so on 30 November 1947 Marlene arranged for a special showing of the film at the Hollywood home of William Wyler, who had won an Oscar for directing *Mrs Miniver* in 1942. Marlene was hoping that with competition from MGM, Lubitsch would agree to giving Gérard Philipe a contract and she persuaded Wyler to invite 'the cream of Hollywood's directors', including her friend Billy Wilder, Otto Preminger and Edmund Goulding. Everyone arrived at Wyler's house except for Ernst Lubitsch. When the director inquired as to his whereabouts, he was told that he had died that afternoon of a heart attack. Marlene was so distressed that she shelved the Gérard Philipe project and everyone else in Hollywood very quickly forgot about him.

Marlene's next film was, again, from my point of view, her best since *The Scarlet Empress*:

> I told her, 'There is one song which you sang in *A Foreign Affair* which I consider belongs to the *réaliste* tradition.'
> ' "Within the Ruins of Berlin"?' she posed.
> 'Yes. Why did you never sing that one on the stage? It was good enough.'
> 'It was too personal,' she said. 'Singing it would only have brought back bad memories – not of the war, but of that film. Believe me, dear, it really was one headache from start to finish.'

A Foreign Affair, shot in 1947 and released by Paramount the following year, was the first of Marlene's two films directed by her friend Billy Wilder. Wilder had recently returned from Germany, where he had directed a startling if not deeply disturbing series of documentaries about the horrors of war – some of the scenes had featured close-ups of rotting corpses – and Wilder had scored a cinema 'first' by actually filming a death. Needless to say, as her hatred of the Nazis was almost legendary, Marlene was the director's first choice to play the central role of Erika von Schlütow, the former mistress of a high-ranking Nazi, who earns an easy living by singing in a Berlin night club. The script was by Charles Brackett and Richard Breen. It showed signs of Suzy Solidor and Léo Marjane, which is probably why Wilder had been reluctant to approach her initially, even though the whole project had been commissioned with her in mind.

'Billy Wilder knew that he was asking too much of me when he gave me the script to read – and at first I didn't want to do it. Then he showed me a test that he had made with another actress. I've forgotten her name.'

'Her name was June Havoc,' I said.

'Well, that doesn't matter,' she returned. 'When I saw the mess she'd made of the part I decided to do it myself. And then all the critics did their usual job of confusing the actress with the part.'

'You were a whore again?'

Marlene laughed. 'Aye-aye-aye! As far as they are concerned, I've always been a whore. What's new?'

The film was released in France as *La scandaleuse de Berlin*, hardly a title to enhance Marlene's reputation, for at the time she described her role not as a whore but as 'a poor girl who didn't have the means to afford a sofa, let alone a parlour'. The leading man was John Lund.

'I thought *A Foreign Affair* to be one of your best films,' I enthused. 'I agree, it must have been difficult playing the part of a woman like Erika von Schlütow but did you really detest the film?'

'I thought you would have been the last person to confuse me with the part I was playing,' she rebuked.

'I didn't mean that,' I said. 'I was thinking of all the things that had happened in Germany during the war . . .'

'But that had nothing to do with it, dear!' she exclaimed. 'I was talking about Jean·Arthur and I was trying to sound polite. That woman was a – well, she was difficult.'

Jean Arthur, whose death was actually announced in June 1991 whilst I was at Marlene's apartment, was an important actress. Her first key role had been in Buster Keaton's 1925 vehicle, *Seven Chances*, and three years later she had starred in the Dale-Arthur comedy, *All at Sea*.

'Okay,' I pressed. 'Tell me about Jean Arthur. I really am surprised that you two didn't get on.'

Marlene chuckled. 'It was amusing, really. Well, it's amusing now, when I think back, even if it wasn't very funny at the time. Jean Arthur wanted her name over mine in the credits, even though I was the one contracted to play the Nazi whore. Billy had asked her to play the part of a stuck-up old virgin. On the set she was anything but. I don't mean that she did anything like *that*, of course! And the director was a dear friend of mine. He knew exactly how to film a scene, but that so-and-so bitch was never satisfied. She never stopped complaining. Each time she had to film a scene with me, she wanted the camera only to be on her mug – and Billy wanted to concentrate on me. In the end we reached a compromise. We filmed all the shots the way he wanted them, then we filmed them the way Jean Arthur had *demanded* them – and that woman had one hell of a temper! And what she didn't know was, Billy hadn't put any film into the camera! That taught her a lesson. Mind you, she still got her own way with the credits – and she never forgave us for what we did. David, why are you laughing? It isn't even funny!'

'Oh, I was just trying to picture the look on Jean Arthur's face when she found out that the film had been taken out of the camera,' I said.

'But it wasn't taken out, dear,' she cried. 'It wasn't even put in! So you see, Jean Arthur was the biggest pain in the backside I ever worked with, and that so-and-so woman didn't have to pretend to hate me, either! And I can assure you, the feeling was very mutual!'

In my opinion, the songs from *A Foreign Affair* were the best that Marlene had ever sung in a film. Billy Wilder had engaged the unquestionable talents of Frederick Hollander to accompany her at the piano during Erika von Schlütow's cabaret appearances in the film. More than forty years on, 'Black Market' may sound dated, with its catalogue of *double-entendres* listing the goods on offer providing one is willing to pay the price, its references to old-fashioned cameras and Spam. Nevertheless, it remains a masterpiece of cunning and precision. 'Illusions', though regarded by many as one of the sexiest songs Marlene ever sang was, if one takes into consideration the nature of the film, tinged with an ironic sadness:

> I'll sell them all for a penny . . .
> They make pretty souvenirs!
> Take my lovely illusions,
> Some for laughs, some for tears . . .

Some forty years after *A Foreign Affair*, the young German night-club entertainer Udo Lindenberg got in touch with Marlene saying that he was thinking of recording 'Illusions' and one of her early Berlin songs, 'Wenn ich mir was wunschen dürfte?', on his new album. For a while she deliberated, then agreed to record an introduction to each song on a personal tape recorder. She actually did this on 23 October 1987, which was in effect, the very last time her recorded voice was heard. The album was called *Hermine* but she is said to have been disappointed with the result. I did not like most of the other songs, though this, of course, was only a personal opinion. When Marlene's original recordings of 'Black Market' and 'Illusions' were released in October 1949, Roy Rich of *Sound Wave Illustrated* wrote:

> Miss Dietrich, with her bluer-than-smoke voice can conjure up for you her particular underground world of broken-down ideals, sweaty night clubs, silver lamé and black lingerie. A world where there is no squealing, no feeling. You will find it all there in that insolent, tuneless voice . . . cynicism, disillusion, innuendo. Your mother will probably say Miss D can't sing, but I didn't say Miss D made records for mothers! My advice to you is to buy this record . . . the day will come when it will rate as a museum piece. The singing of a point number is becoming a lost talent in these days of Moon, June and pint-sized sopranos, but it is an art of which Marlene Dietrich is absolute mistress!

What made the film unforgettable for me, however, was the absolutely sublime 'Within the Ruins of Berlin'. Marlene sang it in English, French and German within the smoke-filled on-set cabaret location, leaning against the piano in a spangled gown into which she had tucked several open-bloomed roses. And one only has to study the overtly harsh expression on poor Jean Arthur's face to detect that the tension was for real – an act of realism which may, in effect, explain why the film was so successful, not just on both sides of the Atlantic, but across Europe as well. The songs, however, did not cut any ice with the star who had created them.

When I was asked by a British record company to do an album of Piaf songs – the ten songs which she had recorded for that company immediately after the war before moving to Pathé-Marconi – the producer informed me that as ten songs were insufficient for any compact disc, I might also include the ten songs which Marlene had recorded for Decca between 1939 and 1944. This to me seemed an excellent idea, considering the intense friendship which had developed between the two. Marlene, however, thought differently.

'Those songs are not my favourites at all . . . Sweetheart, if I've told you once, then I've told you a hundred times. I never, never liked any of the songs from my films . . .'

8

'Une part de bonheur, dont je connais la cause'

Why should I want to read a book about Piaf? I knew her better than anyone – I was her best friend!

Marlene devoted two entire pages of her autobiography to her close friendship with Edith Piaf, whom she 'adopted' at a time in the little singer's life when hope had diminished and when her hitherto indefatigable spirit had begun to fail her:

Terrified of watching her burn the candle at both ends, of watching her take three lovers at a time, I acted like a country cousin. She was a fragile bird, but she was also the Jezebel with an insatiable thirst for love which compensated for her self-confessed ugliness. Unaware of her terrible need for love, I served her well. She appreciated me . . . perhaps she loved me, though she never had the time to give herself exclusively to friendships, and I always respected her decisions. I stopped being faithful when she began taking drugs . . . it was insupportable. I knew my limits. It was like I was banging my head against a brick wall. My love for her remained intact, but it had become useless. I abandoned her like a lost child. It is something which I will always regret. . . .

The *bel amour* between Marlene and Piaf began quite by accident. In 1936, whilst singing at Gerny's, in Paris, Edith had introduced 'Il n'est pas distingué', an anti-Hitler *chanson-revancharde* which had not presented Marlene in a very favourable light. A few months later she had recorded the song, though until the German occupation of Paris it received little or no air-play because the song on the A side proved more popular. One evening, however, the renowned broadcaster, Pierre Hiegel, played it by mistake and the next morning both he and the singer were summoned to the German Propagandastaffel on the Champs-Elysées. Marlene had heard of this and, although she had seen many of the great French stars of the day, either with Gabin or Remarque, she had turned down an invitation to witness one of Piaf's recitals at the ABC.

By November 1947, however, Marlene was not feeling quite so bitter because she had been given a copy of Piaf's recording of 'La vie en rose'. The singer had written 'Les choses en rose' on a restaurant tablecloth for her friend Marianne Michel in 1945. In those days in France, songwriters had to be members-by-examination of SACEM (Sociéte des Auteurs, Compositeurs et Musiciens) before their works could be performed in public and though Piaf did get into the Society later that year, she could not get any of her regular composers to accept responsibility for the song. As a last resort Piaf had taken it to her friend Louiguy, its title had been changed to 'La vie en rose' and Marianne Michel had recorded it. There had also been a cover-version by a crooner of the day, Roland Gerbeau. This had proved so successful that by the end of 1946 Piaf had recorded the song herself. It sold three million copies in just over three months and, following hot on the heels of 'Les trois cloches', which Piaf had sung with Les Compagnons de la Chanson, it had resulted in her being invited to play a season in New York.

Piaf's first recital at the Playhouse on 48th Street was an unmitigated flop. The Americans had expected another Joséphine Baker, or maybe another Mistinguett, drenched in feathers and crooning songs like 'Mon homme' or 'C'est si bon'. What they got was a *maladive* little woman in black, wearing hardly any make-up, and singing songs of despair, death, lost love and fallen women in a language they could not understand. These early audiences were shocked and disturbed and Piaf's problems only increased when she introduced a Master of Ceremonies into her act – the lengthy dialogue in between songs took away all hope of continuity. The little singer fled to her American agent and begged him to book her on the next available passage to France. Virgil Thompson and Marlene came to the rescue. The former, a correspondent with the *New York Times*, devoted two columns to her on the front page of his newspaper and she was offered a contract with the Versailles, where she was met and befriended by the latter. She was also introduced to Judy Garland, Henry Fonda, Orson Welles, Lena Horne and Dorothy Lamour. Only Marlene had any real impact on her.

Piaf's one-week contract with the Versailles proved so popular that the management kept her on for five months. Her salary of $1,000 interested her less than the new friend she had made. The two women, on the face of it, had nothing much in common save their supreme artistry, yet their friendship and devotion would remain solid as a rock for the rest of Piaf's life. They shared two songs – 'La vie en rose' and 'When the World was Young' – and they also shared many happy moments and more than a few sad ones. In a rare but not unprecedented act of devotion, Marlene gave Piaf a precious gift – a tiny gold cross set with seven emeralds. With it was a piece of parchment upon which was inscribed: ONE MUST FIND GOD – MARLENE – ROME – CHRISTMAS. This was something I had never really understood. If Marlene was agnostic, why had she done this – and why did she so often end our conversation with a 'Goodbye and God bless', if she had dismissed the existence of God?

Marlene was close at hand on 27 October 1949 when Edith Piaf suffered the most distressing of her many tragedies. The boxing champion Marcel Cerdan was killed in a plane crash whilst on his way from France to attend her New York première. The news was rushed to the Waldorf Astoria, but Piaf was asleep – the eternal *noctambule*, she would rehearse or simply have fun with her friends all night long, then sleep until late in the day. Only Louis Barrier, her impresario, and Marlene were capable of awakening her to tell her what had happened. For several days the singer shut herself up in her room and, as a form of penance, cut her hair short. But when Marlene suggested that she should cancel her performance that night, she refused, informing her audience that their applause should be for no one but Cerdan. When she collapsed during her recital, Marlene was there to revive her and she continued singing in one of the most emotional scenes ever witnessed on an American stage. In spite of her tragedy, Piaf introduced a new song called 'Monsieur Lenoble', which is the woeful tale of a man who gases himself after being told that his wife has left him for a younger man. The song which thrilled her audience most of all, however, was 'La vie en rose', which even Marlene was not allowed to sing in Europe whilst Piaf was still alive.

Cerdan's death clearly marked the beginning of Piaf's downfall. As a tribute to him she wrote and recorded 'Hymne à l'amour', maybe her most famous song. Within two years she also had become dependent on drugs and alcohol: the former were prescribed after she had been badly injured in a car crash but the latter was Piaf's own surefire means of helping herself to forget. After a brief relationship with the actor Eddie Constantine, and an even briefer one with the racing champion Toto Gérardin – the man whom Piaf dismissed as 'Mistinguett's cast-off' – she fell in love with the singer Jacques Pills. They were married in New York on 20 September 1952 with Piaf's manager Louis Barrier and Marlene as witnesses.

I asked her, 'Marlene, can you remember what Piaf was like on the day of her wedding?'

'Yes, I can,' she replied. 'I kept looking at her, hoping she would be capable of staying on her feet. She was very happy but very sick also. I had arranged everything – her hair and her make-up, and the bunch of white roses which she carried. And she was wearing the cross that I'd given her – you know, the one with the emeralds. She also seemed lost, like a little child. You said you were sending me your book about Piaf. But why should I want a book about her, when I knew her better than anyone? I was her best friend.'

When I explained that the book was written from a fan's point of view, Marlene asked me to take it to her apartment. I did this in February 1990. Later she told me how hurt she had been by the biography written by Simone Berteaut, who in 1969 had claimed to

be Piaf's half-sister. This book had been used for the basis of Pam
Gem's superb play, *Piaf*.

'There was too much rude language for my liking. That's why I
asked them to take my character out of it whilst I'm still alive.
When I began reading your book, I didn't know what to expect. It
was so beautiful that it made me cry. But I didn't care for the
photograph of us together. Every book about Piaf seems to have the
picture of me that was taken at her wedding. Why didn't you use
the one of us kissing? Can you remember where it was taken?'

'It was at Thionville, during the last leg of what the press called
her "suicide" tour on account of her being so ill. It was also her
birthday, ten days before her famous season at the Olympia.'

After their wedding, Piaf and Pills had toured America. This
constituted their honeymoon and the start of the singer's four-year
precipitation into hell. The marriage would be doomed from the
moment the couple set foot in France. Though Pills helped her
with the drugs problem (this had started when, after being
seriously injured in a car crash, a doctor had prescribed large doses
of morphine to which she had become addicted) he had been
content to turn a blind eye to her drinking, even making this worse
by taking her out on binges. But did Marlene desert Piaf in her
hour of need?

'I never really abandoned Piaf!' she cried, when I suggested this –
after reading to her what she had written in her own book. 'I wrote
that, I know. The truth is, Piaf's husband asked me to stay away
from her, and that's what I did. And we always kept in touch on the
telephone. She always sounded so strong, and I thought she'd
gotten over her problems.'

Marlene had a point: even when Piaf's health had been
decidedly fragile towards the end, she had lost none of her
'bantam-cock, fighting spirit', as Maurice Chevalier had called it.
Surviving friends told me that she had still been a tyrant to live,
work and put up with.

Marlene was able to devote so much time to developing her
friendship with Piaf principally because, after the première of *A
Foreign Affair*, she was offered nothing substantial in the way of
work. In 1948 she had a walk-on part as a night club entertainer in

Fletcher Markle's *Jigsaw* and even this somewhat insignificant event caused her a major problem. The 'tough-guy' actor John Garfield, who had been engaged to play a street loiterer in the film, followed Marlene to one of Piaf's parties at the Waldorf Astoria and, when everyone had left, was found naked in the singer's bedroom. Needless to say, the two women manhandled him out of the room – a task made easier because he was drunk – and threw him, still naked, down the stairs. Also, through Piaf's insistence, Marlene accepted a number of television and radio contracts. There was the role of Grusinskaya in *Grand Hotel* which had been portrayed by Garbo in the film and a radio performance in which she played the lead in *Madame Bovary* opposite Claude Rains. This broadcast was celebrated by another party thrown by Piaf but this time without any unwanted hangers on.

The Versailles in New York became Piaf's first port-of-call every time she visited America and almost always Marlene was there to take charge of her every need. She acted as her dresser and helped her with her make-up. If anyone came knocking on the dressing-room door she would put on a formidably high-pitched voice and yell to whoever it was that she was Madame Piaf's secretary and that the star was not available. The plan only backfired on her once when the caller was Robert Bré, a young journalist friend of Piaf's from Belleville. He suggested that if Piaf had engaged someone as elegant as Marlene Dietrich for her secretary, then she might as well take on Maurice Chevalier as her new chauffeur.

Marlene supported Piaf largely via the telephone during her 'years of hell' which ended with her divorce from Jacques Pills and her triumphant comeback at the Paris Olympia. Whenever she was in Paris, she always dropped in at the sparsely furnished apartment on Boulevard Lannes. She was supportive during the aforementioned suicide tour which began at Rheims on 14 October 1960 and exactly three years later, she would be attending her friend's funeral.

Piaf wrote many songs for herself and a few for Yves Montand and Damia. She had been so taken up with 'Mon coin tout bleu' that she had recorded it one year before she had sung it in her film for Georges Lacombe. Marlene had performed it in North Africa in 1944, though so far as I know she never recorded it:

Mais un beau jour rempli d'étoiles,
Mon ciel tout bleu sera sans voile,
Adieux les cieux couverts de pluie,
D'un coup s'éclaircira ma vie . . .

Another famous song, Raymond Asso's 'Mon légionnaire', which Piaf had performed before the war, was re-arranged one evening in the singer's dressing room. This Piaf–Dietrich collaboration, which they performed at a Hollywood party 'on all fours, like a couple of bitches on heat' and which is also said to have been taped, was so filthy that the pair walked around red-faced for days afterwards. On a lighter note, the pair sang 'Les feuilles mortes' at another party and, if Marlene still admitted to hating the song which some claimed to have been responsible for her break-up with Gabin, she was the first to congratulate Piaf when she sang it at a reception for General Eisenhower at the Versailles towards the end of 1951. What did offend her, however, was the fact that she had just heard Marianne Oswald's version of the song . . . in German.

That Marlene made the effort to drop in on Piaf's last tour ostensibly meant that she still cared and put paid to any rumours circulating at the time that she was only interested in making money. In December 1960, when Piaf was rehearsing frantically whilst fighting off ill health to stage a magnificent comeback at the Olympia, Marlene was also taking on a new challenge – her first visit to Germany, artistically at least, for thirty years. She missed the Piaf première, but on Christmas Day she sent a telegram to the Versailles cinema where the singer was rehearsing: IMPOSSIBLE TO COME AND APPLAUD YOU, GOOD LUCK, GOOD HEALTH, I KISS YOU, MARLENE. Piaf told a reporter, 'I've been given Marlene's blessing. Now the show can go on!'

Marlene disapproved of Piaf's second marriage, to Théo Sarapo, the Greek hairdresser who was twenty years her junior. Perhaps she felt that the first marriage had been enough of a disaster without having to put herself through the mill again. She knew, of course, that with Théo it would be a union of love rather than one of gain. Piaf had always been in the habit of spending money before it was earned and now that her doctors had given her but a short time to live, she did not intend letting the grass grow beneath her feet. On this basis, Théo knew that he would inherit a legacy of debts, which is exactly what happened. It may well be that Marlene no longer believed in the sanctity of marriage, the way she claimed she no longer believed in God, because although Piaf sent her a personal invitation, she did not turn up at the ceremony.

'He was a nice young man, but I always thought he married her for the publicity. I later found out that he didn't. But he was also a homosexual, and I couldn't condone that. Piaf was much, much more than a friend and I loved her more than anyone could possibly imagine. Wherever I go, she will always be there inside my heart.'

Piaf died on 10 October 1963 in the south of France and, disapproving or not, Marlene was one of the first to arrive at her Paris apartment to comfort the grieving widower. After Théo she was chief mourner at the funeral. She arrived alone, wearing no make-up and carrying a single rose and was not surprised at all that an incredible two million people had turned out to say goodbye to the Little Sparrow. She was upset, however, that the Pope had refused her friend a Christian burial, claiming that she had lived a life of public sin, in other words, because her divorce from Jacques Pills had never been recognized.

On 11 October 1963 there had followed another tragedy when Jean Cocteau, Marlene and Piaf's great friend, died of a heart attack whilst preparing the singer's eulogy. Thus, kissing Théo goodbye for the last time, Marlene moved on to Cocteau's funeral at Milly-le-Forêt, where she comforted another grieving 'widower' – the actor Jean Marais. From then on there would be no more funerals for Marlene – not even that of her own husband.

It was while she had been in New York, helping Piaf through the Marcel Cerdan tragedy, that Marlene received a call from London to the effect that the eminent British director Alfred Hitchcock was interested in making a film with her. She asked to see the script and it was flown out to her. She glanced through it, took great interest in the proposed part of the musical-comedy star, Charlotte Inwood, and agreed to sign the contract providing she would be allowed to select her own gowns and, most important of all, her own songs.

'I was sick to death of film directors telling me what I ought to be doing all the time. They didn't know a thing about what was good or bad in a song – and as I wasn't getting paid as well as in the past, I wanted to make sure that if I did sing, then it would be something I liked. So I asked Cole Porter, and he gave me 'The Laziest Gal in Town'. I said then that I wanted one other song, and Piaf told me that I would be able to borrow 'La vie en rose'. Neither song made the film any better, did it?'

On different planes but on the same day, Marlene and Piaf flew to Paris – she to be fitted out by Christian Dior and Piaf to appear in a concert at the Salle Pleyel. A few days later Marlene flew into London on a midnight flight and shocked several press photographers by snarling at them when they asked her to pose showing her legs. Things had not improved the next day when she attended a luncheon at the Savoy: she turned up wearing black, smoked constantly throughout the meal and, when reminded by the toastmaster that this was not the done thing in British society, she calmly put out her cigarette and left the room.

Marlene did not particularly enjoy making Hitchcock's *Stage Fright*, though she did get on well with her co-stars Richard Todd, Jane Wyman and Michael Wilding. The latter, it is said, became her lover though there is little evidence to support this other than the fact that they were often seen together in and around London. She was also reunited with her old musician friend Mischa Spoliansky, now a British citizen residing in London.

What is unusual is that for no apparent reason Marlene had Richard Todd's horoscope drawn up by Carroll Richter (the actor was engaged to be married) and he was told that the marriage would fail. (It did!) Another star of the film, Kay Walsh, told reporters of her 'amazement' at how Marlene could put away vast amounts of steak and kidney pie without ruining her figure. Miss Walsh also spoke of Marlene's handbag – a massive Gladstone inside which she had concealed every medication known to mankind and a Hollywood union-card which read, 'You know as much about this business as we do'. Even Hitchcock, who astonishingly kept his distance during filming, apart from the obvious publicity shots for the press, confessed, 'Miss Dietrich is a professional actress, a professional cameraman, art director, editor, composer, make-up woman, producer, hairdresser and costume designer – and she is also a professional director.' This praise came after she had astounded the set technicians and cameramen with lessons in lighting techniques.

Unfortunately, *Stage Fright* was not as successful as some of Hitchcock's earlier films, primarily because the public would not accept Marlene as a murderess. Similarly, some critics disliked it because they were unable to write too much about the plot without giving the ending. Others, like Enid O'Neill in *Picturegoer* emphasized Marlene's taste in fashion, and the fact that her wardrobe for the film was in excess of £1,000:

> One [dress] in white muslin has a billowing fairy-like skirt of frills, each tier lightly picked out with strass embroidery. Another in black muslin has a very full skirt folded into a tremendous handkerchief drape at the back. There is a pale rose-pink organza draped off the shoulder in a shawl line . . . and a grey worsted suit called Acacias which has an extremely tight-waisted jacket with low-cut revers and important hip pocket-flaps . . .

On 30 October 1950, Marlene was invited to sing at the Night of the Stars following the première of that year's royal film, *The Mudlark*. The stars of the film were Irene Dunne and Alec Guinness and they, like everyone else, had especially requested her to sing 'Lili Marlene', which Marlene had agreed to do wholeheartedly because of the presence of King George VI and Queen Elizabeth. Ben Lyon, however, thought he had come up with the ideal alternative – a sketch with Michael Wilding, John Mills, Jack Hawkins and himself, entitled 'We're All in Love with Grandmother'. This, of course, was supposed to allude to Marlene's recently acquired status. What Ben Lyon did not reckon with was her reaction. She had returned to Paris for the weekend for a rest and a brief visit to her friend, the fashion designer Ginette Spanier. When Ben Lyon mentioned his idea, she slammed the telephone down on him. Returning to London, there was a further problem when Marlene was asked to sing her most famous song before a painted desert backdrop.

> 'Ben Lyon wanted me to sing one of his songs in front of the royal family and I wasn't having anything to do with that. And then they

asked me to do "Lili Marlene", standing in the middle of the desert like I did in *Morocco*. So I said, "Who the hell do you think I am, Marie Dubas?" '

Marie Dubas was a famous French chanteuse who, between the two world wars, had becomed legendary in France for her *légionnaire* songs but I was very surprised that Marlene had remembered her.

It would take another two years for Marlene to make the final transition from screen to stage – two years of hard thinking, deliberation and soul-searching. It may well be that Ben Lyon's albeit innocently proposed 'grandmother' sketch pushed her into realizing that though her beauty was intact, she was not getting any younger. Also a new generation of stars had sprung to the fore in Hollywood since the war years, thus making it unviable and unnecessary from most producers' points of view to go on casting her as the eternal siren. Hitchcock had purposely avoided this, though she had come pretty close to playing a vamp when she had purred 'The Laziest Gal in Town'.

After finishing *Stage Fright*, Marlene returned to New York. Maria had given birth to a second son, John Peter, in May 1950, and had afterwards begun losing weight so rapidly – shedding more than sixty pounds – that Marlene had become worried. According to her doctors, Maria's condition was nothing more than a metabolic change and she began to pick up the threads of her stage and television career, aided by Marlene who often sat in on rehearsals to help her with her lines.

At around this time Marlene was also befriended by the young German star Hildegard Knef, whose own career had begun at the Babelsberg studios and whom she met in Hollywood courtesy of Max Colpet. Knef had been invited to Hollywood by Darryl F. Zanuck to appear in the screen version of Hemingway's *The Snows of Kilimanjaro*. Marlene accurately identified her birth sign, as she had with me. Some years later, when Knef starred opposite Don Ameche in the Broadway musical, *Silk Stockings*, Marlene assisted the production company as well as the composer Cole Porter and it was largely due to her intervention that Knef became a sensation. Knef also sang several great Dietrich songs without any hint of emulation, including 'Ich hab noch einen koffe in Berlin' and 'Allein in einer grossen Stadt'.

Early in 1951, Marlene returned to England to star opposite James Stewart in the screen adaptation of Nevil Shute's novel, *No Highway in the Sky*. She played the musical-comedy star Monica Teasdale, lowering her eyelids quite a lot and smoking considerably more. Stewart played the eccentric scientist, Theodore Honey, who is travelling on the same plane as the star when he discovers that it is suffering from metal fatigue and likely to crash. On the face of it, several of Marlene's lines appeared to be autobiographical. When she thinks she is about to die she says to Honey, 'Do you know what I was thinking about? All the people who'll come to my funeral.' Later on she admits, 'I would have stopped working some time ago if I could have figured out what to do with myself.' Then when Honey deliberately sabotages the plane during a stop-over to prevent it from crashing, exclaiming, 'It just folded right up and sat down!' she supports his theory and all ends well. However, in spite of the presence of the man whom Marlene had confessed to being her favourite co-star, making the film was not a particularly rewarding experience.

> 'Marlene, what about the film you made with James Stewart in England?'
> 'You mean the one about the plane which was going to crash. I disliked the film and its German director, but I had to make it ... again because I needed the money. And I didn't like working with Glynis Johns, either.'

The director of *No Highway in the Sky* was Henry Koster, whom Marlene had met in the cutting room at UFA after making *Der blaue Engel*. Fourteen years later in Hollywood, he had worked with Joe Pasternak on *Music for Millions*, the film which had won Margaret O'Brien an Academy Award. In accepting to do a film for purely financial reasons, and stating so in a press conference, Marlene ran the risk of adverse criticism.

Marlene's portrayal of the musical-comedy star Monica Teasdale was generally regarded as unconvincing and little more than an extension of herself. According to some press reports she did initially appear to be suffering from some unexplained form of superiority complex, arriving on the set swathed in more than

£3,000 worth of mink. She was photographed between takes, not in the chair provided by the studio, but in a rich black velvet creation inscribed with her signature in gold. She was also aloof with most of the cast, which may explain some difficulties with Glynis Johns, regarded by many as the most amenable of actresses. It may well be that Marlene was against Miss Johns having the bigger part, and certainly the better lines. Marlene did, however, attempt to make up for her unexplained moodiness towards the end of the shoot, presenting everyone with a half-bottle of gin with a handwritten, personalized label.

Half-way through *No Highway in the Sky*, Marlene was contacted by Billy Wilder and asked to appear in *A New Kind of Love*, an unscripted film which he wanted to be written around the well-known Maurice Chevalier song. The project was doomed from the very start:

> 'I only wish we could have made that film, David! It would have been so wonderful, working with Chevalier. But this was America, and it was 1951. You know what happened, don't you?'
>
> 'The McCarthy thing,' I replied. 'Chevalier wasn't allowed to go to America because he'd signed the Stockholm Peace Proposal against the atom bomb. Then, of course, everybody thought he must have been a Communist.'
>
> Marlene sighed, loudly, 'Oh, God. How could they say such a thing about so wonderful a man? Now, you must write something good about him, here in this book. You must tell everyone how much in love we were . . .'

In 1950, the entire United States was locked in the throes of the McCarthy witch-hunt. Chevalier had recently starred in the film *Ma pomme*, also written around a famous song, and he had signed the technicians' petition without realizing how troublesome this would be to his career. So had 275 million others, including Yves Montand and Simone Signoret, Louis Aragon, and a young politician named Jacques Chirac. In April 1951 he and his entourage left France for Canada. Ten days later he was informed by the Washington State Department that he would not be welcome in the United States. It would take several more years for the American government to forgive him for being something he had never professed to being in the first place.

9

'Here I Go Again,
Taking a Chance on Love'

Some people were shocked to see me dressed as a man, singing men's songs . . . but I didn't care. I was sick of the rubbish they kept churning out for me to do in my films and for the first time in my life I was doing what *I* wanted to do . . .

In December 1951, Marlene returned to New York on the *Queen Elizabeth*. *Stage Fright* had just been released in America, but it had not attracted wholly favourable responses from most of the critics. *No Highway in the Sky* fared better, though by this time Marlene had clearly grown weary of the film world. Rather than travel on to Hollywood she stayed in New York and spent Christmas with Maria and her family and was seen in public with Ernest Hemingway. She was still undeniably close to Erich Maria Remarque, who as usual was suffering from acute melancholia and in need of her attention.

It was Remarque who encouraged her to sign a contract with Leonard Blair of the ABC Network for a series of thirty-minute radio broadcasts called *Café Istanbul*. These were broadcast on Sunday evenings and were based on *Casablanca*, with Marlene interpreting a female Bogart, recounting anecdotes between such well tested Continental favourites as 'Reviens veux-tu' and 'La vie en rose'. She took the enterprise seriously, poring for hours over the scripts and even typing them herself – on the same machine, she alleged, that she had used to type her first letters to me thirty-six years later. The series was subsequently revived and re-named *Time for Love*, always introduced by the song of that name, recorded with Percy Faith. This second series was not as successful as the first and she quickly returned to doing what she was best at – singing on the stage, and acting only as a last resort when she needed the money. She also appeared on the radio with Bing Crosby: they recorded 'La vie en rose' as a duo, perhaps the only time Crosby ever sang in French.

In May 1953, Maria persuaded her mother to participate in a charity show for the Ringling Brothers Barnum and Bailey Circus at the Madison Square Garden in New York. She wore a ringmaster's uniform and looked superb. Immediately afterwards she was inundated with offers to appear on the stage but she turned these down, apparently because the fees were insufficient to meet her needs. But Rudolf Sieber had succumbed to an attack of gastric ulcers and in a subsequent operation to remove half of his stomach he almost died. Therefore, needing the money but very much against her will, Marlene agreed to make a film with Fritz Lang.

'Marlene, what about the film you made with Fritz Lang?' I asked.
'Oh, that was awful.'

Fritz Lang, another stalwart of the Babelsberg studios just outside Berlin, had achieved world fame with one of the most renowned of all the silents, *Metropolis*. What Marlene had said about him in her autobiography had been hardly flattering:

The director I hated most of all was Fritz Lang, with whom I made *Rancho Notorious* in 1952. This man had a sadistic streak which would not have put Hitler out of place – even if he was a German Jew who had fled from the Nazis to take refuge in America. In order to work with him I had to revolt against myself, against the anger which he aroused within me. Lang attempted to replace the genius of von Sternberg by making me go over the same scene a hundred times, and he wanted my body as well as my heart. I knew this because he told me so himself. His Teutonic arrogance repulsed me so much that I almost tore up my contract. Had it not been for Mel Ferrer, I am sure that I would have walked off the set.

Rancho Notorious was a western very much in the *Destry* vein, with Marlene playing Altar Keane, an older and more cynical version of Frenchy, who still dies heroically for the man she loves. The songs, however, were not *Destry* – Ken Darby's 'Get Away Young Man' and 'Gypsy Davey' were mediocre compared to the material she had started to put together for her forthcoming series of one-woman shows at the Hotel Sahara, in Las Vegas.

Incongruously situated in the heart of the Nevada desert, Las Vegas had sprung up shortly after the war and had quickly developed into a boom town. A number of businessmen, it is said, had even cashed in on the nearby testing ground for the United States Atomic Organization. Exploding atomic bombs only added to the general feeling of excitement there and brought in many tourists who might otherwise have travelled elsewhere. Marlene may initially have balked when asked to sing in so opulent a setting, bearing in mind the almost Spartan discipline which she had inflicted upon herself whilst entertaining the soldiers during the war. Two things changed her mind. Firstly, her friend Edith Piaf had already performed in Las Vegas – an extremely unlikely choice for her. Secondly, the fee, $30,000 for a three-week season, was too good to resist. She immediately contacted Jean-Louis, at that time the chief designer for Columbia, and asked him to make her 'something out of furs, spangles and diamonds ... cost immaterial'. She then set about selecting her programme.

'You asked me how I selected the songs for my first concert? Then I'll tell you. You said in your script that in your opinion I had sung "I Wish You Love" better than anyone. Did that include Charles Trenet?'

'I said everyone, and I meant everyone,' I stressed. 'Your version of the song was more poignant than his. You sang it as a love song to a child. It was very moving.'

'I'd heard Trenet performing the song, in Paris just after the war,' she explained. 'I always thought he sang it too fast. There wasn't any sentiment. That's why I decided to sing it slowly, and in

English. "I Wish You Love" was the first song I ever chose for my concerts and I just built everything else around it.'

'Did you admire Trenet? I spoke to him a couple of times on the phone and he sounded grumpy. Maybe he was tired, I don't know.'

'The man was a pig,' she replied. 'He was just one of many entertainers I encountered who gave the impression of being sincere when he was anything but.'

Marlene was even more discerning in her choice of costume for the Sahara. Jean-Louis was commissioned to produce two identical dresses – one in white and another in gold – plus an additional one of black net covered in sequins which, under the spotlight, created an impression of nudity from the waist upwards. She wore this one on her opening night, 15 December 1963, cleverly surmounted by a full-length redingote trimmed with three yards of white fur. The result was a sensation. Photographs of her, taken by John Engstead, appeared on the front pages of newspapers and magazines across the world. During the second half of her show, singing 'male' songs, she appeared in the now-familiar ringmaster's suit, with top-hat and scarlet tail-coat. What was important, of course, was Marlene's voice and delivery. She did not sing her songs so much as speak them, very much in the *Sprechtsinger* style of Marianne Oswald, but without that singer's harshness. The voice was a warm, rich mezzo-bass-baritone, spanning little more than one octave, and because there was no overt straining to reach an upper register, her diction was impeccable. The words, and not the melodies of the Dietrich repertoire, were what counted.

Marlene was not as intense in her performances as she would be during the next decade but as practically everyone who saw her in Las Vegas had never heard her sing live, there could be no comparisons. Even 'Falling in Love Again' and 'Lola-Lola' sounded different. As if anticipating that most people would have by now forgotten the latter song, Marlene planted someone in the audience to shout, when she announced that she was going to sing a song from *The Blue Angel* but not that one, 'Sing "Lola-Lola"!' The ruse worked so well that she adopted it almost every time she sang. At the Sahara, after her admirers had thrilled to this song and been seduced by 'The Laziest Gal in Town', she gave them 'I

Wish You Love' and more often than not there was hardly a dry eye in the house.

Over the next twenty years, her act would vary only slightly: she would attempt the odd comedy number, such as the absurd Australian ditty, 'Boomerang Baby', but by and large she would only add a new song to her repertoire if she thought that it contained an important message.

The previous year, in 1952, she had recorded two songs – 'Good for Nuthin' ' and 'Too Old to Cut the Mustard' – with Rosemary Clooney, not because she had wanted to but because a hit record had seemed a good idea at the time. The latter song had featured Stan Freeman on the harpsichord and had proved so popular that many people expected Marlene to team up with Rosemary Clooney for at least one concert. She refused to do this and one wonders why, but during rehearsals for her show at the Sahara she took time off to record two more songs with Clooney and two more the following year.

Early in 1954, after being bombed during the war, the Café de Paris re-opened in London and its owner, Major Donald Neville-Willing, hit on the idea of what he thought would have been the show-business sensation of the decade – Greta Garbo, in cabaret. Apparently, this was not as ridiculous as it seemed at the time for the great Swedish legend was reputed to have had more than a passable singing voice and is also said to have insisted on using her own voice whilst interpreting the role of a chanteuse in *As You Desire Me*. Neville-Willing therefore went to New York where Garbo granted him an interview and even seemed interested in the idea of earning £1,000 per week for standing in a night club and doing exactly what she wanted, even nothing at all, if need be. She then asked the entrepreneur if, whilst she was on the stage, the public would be able to see up her nostrils. Neville-Willing replied that they probably would and the interview ended abruptly – Garbo would not be making her cabaret début.

Undeterred, Neville-Willing contacted Marlene in New York (they had apparently met at the Ruban Bleu, twenty years earlier, in the company of Tallulah Bankhead) and the deal was clinched a week or so later over tea in Marlene's Park Avenue apartment. She would open at the Café de Paris on 21 June 1954, for a fee estimated to be around £2,000 per week, twice the amount Neville-Willing had been prepared to pay Garbo. To coincide with her première, Philips released two of her songs on record – 'Time for Love' and Mitch Miller's 'Look Me Over Closely', which she had anticipated including in her routine.

With typical flamboyance and showbusiness hype, Marlene was met at London airport by Noël Coward and escorted to a press reception at the Dorchester, where Neville-Willing had booked her the most expensive suite they had. Here, she went through her songs with her new musical director and arranger and a man whom she once described as the most important human being in her life:

> One day, there was a knock on my door, and I saw this masculine silhouette. 'My name is Burt Bacharach,' he told me. He was very young, very handsome, and had the bluest eyes I had ever seen. He walked up to the piano and asked to see my first song. It was the Mitch Miller number. He studied the music and said, 'You can't sing it like this!' Then he played the song the way he thought it should have been before declaring, 'I'll see you in the morning, ten o'clock sharp!' From that day forth I lived only to sing for him, and to please him. He had seen so little of the world, and we travelled far and wide together – he working on my arrangements, and myself washing his socks and shirts.

Marlene disapproved of the Café de Paris's modernized sound system, which included a cordless microphone. That same week in Paris, Damia – who in a career spanning forty years never used a microphone once – announced her retirement from the stage on account of 'that damned metal contraption taking over'. Even Mistinguett, whose singing voice was less powerful than Marlene's, had only used a microphone once and in doing so had tripped and fallen down her famous staircase. Needless to say, Marlene threw more than a few tantrums during rehearsals for her show – and more than once, during a song, the microphone began picking up messages from local police patrol cars. Her opening night was even more sensational than the one in Las Vegas. When she arrived at the theatre clinging to Noël Coward's arm, the crowds outside the building became so unruly that the police had to be summoned to restore order. She did not make her appearance until after midnight and her introduction by Coward was so witty, camp and absolutely brilliant that it was included on the album of the première, whilst several of her better songs were omitted:

> We know God made trees
> And the birds and the bees
> And the seas for the fishes to swim in
> We are also aware
> That he had quite a flair
> For creating exceptional women.
> When Eve said to Adam
> 'Start calling me Madam'
> The world became far more exciting,
> Which turns to confusion
> The modern delusion
> That sex is a question of lighting
> For female allure
> Whether pure or impure
> Has seldom reported a failure
> As I know and you know
> From Venus and Juno
> Right down to La Dame aux Camélias
> This glamour, it seems,
> Is a substance of dreams
> To the most imperceptive perceiver
> The Serpent of Nile
> Could achieve with a smile
> Far quicker results than Geneva.
> Though we all might enjoy
> Seeing Helen of Troy
> As a gay cabaret entertainer
>
> I doubt that she could
> Be one quarter as good
> As our legendary, lovely Marlene.

Then, to a standing ovation, Marlene descended the stairs, touched Coward's hand and stepped into the pink spotlight, her Jean-Louis dress causing everyone to catch their breath in astonishment, for she had had it taken in, revealing even more of her fabulous figure beneath the $8,000 worth of black net. Her act was relatively short – around forty-five minutes – and comprised just twelve songs. Most of these were, for the time being, from her films. One, Frederick Hollander's 'Lazy Afternoon', which Marlene drawls so much in the recording that she gives the impression that she is falling asleep, caught the emotions of Kenneth Tynan to such an extent that he wrote many years later, 'For me, she was the widow of every soldier who had died in the war. I simply had to meet her!' Meet her, he did. Then perhaps the most acclaimed critic in England, Tynan only had to send a message to her dressing room after the show and Marlene was putty in his hands. She even agreed to dine with him and rumour very quickly had it that she was interested in having an affair with him, until Noël Coward informed her that Tynan was married. Even so, they remained good friends until the end of Tynan's life and, in her autobiography, Marlene includes a tribute of several thousand words which he had written in her honour.

Spending so much of her time with Noël Coward during the early and mid-Fifties led to some of the silliest rumours, none probably more so than the one which suggested that their friendship might, if Marlene could have had her way, have progressed beyond the platonic.

Noël Coward's famous introduction set a precedent for the remainder of Marlene's Café de Paris run. On subsequent evenings she was introduced by such renowned personalities as the magician David Nixon, Laurence Harvey, Sir Donald Wolfitt (quoting Shakespeare), Van Johnson, Herbert Lom and Robert Morley, whose speech went on for so long that the star of the show cracked, 'Has he forgotten that I'm supposed to be on the bill as well?' The shows were, of course, aimed to please the high society of London, for the average man in the street would never have afforded the steep prices of the establishment. Each morning the newspapers listed a Who's Who of celebrities: Laurence Olivier and Vivien Leigh, Sir Alexander Fleming, Mischa Spoliansky and his wife, Princess Margaret and the Member of

Parliament for Liverpool, Bessie Braddock.

The Café de Paris season was not without its share of drama. Marlene agreed to participate in Coward's Night of a Hundred Stars and afterwards told him that she would be delighted to attend a garden party in Regent's Park to help raise money for the Blind Babies' Sunshine Homes. While performing, she tripped over a cable and broke two toes in her left foot. Rather than cancel her performance, she sang for several nights in great pain wearing odd shoes, hidden by the hem of her Jean-Louis gown. During the last week of her season she also attended a luncheon to launch the People Against Polio campaign, sparking off a minor panic by telling a group of mothers that an ordinary cold in a child could well be the initial symptoms of infantile paralysis. The third drama took place when a young Cypriot woman called Hella Christofis was murdered and her body burned by her mother-in-law. The woman's husband, Christopher, worked as a waiter at the Café de Paris, and Marlene was very distressed to learn that he had been left with several small children. Putting on a disguise, she visited him at his home and gave him some money to pay for the children to stay in the country until the publicity over the trial had died down. Several months later, Donald Neville-Willing rang Marlene in New York to inform her that Christopher's mother had been found guilty and hanged.

In London that year there were many more devoted acts of charity. When a young man wrote to Marlene to inform her that he and his lover had booked tickets for her show but that since then his lover had been diagnosed as suffering from terminal cancer, she made a point of visiting the dying man in hospital and singing for him the twelve songs from her show. A few days later, the young man died. She also accompanied the children from the Sunshine Home to Victoria Station, where she saw them off on a day trip to the seaside: she had arrived armed with boxes of sweets and each child received a kiss and her autograph as he or she boarded the train. Many of those waiting outside the Café de Paris had had to be content with a mere smile or a wave, for even then it was alleged that she had begun to loathe that small, indefatigable section of her public who, programmes in hand, would wait patiently for hours for their idol to leave via the stage door.

'There were the fans,' Marlene said. 'And there were all the others – the parasites. The genuine fans were content just to wave at me, or shake my hand. Some of the others went too far. Just because they'd paid to hear me sing, they thought they had the divine right to push their books and programmes under my nose. They didn't understand that I might have had my reasons to get away from the theatre to keep up another appointment, or that I had a life of my own. And if I didn't feel like doing an autograph, some of them were very rude. Mind you, I could never resist signing one of my photographs for a child. There is nobody on this earth as innocent as a child.'

Marlene's success on the world stage can never be over-estimated. In dealing directly with her public she was able to monitor her appearance and her appeal – there was no more waiting for weeks and even months to find out if a film had failed or not. Performances could be judged on the spot and if a particular song did not work out, then it could be set aside for the time being. The money was better too, though I tended to doubt Marlene each time she told me that she had sung solely for money. Her films, yes, but never her one-woman shows. They contained too much of her real self to be anything but personal crusades for love and, during the next decade, world peace.

During the first week of August 1954, Marlene met the staff of the Café de Paris at a private backstage party, offering everyone something to remember her by. These gifts ranged from personalized bottles of whisky and gin similar to the ones she had doled out after making *No Highway in the Sky*, to pairs of gold cuff-links. Then, in the company of Major Donald Neville-Willing, she flew to Paris, where she rested for a while before travelling down to Monte Carlo. She had been booked to top the bill in an extravaganza called 'La Nuit d'Août', aimed at raising money for the United French Polio funds, probably appropriate after her gaffe in London – at the famous Sporting Club. Still wearing the Jean-Louis gown, on 17 August she was introduced to a selected audience of 1,600 by Jean Marais, who recited an appraisal that could only have been penned by Jean Cocteau, himself too ill to attend her recital:

Marlene Dietrich. Your name begins with a caress and ends

with the lash of a whip. You wear feathers and furs which seem to belong to your body as they do to the beasts and the birds. Your voice and gaze are of the Lorelei, but the Lorelei was dangerous . . . you are not, for the secret of your beauty is the secret of your heart. It is your heart which places you above elegance, above fashion and style, and even above your reputation, your courage, your walk, your films and your songs. Your beauty asserts itself. It is not even necessary to mention it . . . it is your kindness that I salute, illuminating from within the long wave of glory that is you, a transparent wave which comes from far away and which condescends to generously unfold before us. From the spangles of *The Blue Angel* to the gown of *Morocco*, from the poor black dress of *Dishonoured* to the plumes of *Shanghai Express*, from the diamonds of *Desire* to the American uniform, from port to port, from reef to reef, from surge to surge, and from dam to dam there comes a frigate in full sail, a valiant figure, a Chinese fish, a lyre-bird, and an incredible, wonderful Marlene Dietrich . . .

Marlene had included Cocteau's speech in an appendix to her memoirs, though this had represented more a tribute to his memory and friendship than actual admiration of what he had said about her.

The section of my book, *Les Grande Dames de la Chanson*, which included Marlene, was 'Les visiteurs du soir', which was also the title of a famous French film made during the Forties and starring Arletty, an actress of some renown who had been suspected of collaboration just a few years before. Needless to say, I changed the title but Marlene still was not content.

'I don't like being called an invader from another land, dear. It gives me the impression that I've just descended from outer space, for God's sake. How many times have I told you, David, that I don't belong in one of your categories. You're almost as bad as Jean Cocteau – he called me a Chinese fish. But whilst we're talking about your book – who was that woman who was singing in Monte Carlo when I was there? She sang the most beautiful song. I rehearsed it for my show but they stopped me from putting it in. A lovely song about a couple taking a holiday in Spain.'

'That was Patachou,' I said. 'The song was called "Voyage de noces". It means "honeymoon".'

'I know what it means,' Marlene returned impatiently. 'What I would like to know is, could you sing it . . . with me?'

'*Vous avez du en faire des beaux voyages de noces, en montagne. Et vous avez du en faire des châteaux comme deux gosses – comme deux gosses en Espagne . . .*'

I told her that her singing voice was still near-perfect, and this made her chuckle. 'Well, I'm pleased I got it right. That woman was brilliant. But why did Mistinguett hate her?'

'She called her Patamerde,' I began.

'Patashit,' Marlene repeated. 'Was it because of her involvement with Chevalier? Aye-aye-aye. Anyway, that was the song I wanted to sing more than any other at the time and I was very, very sad that I never could.'

After Monte Carlo, Marlene sang in Amsterdam. Here there was a problem with the stage when, during a rehearsal she tripped over a loose board. When the manager told her that there was no one around to rectify the situation she borrowed a hammer and a workman's overall and did the job herself. Before the actual performance, she found her dressing room overflowing with dozens of bouquets of flowers. She had these transferred, with as little fuss as possible, to Anne Frank's house, and spent half an hour meditating in the room where the famous diary had been written.

In October Marlene returned to play another short season in Las Vegas, appearing in a ruby-coloured diaphanous creation which covered 'only where it touched' and which at times during her opening number, 'Look Me Over Closely', seemed as though it would be blown off by the wind machine. She then returned to New York, where she spent the next few weeks with her family, writing magazine articles in her spare time under the collective title 'How To Be Loved'. Thus the Dietrich 'doctrine', for a modest fee of £20,000, could be observed to be strangely but accurately philosophical:

To make a man happy is a full-time job with no holidays. It leaves us very little time to take ourselves too seriously, and if you have children you have no time at all. Men tell you many things. His desires of each day and night, and his dislikes. When to talk when to be quiet, when to give an opinion on his problems and when just to listen, when to ask questions – when to welcome him with kisses, and when your hand in his is quite enough . . .

Marlene arrived in London at the end of May 1955 to rehearse for a new season at the Café de Paris. This time her salary had been fixed at £6,000 per week without so much as a murmur from Neville-Willing, who as well as being a close friend clearly knew when he was on to a winner. The Café even put up a plaque: affixed to the pillar where she had leaned to listen to the rapturous applause of her last première it read, 'Dietrich rested here'.

There was a slight problem with the Dorchester: the actor and entertainer, Danny Kaye, had booked into Marlene's favoured Oliver Messel suite on the hotel roof. He was asked to give it up, and did so willingly, or so it would appear. Marlene's première, a few days later, was little different from most of the others. The auditorium was packed with celebrities, including the Sultan of Johore, Tyrone Power, Leslie Caron, and the actor Clifton Webb whom, it is said, had once humiliated Marlene by fighting at the Ruban Bleu with Tallulah Bankhead over a handsome young Austrian army officer. Needless to say, Tallulah had walked off with the prize. Marlene's dress, a copy of the one she had recently worn in Las Vegas, raised more than a few eyebrows as she was introduced by her friend, Douglas Fairbanks Jnr, with a speech penned by playwright Christopher Fry. The songs, too, were from her Las Vegas show, but with one entirely remarkable exception. After her curtain call, she returned to the stage and, in a quaint but convincing Cockney accent, sprinkled with a subtle hint of Berlinese, she hit them for six with 'Knocked 'em in the Old Kent Road'.

As with her previous season in London, Marlene was introduced by a different celebrity each night. Dame Edith Evans, Lady Violet Bonham Carter (later Lady Asquith). Eva Bartok, Orson Welles and MP Bessie Braddock were but a few household names who stepped forward to become bathed in the famous pink spotlight. The latter, a somewhat hefty woman, found herself laughed at by some of the audience, particularly when Marlene asked her about the various badges on her coat. Mrs Braddock surprised her by revealing that she was Honorary President of the Professional Boxers' Association. She then gave the audience a taste of their own medicine, in effect, by inviting Marlene to spend an afternoon with her in the House of Commons. One week later, this extraordinary event took place. Marlene and her host ate lunch in the Strangers' Dining Room so as not to give any indication that Marlene might have nurtured Labour Party tendencies, surrounded by a large group of excited politicians, begging her for an autograph. Later on, she listened intently to a debate by the Opposition members Herbert Morrison and Clement Attlee and to a heated tirade concerning unemployment in Jamaica and the arrowroot industry in St Vincent. She also met Manny Shinwell and only narrowly missed meeting Harold Wilson. She told the press, outside the House, 'Today I have learned something about arrowroot. I'll have to find out a little more, won't I?'

Whilst appearing at the Café de Paris, Marlene attended the Rose of England Ball, a charity event at the Dorchester put on to raise money for Gosfield Hall. She had agreed to sing but at the last moment was prevented from doing so because of a clause in her contract. Instead, she auctioned herself as a dancing partner and by the end of the evening had raised over £5,000. A few weeks later she did sing, at a party given by Lady Astor in Upper Grosvenor Street. The guests of honour were the Queen and Prince Philip and the Princesses Margaret and Alexandra.

Marlene's companion at this time was the actor Mike Todd, a handsome young man with the physique of a Remarque and a passion for spending money and living life to the full. The Hollywood star Joan Blondell had divorced him in 1950 and for a while he had submitted to severe bouts of depression, until launching himself back into the limelight with a recklessness which had surprised even his closest friends. In 1952 and 1953 he had presented 'A Night in Venice' at the Jones Beach Stadium – an extravaganza featuring the entire company of the Metropolitan Opera, plus a supporting cast of three hundred, staged on a massive revolving proscenium and set to the music of the Strauss family. Each production is said to have cost something in the region of half a million dollars. Needless to say, when Todd asked Marlene to star in his latest project – a celebrity-packed film version of Jules Verne's *Around the World in Eighty Days* – she did not hesitate for a second. The principal stars of the film were David Niven, who played Phileas Fogg, Robert Newton, Shirley MacLaine and Cantinflas. But what really made it work was the clever succession of vignettes, each headed by famous names playing parts set in the minor key. Many of these were friends or former co-stars, including George Raft, Cesar Romero, Charles Boyer, Robert Morley, Ronald Colman, Victor McLaglen, Glynis Johns, Fernandel and Noël Coward. The music was by Victor Young, who had recently directed her in the recording session for Brunswick that had produced what I have always regarded as the definitive versions of 'Falling in Love Again', 'The Boys in the Backroom' and 'Lili Marlene'. In the film Marlene played a San Francisco dance-hall queen and, although she was only on screen for a few minutes, she excelled as usual.

> I asked her, 'Is there anything you would like to say about *Around the World in Eighty Days*?'
> 'Oh, yes,' she replied. 'That was a wonderful film because it gave me the chance to work with Frank Sinatra – he played the part of my pianist. He's my very favourite American singer and he and I have a lot in common. Frank doesn't like all those so-and-so journalists poking their noses into his affairs. That's why he always appears to be tough. In reality he's a gentle, gentle man . . .'

Towards the end of 1956, Marlene was approached by the playwright and film director, Samuel Taylor, with the script of *The Monte Carlo Story*. She was reluctant to accept at first but when Taylor told her he had signed up the Italian actor Vittorio de Sica to play the male lead, she acquiesced. De Sica was, she claimed, 'the most exciting and romantic middle-aged man in the world'. In spite of the magnificent location shots, it was not one of Marlene's better films. She played, with what appeared to be incredible boredom, the poverty-stricken Maria, Marquise de Crevecoeur, who has arrived in Monte Carlo in search of a wealthy husband. De Sica, in the role of Count Dino della Fiaba, has arrived with pretty much the same idea, and during the film the couple are attracted to one another by pursuing each other's imaginary wealth, until eventually they do fall in love. The film was hammered by the critics: one described it as 'all icing and no cake'. It did, however, contain a trio of fine songs which, sadly, Marlene refused to record. Michel Emer had achieved world fame writing for Edith Piaf: 'L'accordéoniste', which he had written in 1940, had been her first million seller. For *The Monte Carlo Story* he came up, appropriately, with two gambling songs, 'Rien ne va plus!' and 'Les jeux sonts faits'. Marlene also sang the beautiful 'Back Home in Indiana', which Susan Hayward had mimed to Jane Froman's voice in *With a Song in My Heart*.

Although Marlene is reputed to have enjoyed making *The Monte Carlo Story*, she never became too attached to Vittorio de Sica and, according to the German actor Helmut Berger, she 'renewed her acquaintance' with Luchino Visconti, 'sending him bunches of roses and begging him to marry her'. This was just one of the fabricated stories which followed her around. She did not, however, get on with Natalie Trundy, who played Jane Hinkley in the film, and refused to pose with her for publicity photographs.

The next film, Agatha Christie's *Witness for the Prosecution*, was considerably more interesting and a great commercial hit on both sides of the Atlantic. It was also Marlene's second film with her friend Billy Wilder, who rang her in New York after a mutual friend told him that she had enjoyed the original play enormously. In a recent interview, the octogenarian but still sprightly director said of Agatha Christie, 'For every five hundred great dialogue writers, there are only five great constructionists.' Of Marlene, he said with the utmost sincerity, 'To me she was more like a man, a fellow fighter. We talked a lot about illusion and truth. She was one of the great faces in the cinema. I'm going to miss her – or if I go first, she'll miss me.'

Marlene played the part of Christine Vole – in the German version of the film, in which she dubbed her own voice, this became Wohl – the beautiful wife of Leonard Vole (Tyrone Power), who has been charged with the murder of a wealthy widow. Christine, in an attempt to save her husband from the hangman's noose, pretends to be his enemy by testifying against him in the witness box, but she also disguises herself as a foul-mouthed Cockney informer who supplies vindicating evidence to the defence which proves Christine's testimony to be invalid. Two lines are repeated twice – once by the Cockney hag and secondly by Christine Vole as she takes the stand: 'Ah'll give yer somethin' ta dream abart, Mister! Want to kiss me, duckie?' The flawless Cockney accent was perfected by Charles Laughton, who played the judge, Sir Wilfrid Robarts, and his wife Elsa Lanchester, who also starred in the film. Marlene spent a lot of time at their house, going over the same lines hundreds of times. Cockney, she said, was the English equivalent of the Berlinese she had heard spoken by the servants back home and not too unlike the quaint but infectious Bellevilloise of Piaf and Chevalier. It was the language of the people. She also said that Christine Vole was a woman after her own heart because she had risked her life for the love of a man. What she did not add was that when Christine discovered her husband's guilt, she stabbed him to death. For myself, the film's greatest moment was when, exposed by Robarts, she screamed, 'Damn you! Damn you!'

Billy Wilder later admitted that the only reason why Marlene did not get an Oscar for the film was because he had been reluctant to allow the nomination to go ahead in case too much of the plot should have been revealed to the critics. The statement seems just as baffling now as it did then. *Witness for the Prosecution* also contained the most interesting song that Marlene had sung in a long while – an almost English rendition of a German *bier keller* song, 'I May Never Go Home Any More', written by Jack Brooks and Ralph Arthur Roberts and sung with a roisterous male choir.

Also in 1958, Marlene appeared with Orson Welles in *Touch of Evil*, which he also scripted and directed. It was the only one of her films that I did not try to discuss with her, principally because it was the only film she had starred in that I had disliked . . . even more so, I had loathed it, apart from the brief scenes she appeared in. In his book *Marlene*, Alexander Walker described her unnamed role as 'a cigarillo-smoking brothel madame, wearing a tentacular black wig that she had found in a closet'. This was very apt and almost certainly was one of the phrases that had caused Marlene to lose her temper and burn Walker's excellent book. What I did not like about the film, apart from Orson Welles's gross, perspiring Hank Quinlan and the Charlton Heston character, was the curious way in which it had been shot – all from unusual angles. The scene where Welles squeezes an egg I had found disgusting. It had, however, contained a couple of classic one-liners from Marlene: 'Lay off the candy bars', whilst gazing at Quinlan's huge, bloated face and, at the end of the film when he has been shot dead, comes what may be regarded as one of her major philosophies on life when she says laconically, 'He was some kind of man, but what does it matter what you say about people?'

What Marlene said about this actor, however, was important, for she dedicated six pages of her autobiography to him and when interviewed for Maximilian Schell's 'heard-but-not-seen' documentary she snarled, 'If you're going to talk about Orson Welles, then make sure you cross yourself first!'

In France, Welles was regarded as Christ, returned to the earth to make films – that is because France is a cultivated country. Orson Welles revolutionized the Seventh Art by becoming its lighthouse, and yet he was not always appreciated in America. Today, *Touch of Evil* is an international classic, but in 1958 Universal made fun of it. Many years later (in 1975) Orson Welles won an Oscar, and I did not agree with Universal's hypocrisy. I would have loved to have dropped a bomb on them to send them to heaven – or rather, to hell.

Early in 1959, and accompanied by the by-now-faithful Burt Bacharach, Marlene set off on a series of engagements which would take her to far-off locations not usually visited by cabaret entertainers. Her first stop was at the Copacabana Palace in Rio de Janeiro. She flew via Varig Airlines, the only one who had ever supplied her with a bed so that she could sleep throughout the long journey. The 'Anjo Azul' (Portuguese for blue angel) – as the people of South America had baptized her after seeing her in the film – received a fanatical, if dangerous, reception when the plane touched down after one of the biggest publicity campaigns Brazil had ever known. Twenty-five thousand screaming fans streamed on to the tarmac, into the pathway of the plane, causing the pilot to swerve off the landing strip. Marlene was moved to tears. Five years later, the world would be swept by Beatlemania –

in Rio, it was Marlene-mania, so it came as no surprise to me when she included several songs from the *Dietrich in Rio* album in her list of favourite songs.

Wearing an ultramarine diaphanous dress which barely covered her breasts and which appeared to be held together at the groin by a clasp of pearls, she opened with 'Look Me Over Closely' and went straight into 'You're the Cream in My Coffee' and 'My Blue Heaven'. Her gown, she had claimed, was designed to titillate the *men* in her audience and yet she was shocking when she came to the line, 'Just Molly and me'. The management had asked her to change it to 'Just Johnny and me', but she had refused. She also sang 'Das lied ist aus' (Warum) known to the English-speaking world as 'Don't Ask Me Why I Cry' and meant as a tribute to Richard Tauber, whom no one in Rio had ever heard of. In this song, Marlene really went over the top, and slightly out of tune, on account of the emotion, driving the audience at the Copacabana into an unaccustomed frenzy. Some of them rushed up to the stage, others climbed on to their tables – and began chanting. After the last song in her first half – 'Je tire ma révérence' there was the now-familiar, noisy drumroll which enabled Marlene to leave the stage and change into her male attire. The whole process took her exactly sixty seconds and when she sang 'I've Grown Accustomed to Her Face', as a man singing to a woman, sitting astride a chair, everyone began banging their cutlery against their plates. She then sang Harold Arlen's 'One for My Baby' made famous by Frank Sinatra and instead of ending her show with the usual 'Falling in Love Again', she opted for a rarely heard upbeat number called 'I Will Come Back Again'. For a curtain-call, she sang several verses of 'Luar do sertão', a *fado* popularized that year by Amália Rodrigues, the Portuguese singer known then as the Queen of Fado, in flawless Portuguese.

Marlene repeated her success in São Paulo and in Buenos Aires. In Buenos Aires, the crowds outside the theatre were so vast that she had to be carried into the building on the shoulders of four armed policemen whilst everyone chanted 'Marlene divina'.

Her mood, however, was somewhat subdued when she arrived in Paris in November 1959 to be greeted by a delegation headed by Bruno Coquatrix, the director of the doyenne of the French music halls, the Paris Olympia, who had agreed somewhat reluctantly to act as her agent while she was being presented not at his theatre, but at the more affluent Théâtre de l'Étoile. At the press conference, unable to get her cigarette lighter to work she said gruffly, 'What are you all staring at? Give me a light, for God's sake!' And when asked to kiss Coquatrix whilst posing for photographs, she snarled, 'Why should I? I don't even know the man!' The ensuing questions did not help her bad mood. When asked to divulge the new songs in her repertoire she snapped, 'Come to the show and see for yourself . . . if you can afford it!' She then delivered a point-blank message to the reporters gathered outside the airport: 'From now on, I want to work. If you don't allow me to rehearse in peace, I shall ask for the protection of the gendarmes.'

There were further problems when she examined the theatre. Claiming that she could not be seen properly from the back of the auditorium, she brought in additional lighting which she herself positioned and told the stagehands to move back the first five rows of the stalls – by no means an easy task.

Marlene was paid an estimated £30,000 for her two weeks' stint at the Théâtre de l'Étoile, putting her almost on a par with Edith Piaf, at that time the highest-paid female entertainer in the world. Piaf was not present at her opening night due to ill health – she had recently been hospitalized with double bronchial pneumonia and had almost died – but she did manage to attend one of the shows during the second week. Jean Cocteau and Jean Marais were there and so were the Aga Khan, Maurice Chevalier, Lena Horne, Alain Delon and Martine Carol. Cocteau told his friend, the revue writer Jacques-Charles who, with Michel Guyarmathy of the Folies-Bergère had wanted to engage her, 'Marlene, like children playing at knights in armour, entered into legend on horseback astride a chair.'

It was around this time that Marlene met Roger Normand, in Parisian music-hall circles something of a cornerstone. Born in the Auvergne in 1920, he had joined Mistinguett's company in 1942. After the war, Normand had left Mistinguett to make a film called *Gueule d'ange*, and some years later he had written one of Colette Renard's biggest songs, 'Lili-Vertu'. At the time of Mistinguett's death his pianist had been Charles Dumont, the man responsible for many of Edith Piaf's later hits, including 'Non, je ne regrette rien'. Roger told me:

Marlene gave me the impression that she was very tough . . .
this was because of all the things that had happened to her
during the war. Underneath, she was a soft touch. She was
much more generous to her friends than Garbo, whom I had
met at around the same time. I remember her dinner parties.
She would present everyone with a gift and put on the most
magnificent meal, then sit in a corner and munch an
artichoke or a poached egg! So far as I know, she no longer
entertains, though she still gets the occasional visit from her
butcher. She's used him for years. But she and I got on very
well. She once told me that the Auvergnat soul had much in
common with the Jewish one. If Marlene could have been
born in France, she would have chosen the Auvergne.

Roger Normand also wrote Marlene a song, a poignant number
called 'Au dernier moment', which she is thought to have 'test'
recorded at the same time as 'J'aurai toujours une chambre à
Berlin'.

Paul Tanfield, writing for a French newspaper, attempted to
take a leaf out of Cocteau's book by penning a glorious, almost
surrealistic, account of Marlene's first appearance in Paris since
the war. Indeed, one theatre critic even suggested that Tanfield and
Cocteau might have been one and the same:

She swayed up to the microphone with a lubricated walk as
old as Eve, with her hair a cascade of spun gold – and
Shakespeare was speaking of Cleopatra when he said, 'Age
cannot wither her!' But the same can be said about Dietrich,
the soignée, indestructible fifty-four-year-old butterfly – a
grandmother, a rarity, and a legend in her lifetime . . .

'Yes, of course I can remember Roger Normand and the song he
wrote for me,' Marlene said. 'He wrote it with the man who was
musical director at the Paris Olympia. But I don't think I did it at
the Étoile, and I know I wasn't allowed to do "La vie en rose". I
sang "Where Have All the Flowers Gone?" in French – the words
were by Francis Lemarque. I'd first heard that song done by a
group. It sounded lousy – they hadn't taken it seriously enough, so
my daughter helped Burt Bacharach with the arrangement. I sang it
in French in 1959, then recorded it in all three languages the

following year. Unfortunately, everybody seemed to prefer the German version.'

'I like that version, too,' I admitted. 'Sag mo vir die . . .'

'You don't even know any German,' she suddenly bellowed and the receiver seemed to rattle in my hand. 'You can't even begin to pronounce the title, let alone understand any of the words. It's "Sag mir wo die Blumen sind?" for God's sake.'

'Well, that isn't important,' I said quickly, trying to compensate for my mistake. 'What I mean is, your songs transcend the language barrier, so I don't need to understand what you're singing about to get the feel of the song, to experience the emotion.'

Marlene muttered something under her breath at this.

The original version of 'Where Have All the Flowers Gone?' had been recorded by the Kingston Trio. Although a massive commercial success in the United States – not necessarily proof of quality in a world governed by revolutions per minute – it had lacked any sense of propriety. In my opinion, it had sounded bland and uninteresting. As 'Où vont les fleurs?' it had been covered during the Sixties by Eva, another German *Sprechtsinger* who had cut an absolutely first-class version of 'Lili Marlene', and there had been a passable version by Tino Rossi. As 'Sag mir wo die Blumen sind?' however, it could not even have been attempted by anyone but Marlene.

Her interpretation begins as little more than a whisper, very gradually building up to a climax wherein the voice suddenly breaks and she cries out, quite literally, the German equivalent of 'Gone to graveyards every one!' before relaxing, almost nonchalantly returning to the point where the song has opened. She had erred, however, with the actual date of the recording session – this had taken place in Paris in 1962, when she had dined with Edith Piaf and Théo Sarapo. Colpet had also adapted another Piaf song, 'Le chevalier de Paris', into German for her and this was recorded on the same day.

'You said that you couldn't sing "La vie en rose", certainly not in France, because Piaf was still singing it,' I commented to her. 'But what about "When the World Was Young?" '

'I never sang that one in French,' she replied. 'The French lyrics have nothing to do with the English one.'

'And what about the Prévert and Kosma song?' I pressed. 'It was originally called "Sans me parler", but you insisted upon it being changed to "Déjeuner du matin" – "Dinner in the Morning". Why was that?'

'Because it was a Marianne Oswald song!' she cried. 'You know that already, for God's sake! Why do you keep mentioning her?'

'I only wanted to talk about the song.'

'But the lyrics were so simple. The woman is sitting at the table when the man comes in. He pours the coffee into the cup, then adds the milk and sugar. "*Il a mit le café dans la tasse. Il a mit le lait dans le café.*" But I can't remember what he did with the spoon.'

'He stirred his coffee?'

'No, that can't be right. He picked up his hat first.'

'That was after he'd drunk the coffee and smoked the cigarette.'

'Yes, you're right. That was the theme of the song. He was about to leave her, so he kept blowing smoke-rings. Then he put his cigarette out and walked out into the rain, without speaking. Prévert said that the couple must have had a row, but how could that be if he never spoke? And then, at the end of the song the woman sings, "*Et j'ai pris la tête dans mes mains, et j'ai pleurée.*" To tell you the truth, I hadn't heard my version of the song for years.'

'You said that you'd thrown away all your records. Some of those were extremely rare.'

'And they'd started to clutter the apartment,' she levelled, as though committing an act of what amounted to sacrilege had been but an exercise in tidying up, adding to her alleged mania for cleanliness. 'And sweetheart, I never listen to myself unless I have to. I never watch any of my old films, and if I want to hear one of my old songs – if it's necessary, that is, then all I do is wait until I am alone. Then, if I don't have it on tape or compact, I try singing it to myself.'

'Well,' I said. 'You still have a good voice.'

Marlene laughed at this. 'Aye-aye-aye! Did I ever have such a thing, dear?'

10

'Annie Doesn't Live Here Any More'

If I don't want to speak to anybody, I'm always in Switzerland. In the past, if I didn't want to meet anybody after a show and be bored out of my head, I had nothing to wear. Even famous people can sometimes be parasites.

The morning after her Théâtre de l'Étoile première in November 1959, Marlene was interviewed in her Paris apartment by the journalist Nancy Spain – one of the many celebrities who had introduced her at the Café de Paris and whose endless list of close friends included Gilbert Harding, Noël Coward, Hermione Gingold and, particularly, the French couturier, Ginette Spanier. Nancy had been one of the handful of people allowed inside Marlene's dressing room before her performance and the star had found the similarity of their jackets so hilariously amusing that they had gone out on the town. Her interview with Nancy Spain is thought to have been her most explicit ever, primarily because the journalist had 'sworn on her own life' never to reveal a single word of what had been said. Instead, she composed a glowing retrospect of her career, filled with superlatives, and in doing so enabled Marlene to begin to trust journalists again. Four years later she was devastated when Nancy was killed in a plane crash whilst on her way to Aintree Racecourse to cover the Grand National. Upon hearing the news of her death, Noël Coward wrote, 'It is cruel that all that gaiety, intelligence and vitality should be snuffed out when so many bores and horrors are left living.'

> 'Most journalists are not even fit to be called human beings. That's why everybody always got me wrong. They never bothered contacting me to ask for my opinion, and in any case I never would have told them anything because they would only have twisted everything I said. The woman who spoke to me after my Paris début didn't. Her name was Nancy Spain, and she kept a lot back. She was very, very kind. It was through her that I got to know Gilbert Bécaud – the man who wrote me "Marie-Marie". I was looking for a song to take with me on my tour of Germany, and the theme about the prisoner asking the girl to write to him was so wonderful. "*Marie-Marie, écris donc et souvent, au Quatorze-Mille-Deux-Cent.*" The first time Bécaud heard me singing his song, he burst into tears. I knew straight away that I would be singing it for a long, long time. Then Henri Salvador gave me "Cherché la rose", another lovely song. The other French song I took with me was the one that Marianne Oswald had done. I thought, "What's so remarkable about somebody drinking a cup of coffee?" But they loved it. Then I wanted to include the German version of "Annie Doesn't Live Here Any More". The words were appropriate to the way I felt about Germany. Max Colpet advised me not to do that.'

Marlene flew to Berlin in May 1960, extremely apprehensive about her reception. Although she had agreed to sing almost anywhere in West Germany, she had dismissed any idea of crossing the border into the East, even when an East Berlin theatre offered her the equivalent of £2,000 a night for just ten songs. She was met at the airport by Willy Brandt and Hildegard Knef and was observed descending the steps of the plane somewhat tremulously. The two thousand people waiting on the tarmac were mostly on her side, particularly an elderly admirer who clutched her to her breast and said, 'Well, can't we be friends again?' This adulation continued whilst she was being escorted around the UFA studios at Babelsberg, although in the newsreel clip she still seems very much on edge, as though expecting someone to rush out of the crowd and attack her. She later admitted that she had actually anticipated someone hurling a bomb. Such threats were taken very seriously indeed: on the first evening of her tour, her car was pelted with tomatoes and rotten eggs as she got out and dashed into the theatre. Later, she was faced with a sea of angry banners that implied that she had forgotten her mother tongue, with the words 'Marlene Go Home' scrawled in English.

Even so, her recitals were triumphant, particularly the one at the Titania-Palast in Berlin, where she took sixty-four curtain calls. Many critics regard this as the greatest performance of her career, although the quality of the live recording is not as good as it could have been. As she had told me, Max Colpet had reworked several of her old songs. 'Allein' was perhaps her most popular song, apart from the ones from *The Blue Angel*. Instead of singing 'Marie-Marie' in French, she sang it in German as a reminder, perhaps, of what had happened in the past. She also sang 'Ich hab noch einen koffe in Berlin' ('I still have a trunk in Berlin'), which certainly was not true at the time, and never would be.

These songs, along with 'Jonny', 'Peter', 'Mein blondes Baby', 'Ich weiss nicht zu wem ich gehöre' and 'Wer wird den weinen' (the very first song she had sung in Berlin in the Twenties and at sixty-one seconds the shortest), she recorded in a single session with Burt Bacharach in Berlin.

Afterwards, she met Josef von Sternberg, now well into his sixties and ailing. Their conversation, unfortunately, was not recorded and whenever they did speak, their voices were kept to a discreet whisper.

Marlene's tour had been partly organized by Norman Grantz who, instead of accompanying her, had decided to tour South America with Ella Fitzgerald. Marlene had made few comments about this, though she had been far from pleased, but during the tour she leaned heavily on Burt Bacharach. According to some sources, her musical director could do 'absolutely anything' with her. So, when Bacharach expressed a desire to hear the East German Opera, in spite of her own convictions, Marlene allowed him to 'cross the Wall'. A few days later he publicly defended her at Rhenanie when a young woman rushed up to her, spat in her face and said, 'This is for Germany, and what you did to us.' He then persuaded her not to cancel her show and again there were dozens of curtain calls. At Bad Kissingen, when she was harassed by a street-gang outside the stage door, he threatened several of the thugs with physical violence, and managed to get her into her car before they began throwing bricks. And although she never mentioned anything even to her closest friends, one only has to read between the lines of Marlene's autobiography to realize that Burt Bacharach was very probably one of the greatest loves of her life . . . artistically, spiritually and physically.

> With Burt Bacharach, I was in a seventh heaven . . . but until now I have only spoken about the artiste. As a man, he represented everything a woman could desire. He was tender and affectionate, bold and courageous, strong and loyal. Above all he was adorable, thoughtful, and magnificently delicate. . . .

At Wiesbaden, Marlene was greeted with more GO HOME banners, though by this time she was used to them. The majority of people who bought tickets to see her were only interested in hearing her sing her famous songs and in witnessing a legend in the flesh. Her recital was very much like the ones she had given in London and Paris. The material was slightly more on the German-language side, although most of the songs she sang in tails during the second part of her act were in English. 'One for My Baby' was always performed straddled across a chair (in her own words, 'horse-fashion') and towards the end of the song she would get up and make for the wings, hand in pocket and trailed by the spotlight. On this particular occasion she tripped and fell behind the side curtain, banging her shoulder against the boards. In spite of the pain, she returned to the stage and sang two more songs before launching into a high-kicking routine with half a dozen tuxedoed chorus girls, although she did keep her left hand in her trousers pocket.

After her show, she and Bacharach met Josef von Sternberg and his son for dinner and it was then that Bacharach realized that there was something wrong. The next morning he drove her to the American Army Hospital where a surgeon diagnosed a fracture of the left humerus. When the surgeon added that he had seen many such injuries on English and American parachutists during the war, Marlene laughed. Bacharach passed out cold! She refused to have her arm set in plaster, but allowed the surgeon to strap it close to her body. At her next rehearsal, she allowed her mentor to teach her how to perform on stage using just one arm. Interestingly, for the rest of her career, Marlene used the full-arm swing much favoured by Piaf and her genre to a distinct advantage, particularly in lively numbers such as 'The Boys in the Backroom'.

The tour ended at Munich, when Marlene's penultimate farewell to Germany was taped for posterity. She had already made it clear that she would never sing there again publicly unless the people, or at least a great many of them, changed their attitude towards her. Considering the fact that she held almost every German who had drawn breath responsible for what had happened during the war, this seemed unlikely at the time. Therefore, when she flew out of Germany – alone, because Burt Bacharach had agreed to stay on for a week to supervise the pressing of the *Wiedersehn mit Marlene* album taken from the Munich tape – there were a few tears maybe, but certainly no regrets.

Immediately after her German tour, Marlene flew to Israel and into yet more controversy. The authorities told her, on the eve of her press conference, that she would not be allowed to sing any of her German songs. The same ruling had applied a few weeks before when Sir John Barbirolli, conducting a series of special performances of Mahler's *Second Symphony* in Jerusalem and Tel Aviv, had been ordered to remove the German vocal sections. But if Barbirolli had acquiesced without too much of a fuss, Marlene refused even to consider the idea of not singing in her native language.

'Israel was the most rewarding country I ever toured. The people were wonderful. And you know, the authorities tried to stop me from singing my German songs, so I told them, "That is ridiculous. I've always sung in English, French and German, and I'm not going to stop now." Then I said, "I was born German but I'm an American citizen, living in Paris. And you all know whose side I was on during the war." That didn't make any difference, so in the end I just pleased myself.'

The tour opened in Tel Aviv. Marlene walked on to the stage and sang 'Look Me Over Closely', 'My Blue Heaven' and a selection of songs from her films before launching into her German repertoire, with such conviction and sincerity that she got away with it. Then she announced, 'Here's a song about the child in the night who is crying because he's hungry.' And turning the tables on her own country, so to speak, she sang 'Shir hatan', a Hebrew lament that had been especially written for her by Zaria Sahar. After the song she was awarded a thirty-five minute standing ovation. When she later performed it in Haifa and Jerusalem, the adulation excelled anything she had ever known. These, and not her German recitals, were the greatest of her career.

It was because of her attitude towards Germany that, at the end of 1960, Marlene was approached by Stanley Kramer to play the part of Madame Bertholt, the widow of a Nazi general, in his production *Judgment at Nuremberg*. The film's strident message was that all the Germans had been responsible for the war and not just the leaders. When Kramer explained this to her, she is alleged to have accepted to do the film without so much as glancing at Abby Mann's script, although her decision almost certainly must have had something to do with her desire to act opposite Spencer Tracy, whom she later described as 'the only truly admirable actor I ever worked with'.

Marlene chose her own clothes for the part – a brown-black suit with matching hat, which she had made up in Vienna. Then, to complement her 'widow's weeds' she sent to Germany for a box of heavy silk stockings and several pairs of old-fashioned square-toed shoes. She then flew to Hollywood to begin filming.

The cast list was impressive. Besides Spencer Tracy there were Judy Garland and Montgomery Clift – the former trying desperately to cope with her weight problem and the latter suffering with his nerves. There was Burt Lancaster, marvellously portraying a character named Ernst Janning and the German actor Maximilian Schell played Hans Rolfe as though his life depended upon it.

I asked Marlene what it had been like working with Schell. 'He was absolutely terrific! Such wonderful acting!'

'And Montgomery Clift?' I posed. 'Some of the others?'

'I don't want to talk about Spencer Tracy, if that's what you mean,' she furthered. 'Well, other than saying that he was such a wonderful man. I didn't have much to do with the other one – with Montgomery Clift. He was an absolute bag of nerves. It was something to do with his drinking, and a man he was having some trouble with. And Judy Garland was a mess, too. Sometimes you

can talk to people – you advise them what to do, and in the end
they only please themselves. Judy Garland was like that. She didn't
know anything about how to take care of herself. I knew that
within a few years she'd be dead . . . and you know, I felt happy
when she died because for the first time in her life she was actually
doing something she wanted to do. We only have one life, David,
and if we decide to end it all, that's our business. Everybody has a
right to put themselves out of their misery if that's what they want
to do.'

'And the film,' I pressed. 'You didn't like most of your old films.
What about this one?'

'I think the script was one of the best I ever had,' Marlene
admitted. 'Yes, I liked the film. But who wouldn't have loved
working with Spencer Tracy?'

As with most of her later films, Marlene monopolized the set –
arranging all her own lighting, poring laboriously over the script,
and making suggestions and alterations where she thought fit.
Some years later, in *Marlene*, Maximilian Schell's award-winning
documentary of her life, she actually tore a strip off him for
suggesting that actors could improve a scene by ad-libbing, which
was why every single one of her own improvements had to be
written down before she even considered facing the camera.

The Madame Bertholt role was not a sizeable one but it did
contribute enormously to the film's human edge and her lines
expressed her own sentiments exactly. For once, the actress did
have a great deal in common with the character she was
portraying on the screen. One only has to listen to what this
character is saying to work out which of the lines Marlene wrote
herself. She tells Tracy, whilst they are sitting in a noisy *bier keller*
surrounded by a crowd of drinking Germans:

'There are things that happened on both sides. My husband
was a military man all his life. He was entitled to a soldier's
death . . . he asked for that. I tried to get that for him, just
that, so that he would die with some honour. I went from
official to official. I begged . . . that he should face the dignity
of a firing squad. You know what happened? He was hanged
with the others. After that I learned what it was like to hate
. . . I hated with every fibre in my being, every American I

knew. But one can't live with hate. We have to forget, if we are to go on living.'

Later, she and Tracy take a stroll through a street. Ironically, the song emanating from a nearby bar is 'Lili Marlene' and she explains what it is about. then, as she serves coffee in her room, she explains not the philosophy of Madame Bertholt, but the philosophy of Marlene Dietrich:

'I'm not fragile, I'm a daughter of the military. Do you know what that means? It means I was taught discipline . . . a very special kind of discipline. When I was a child we used to go for long rides into the country in summertime. I was never allowed to run to the lemonade stand with the others. I was told, "Control your thirst, control your hunger, control your emotion!" It has served me well.'

Judgment at Nuremberg was a massive commercial success and as such may be deemed the very last of the great Dietrich films. In Marlene's own words, the two productions that followed were 'money-making jokes'. Considerably more important was the proposition put to her by the documentary film-maker, Louis Clyde Stoumen, who had scripted *The Black Fox*, a very hard-hitting chronicle depicting the rise and fall of Hitler. In searching for a narrator for his work, Stoumen had to look no further than Marlene. He pieced together three reels and arranged for her to see these and the script. She signed the contract without even asking how much she would be paid for the probject. *The Black Fox* remains an extraordinary and intensely moving document and a fine tribute to Marlene's innermost feelings. Once she had accepted to read the script over the film footage, she made minor adjustments which, upon the film's release, would create a lasting impression on the generation that had sprung up from the war. When she read during one of the concentration-camp scenes, 'And Hitler did not even spare the children,' she broke down and wept. This was left in the narration and almost certainly was responsible for the film winning a Hollywood Oscar for the best documentary of 1962. Many years later, Marlene's and Stoumen's paths would cross again when her grandson, John Michael Riva, went to UCLA, where Stoumen was teaching.

In May 1962, Marlene flew back to Paris to begin rehearsals for a new season at the Olympia and this time she was friendlier with the press, not objecting at all when asked to pose for pictures. She spent time with her closest friends in the city – Ginette Spanier and Edith Piaf – and on 12 May she finally got around to recording 'Sag mir wo die Blumen sind', beautifully reworked by Max Colpet and Burt Bacharach. On the other side of the disc was 'Die Welt war jung', the German version of 'Le chevalier de Paris' which she had recorded only after Piaf had given the new arrangement her blessing. What is strangely and tragically ironic is that during Marlene's visit to Paris, Piaf suffered a horrific recurrence of her 1949 nightmare when she had lost Marcel Cerdan. Douglas Davies, a handsome but fragile young American painter who had seen her through her brush with death in New York during the winter of 1958-9 and with whom she had fallen head-over-heels in love, only to have him walk out on her after she had brought him back to France, was killed in a plane crash just outside Orly airport on 3 June 1962. This time Marlene was not there to comfort her friend, which probably explains why she wrote in her autobiography that she would always regret abandoning Piaf 'like a lost child'. Marlene was also still mourning the recent deaths of her friends Gérard Philipe and Gary Cooper, and Erich Maria Remarque had just suffered a stroke.

When Marlene opened at the Olympia, the audience observed that her repertoire had been modified, though only slightly. She was still performing what she called the third-rate songs from her films – strictly due to public demand – but there had also begun to appear the songs with meaning, such as 'Marie-Marie'. Gilbert Bécaud had sung it on the same stage that same year, a far cry from his first appearance at the theatre in April 1954, when mass hysteria had resulted and many thousands of francs' worth of damage had been caused when his fans had begun smashing up the seats. Marlene also sang 'Où vont les fleurs?' and 'Je tire ma révérence', as well as 'Déjeuner du matin'. All of these songs went down remarkably well in this, the middle of the 'yé-yé' age. Indeed, Marlene had been so baffled by this sudden incursion of noise that when, as a joke, Bruno Coquatrix invited her to Claude François's opening night, she accepted without hesitation.

'Why sound so surprised – just because I went to the Olympia to see Claude François?' Marlene asked.

'Because I am surprised,' I replied. 'You're the last person I'd expect to be interested in rock and roll.'

'Well, you needn't be,' she levelled. 'He was terrific because he was one of the first to do what he did. Johnny Hallyday was another. I adored him! The man had so much talent, and he was so beautiful! God, he was so very beautiful! Mind you, I didn't care for his wife. She was what the French call "une mangeuse du micro", and I don't mean that to sound like I'm being offensive. In my opinion she was just another pretty face.'

For fifteen years, theirs had been the most talked about marriage in French showbusiness. Johnny Hallyday, whose lean, hungry looks and moody mien had caused his fans to hail him as a French James Dean, and Sylvie Vartan, blonde and beautiful, the envy of a whole generation because she claimed to have tamed the beast within the man. These two and Claude François had ruled over the French yé-yé wave.

'And today?' I asked. 'I'm surprised you never sang anything by Aznavour. Why was that?'

'He never wrote me anything! As for today, there is so little genuine talent in France. Gainsbourg's gone, and Piaf. There was a girl on the television the other night, and when I read all the hype about her in the newspaper, I decided to watch her show. She was miming! Maybe I'm old-fashioned, dear, but I just don't care for pop-singers, or their songs.'

'You adapted Bruce Welch's Theme for Young Lovers in 1963. That was a pop-song.'

'Yes, but in those days pop-songs were better than they are now. It wasn't all bompity-bomp and a lot of noise. I heard the Shadows playing that song when I was in London that year. I wrote the German words at the same time as I adapted "Mutter hast du mir vergeben". But I never sang it on the stage because I had difficulty remembering the words. My own words, would you believe it!'

In the summer of 1963, Marlene was awarded the prestigious Knight of the Léopold Order of Belgium for helping the Allies during the war. No one knows quite why this had taken nearly twenty years but she was suitably moved to tears. Soon afterwards she sang 'Where Have All the Flowers Gone?' and 'Lili Marlene' in front of the Queen Mother at the El Alamein Reunion.

Two weeks later she witnessed mass hysteria when she appeared in the Royal Variety Performance but this was not just for herself as the Beatles were included in the very same programme. Marlene was perfectly willing to pose for several publicity photographs with the Fabulous Four from Liverpool, although she declined when asked to do joint signings, later doling out the customary batch of autographed photographs and even climbing on to the roof of her car in the most unladylike manner so as to enable her friends to get a better glimpse of her. Truly, she was in her element.

In November 1963 she also paid a brief visit to a London recording studio to cut 'Paff der Zauberdrachen', the German-language version of 'Puff the Magic Dragon', which she had first heard sung by Peter Paul and Mary. She had anticipated this as her new single, with another folk song on the flip side, 'Die Antwort weiss ganz allein der Wind', the German almost word-for-word translation of Bob Dylan's 'Blowin' in the Wind'. When Marlene sang this magnificent song in English, it proved so tremendously successful that she recorded it in the language, and the following year it was issued on the flip side of 'Where Have All the Flowers Gone?' This, many people considered, was her new theme-song:

> Where have all the soldiers gone?
> Long time passing . . .
> Gone to graveyards, every one!
> When will they ever learn?

In the spring of 1964, Lord Harewood announced that Marlene would be taking part in that year's Edinburgh Festival, while she herself surprised many people by announcing that she had signed a contract to sing in Russia. At a London bookshop she had bought a bilingual edition of Konstantin Paustovsky's *The Telegram*. Although a bestseller in Russia, the work had only a moderate success in Europe and was printed with the Russian text and the English translation side by side. It was not easy to read, although Marlene does not appear to have had much difficulty reading anything. Her attempts, however, to buy Paustovsky's other

' "Moi, je m'ennuie". I don't know why I'm reminded of that old song
every time I think of that film. I guess it must be because I really *was* bored!'
From *Seven Sinners*, 1940.

'This is me, impersonating Tallulah in 1948, wearing my favourite Balenciaga outfit.' After she died, Marlene was dressed in this costume.

'Cybulsky was probably the most beautiful man I ever knew. I shall always hold myself responsible for the way he died. That day will haunt me for the rest of my life.'

'Piaf and Cocteau shared the same soul. They even died on the same day and after I'd said goodbye to them, I swore that the next funeral I'd attend would be my own.' This photograph was taken in 1939. Marlene was good to her word and did not even attend her husband's funeral.

'This photograph with Mae West was taken in 1936 when I was making *Desire* with Gary Cooper. I loved that costume. I called it "the beginning of today's good taste".'

'This was taken in 1950, whilst I was doing *Stage Fright* with Hitchcock.
The only problem I had making the film was being forced to listen to all
those English actors talking about the weather!'

'I know this was taken in the late forties, but I called it "Cherché la rose" because it reminds me so much of the beautiful song by Henri Salvador.'

works were unsuccessful and when she touched down in Moscow in May 1964 she immediately asked her translator – a woman called Nora – to put her in touch with the writer. Because of this, the waiting press committee were not quite as interested in her private life and film career as they were in her cultural tastes. For more than an hour she spoke about her literary favourites, among them Rainer Maria Rilke, Knut Hamsun, Goethe, and of course Hemingway and Remarque. She was then told that Paustovsky had recently been laid low with a heart attack, so her nursing instinct took over at once: the writer was sent a number of gifts, bottles of pills and medicines, and the usual roses.

Russia was in itself a tonic for Marlene. Burt Bacharach had begun to express a certain amount of dissatisfaction at spending so much time on the road. He had recently teamed up with the lyricist Hal David, composing the first of many pop songs that would very soon bring him more money and fame than he had ever achieved working with Marlene. One of the most popular recordings in Britain, early in 1964, was Cilla Black's 'Anyone Who Had a Heart'. Almost certainly, this was why Marlene hated pop singers, for it was a series of pop songs that had inadvertently forced a parting of the ways. Bacharach even composed a song for Marlene, 'Kleine treue nachtigall', for which Max Colpet supplied the lyrics, but she did not sing it at once and showed little interest in recording it until 1974. In 1964 the song was given English words by Hal David and, as 'Message to Martha', was a big hit for Adam Faith. Thus, while preparing for her Russian tour, Marlene admitted to feeling despondent because, it is said, Bacharach had announced that this would be his final tour.

This despondency, of course, soon left her once the curtain rose at the Estradi Theatre, facing the river directly opposite the Kremlin. She sang in English, French and German. Her new songs included 'Wenn der Sommer wieder einzieht', a sultry but effective adaptation of 'A Little on the Lonely Side' and two stirring military songs, 'Wenn die Soldaten' and 'In den Kasernen'. The Russians were impressed – so much so that they made her take thirty-seven curtain calls. She was showered with roses, and one young soldier was so moved by 'Wenn die Soldaten' that he asked his girlfriend to throw Marlene her gold-plated necklace. The trinket was virtually worthless when compared to the rest of

Marlene's jewellery. Even so, she rushed off the stage in tears and the theatre manager ordered the hapless soldier to fetch her back. His reward was a kiss in front of two and a half thousand people . . . and she kept the necklace. She then sang several more songs, removed her shoes and, dangling them in her hand, gave an encore of 'Falling in Love Again' to perhaps the most emotional scene that had ever been witnessed on a Russian stage. She told the audience, in English, with Nora acting as her translator, 'I love you so very much. This is because there are no lukewarm receptions here . . . you are either very sad, or very happy. I myself have a Russian soul.'

Marlene's greatest, and proudest, moment in Russia occurred whilst she was appearing in Leningrad in a special series of concerts for smaller audiences of poets, writers and actors. Within a twenty-four-hour period she did four separate shows: each programme was considerably shorter than her regular recitals, though this did amount to fifty-six songs in all. During the afternoon, Nora informed her that a still very ill Konstantin Paustovsky was sitting at the back of the hall but that he was apprehensive about meeting her because he had heard that at times she could be indifferent towards strangers, if not actually hostile. Marlene sent him a message, asking him to meet her in her dressing room. Paustovsky did one better than this – he walked on to the stage after she had just sung 'Lili Marlene'. Marlene was so overwhelmed that she sank to her knees at his feet and kissed his hand. Paustovsky started to cry and so did most of the audience. A few months later the great writer died but not before his wife had given Marlene a copy of each one of his books.

In Russia, Marlene was unbelievably generous towards not just her musicians, but everyone who came into contact with her – stagehands, doormen, porters and cleaners were allowed to bypass protocol when invited to her parties and, as she was not allowed to take any of the money which she had earned in Russia away with her, she spent every last rouble on those who had helped to make her tour a success. As Leslie Frewin wrote in his book *Dietrich: The Story of a Star*, 'She seemed to have conquered all Russia where Napoléon had failed.'

In August 1964, Marlene opened at the Royal Lyceum Theatre in Edinburgh in what would be her penultimate series of recitals with Burt Bacharach. Her fee was not disclosed, though it is reputed to have compared with what she had been paid ten years before at the Café de Paris. She was pleased when, telephoning Lord Harewood to ask how many seats had been sold, she was told all of them . . . and not to the tourists, but the locals. She was even more delighted when, during the Festival itself she met Svietoslov Richter, the famous Russian pianist. She is also said to have been 'tickled' by a piece which appeared in *The Times* several days later:

What more is there to say about Marlene Dietrich? She DEFIES change! To watch her work is a lesson of sheer professionalism. The pencil-slim silhouette sways in a glittering peach-coloured creation which catches the spotlight at every movement . . . and just about the biggest thing in faces since the Mona Lisa. And she knows it!

11

'Don't Ask Me Why I Cry'

You're a very innocent man, dear, because you don't know the world, or that love affairs are more important than marriages! That's why I slept with all my partners – well, all except for Emil Jannings . . .

In September 1964 Marlene flew to London to record nine songs for her new album, *Sag mir wo die Blumen sind*. These included several of the *chansons* she had performed in London, a brand-new one by Mischa Spoliansky called 'Auf der Mundharmonika' and her very first Christmas song – 'Der kleine trommelmann' – a German adaptation of 'The Little Drummer-boy', which she had first heard being performed by Gracie Fields. And for the first time in more than a decade most of these songs had not been arranged by Burt Bacharach – popular success had changed him, just as as her world had transformed Marlene. At the last minute, she asked for the album's title to be changed to *Die neue Marlene* – the new Marlene. Nothing could have been more appropriate.

Engaged by her friend the theatrical agent Binkie Beaumont, Marlene opened at the Queen's Theatre, London on 23 November 1964. She was accompanied for the last time in a major season by Burt Bacharach, probably reluctantly so, yet still earning her immense respect when she announced, 'He is my teacher, my critic, my accompanist, my conductor and my arranger. I wish I could say that he was my composer . . . but he's everybody's composer!' The songs, twenty-two in all, were little different from the ones she had sung at the Café de Paris, though their order had changed. Edith Piaf had advised her exactly where to position each song in her programme, sound advice which would hold good for another decade and, to prove the point, there were just four songs from her films. The final show, on 12 December, was recorded and fourteen of the numbers later issued on the album, *Dietrich in London*. One of the most-played songs was J.J. Niles's 'Go 'Way from My Window'. Half-way through this Marlene broke down and this moving moment was not edited out of the album. Penelope Gilliat of the *Observer* wrote, 'She is the only performer alive who can make an erotic number sound like a lullaby – you have to be a thousand years old to do it, which she is.' One of the few critics Marlene actually admired, Harold Hobson of the *Sunday Times*, wrote:

At her best she is better than Chevalier, because more tender in feeling – better even than Piaf, whose thrilling voice was uncomfortably enormous for the sorrows she used to sing about so memorably. Grief is not ideally a theme to announce on the trumpet and drums. It is better suited by the wounded notes of the nightingale, with what it has of mutiny and defiance poignant, and quiet. Miss Dietrich shows us the height and depth of love by catching it with infallible precision in the very moment of its defeat, rejecting because rejected ('Go 'Way from My Window') – or when it is killed ('Don't Ask Me Why I Cry') – or when it feels itself neglected, as when the prisoner begs Marie to write to him more often . . .

It was not by coincidence that five tracks from the *Dietrich in London* album appeared on her list of favourite songs – the coincidence is that the success of this album, particularly in Britain, caused the country to miss out on *Marlene singt Berlin-Berlin*, her favourite album. One number from this, 'Solang noch Untern Linden', was familiar to me because it had been used as the theme for the Agnes Bernel cabaret series, which had been broadcast some time before by the BBC. The other songs were, most un-Marlene-like, written by largely unfamiliar composers such as Walter and Willo Kollo, Jean and Robert Gilbert, Robert Katscher and a number of others.

One of the titles on Marlene's list, 'Alles tun auf diese Welt', caused me a few problems when I asked her to hum a few bars. The list had been typed up by Mrs Colpet, who had included somebody else's song by mistake.

> 'I've never even heard of it, so how the hell can I sing it? Really, David, you should know all of my songs by now! I wanted the album to end with a funny song, and that's what should have been at the bottom of the list. "Nach meine Beene ist ja ganz Berlin verrückt" . . .'
>
> 'That's on the *Marlene singt Berlin* album.'
>
> 'Not Berlin, sweetheart, Berlin-Berlin. You're supposed to say it twice! And I didn't record the album in London or Paris, as you wrote in the script. I did it in Munich.'
>
> 'You returned to Germany . . . really?'
>
> 'I said to Max, "If I'm going to record fifteen songs about Berlin, then why the hell should I do it here in Paris? He produced the album, and Bert Grund did all the arrangements. And you know, it's my favourite album of all time.'

In January 1965, probably a few days before her clandestine visit to Germany, Marlene sued Air France for £3,000, holding them responsible for the loss of her luggage which had included a mink coat. As if to hammer home a point she accepted an offer from another airline to publicize the leg-room in their jets. Their earlier advertisement had featured a girl basking on a beach with the electioneering slogan 'Let's Go With Labour', which many MPs had found shocking. Marlene's photograph, promoting the company's VC10, was 'seductive but not suggestively so', and is reputed to have cost them £70,000. The advertisement was, by and large, aimed at the American market and appeared in *Time* and *Life* magazines. But when BOAC's European publicity director, Paul Breuer of Frankfurt, learned that Marlene's photograph would be used for direct-mail advertising in Germany, he issued a stern warning. 'No chance. She's too unpopular over here.' Then, quite suddenly Breuer decided that as he did not wish to incur Marlene's wrath – or that of her lawyers – he issued another statement to the effect that during the war he had only been a child. Marlene's unpopularity was disproved soon afterwards when a reporter conducted an independent survey in Bonn. However, when Marlene was asked what she thought of the Germans, she did not hesitate in saying, 'There are still too many Nazis who are sitting around over there, and nothing delights me more than their dislike of me! Who cares if the Germans hate you when you have the affection of the British?'

Something else which generally displeased Marlene at this time was the publication of Josef von Sternberg's memoirs, *Fun in a Chinese Laundry*. Until the summer of 1965, Marlene had telephoned him every now and then to inquire about his health. Often it had been an effort but it does seem that until this time she was still fond of him. The book changed all that. Von Sternberg's attitude towards her was harsh and unflattering on the printed page. He never referred to her as Marlene, but Frau Dietrich or simply 'the Fräulein' in the German translation. Marlene burned the book and swore never to speak to her former mentor again.

Towards the end of the year, Marlene visited Australia. She had been engaged to open at the Princess Theatre, one of the most prestigious in Melbourne, on 7 October, and two days prior to this she booked into the Southern Cross Hotel. At a press conference, where the word 'hype' took on a new meaning, she discovered that the journalists' chairs had been arranged around a dais, 'like in an interrogation room', and she was particularly annoyed by the photographers, one or two of whom tried to get close-up shots of her face. Her Australian impresario, Kenn Brodziak, managed to sort out the situation, and Marlene attempted to make up for her bad mood by cracking jokes. When a Tasmanian reporter explained that the island was off the coast of Australia, she retorted, 'I know that, although I used to think that Ernst Lubitsch had invented it!' (She was referring to his film, *The Princess of Tasmania*.) She did snarl at another reporter, however, when he asked her if she was wearing a wig, 'Why – are you?' Matters were made worse when a young waiter stepped up to the dais and presented her with a 'Madame Marlene' – an ice-cream in the shape of an apple. The real Marlene placed it on the floor next to her handbag, and it stayed there.

Her opening recital at the Princess Theatre was as splendid as everyone expected, although there were problems afterwards when the time came for her to sign photographs in the theatre foyer. Her aide failed to rush these around to her dressing room on time and Marlene attempted to leave the building with out them. Some of the crowd near the stage door became hostile. Surging forwards, they tried to prevent her climbing into her car and, when one of the theatre staff slammed the door, a small boy had his hand badly crushed. Marlene's concern was only too obvious. She would have loved nothing more than to get out of the car and tend to the injured child but the thought of what could have happened to her, with or without the protection of her bodyguards, only terrified her. Her assistant, with some difficulty, shouldered his way through the crowd. The car window was opened a fraction, enabling the troublesome photographs to be pushed through. It is not known how many of them were signed, if any, but Marlene instructed her chauffeur to start the engine and as the car moved off, the photographs were flung into the middle of the car park, where the now frantic crowd pounced upon them like beggars squabbling over coins.

Marlene was so disturbed by this incident that she vowed never to sign another photograph. She changed her mind exactly one year later when mobbed by adoring fans outside the Golders Green Hippodrome in London. Then, the police were brought in to prevent matters from getting out of hand and, if the photographs of the event revealed Marlene as 'the laughing legend', deep inside she was far from content:

'Genuine fans should never behave badly, David. It was all too frightening. I would rather they write to me than mob me.'

'But you don't like receiving fan mail,' I said.

'All right,' she returned. 'So there are the genuine fans and there are the ones who make nuisances of themselves writing to me all the time. Some of them ask for my autograph, or maybe a photograph – the journalists are worse than anybody. A few weeks ago I sent a journalist a photograph because he'd asked for something to remember me by. It turned up in a Berlin newspaper, with more lies! That's why I sometimes tell Manuel to tell people I don't live here any more. Even he gets fed up with being pestered by journalists. And then you have the radio and television announcers. They're always telling people where I live. If I'd have known what

Mitterrand was going to tell everyone, I never would have made that blasted tape.'

Marlene was not referring to the French president but to his nephew who had been engaged as Master of Ceremonies at the 1989 European Film Awards. She had agreed to express her best wishes on tape and this had been relayed to the nearby Théâtre des Champs-Elysées, along with a clip of film from her farewell concert at the same theatre in 1965. Mitterrand had announced, perhaps innocently, that Marlene lived 'just up the road' from where the audience had gathered and that for the first time in ten years she had decided to 'break her silence'. The next day, the apartment block on the avenue Montaigne had been besieged by press photographers and reporters.

'The photographs they used during the Film Awards were very beautiful,' I told her. 'They're the kind of photographs that I would like to use for my book.'
   'No,' Marlene exclaimed. 'I'll send you some private photo-graphs for the book. I know that I can trust you not to let it out of your hands – I'm a pretty good judge of character, and I've lived long enough to be able to tell when somebody's sincere or not. I'll send you one photograph, then you'll tell me what you think before I send any more. You give me a call, tell me what you want, and I'll decide if it should go in the book. It's much better if I choose the photographs myself than rely on any publisher. I mean, they never seem to get anything right . . .'

The first photograph arrived a few days later – it had been taken in 1934 and depicted her wearing a hat and spotted scarf, leaning against what appeared to be a radiator. I did not know the name of the photographer, though the printing on the reverse told me it was from the Kobal Collection, which I found amazing considering how she disapproved of collectors. Later she sent me a photograph which had never been seen before for the back of the book jacket, with an accompanying note instructing me to 'blacken out the cigarette with just a bit of ink'.

I asked her if she was a reformed smoker, adding, 'I remember seeing you in the film, *No Highway*. You kept lighting up one cigarette after another. Each time the scene changed, you lit up.'

'That's true. I used to smoke like a chimney, sometimes up to three packs a day. I gave up after making a bet with Noël Coward. He said I wouldn't last the year out, but stopping smoking was so very easy. And you told me, David, how you sometimes get through fifty cigarettes a day. You've got to promise me you'll stop, if not for yourself then for your wife's sake. Think of what you must be doing to her asthma! All you need is the willpower, and I'm sure you've got plenty of that!'

That very day, I threw away my cigarettes, and I have never smoked since.

Marlene continued, 'As for the photograph – well, maybe you should leave it as it is, and I'll make sure that I don't send you any more pictures with cigarettes on them. I also have made up my mind about the other photographs for the book. There's the one I told you about earlier, when I'm kissing Piaf, and the one that I had taken in Poland. Then there's the one with Cybulsky, and the one with the soldier that you spoke about. I want nothing from my films – well, maybe the one with Jimmy Stewart, one with Gabin, and the one you liked from *A Foreign Affair*, so long as Jean Arthur doesn't get her mug in the book. And I want no photographs that were taken in Germany, in Southport, or when I made that terrible television show . . .'

The photographs arrived one at a time: a small one signed by Christa Vogl which had been taken in Warsaw in 1966, one of her in a ringmaster's uniform, another with Judy Garland, one of her 'pretending to be a whore'. There was also a large colour study of her reclining in a chair.

She explained, 'I was sitting in that chair the very first time I spoke to you on the telephone, so I think it appropriate that that particular photograph should go on the front of the book, don't you? And I can't find the photograph of Cybulsky that I was looking for, so you'll have to get it yourself . . .'

Marlene had mentioned this man's name several times before but each time I had asked her to elaborate she had clammed shut, which ultimately made me suspicious that there might have been more to him than met the eye. Zbigniew Cybulsky was a Polish actor who had starred in a film called *Ashes and Diamonds* and who had been referred to in Marlene's autobiography under the sub-heading 'Actors' Styles'. John Barrymore, with whose sad but inevitable decline that of Cybulsky had been later compared, was hailed by her as 'a champion in every category'. That fine British actor Brian Aherne, with whom she had made *Song of Songs*, had had a caustic sense of humour which had been appreciated – and I knew, of course, how important such things were to Marlene! James Stewart had played a love-scene 'as though he had put on one shoe and was thinking about searching for the other'. Her true feeling for Cybulsky, however, she had hidden from her readers by keeping what little was known of their friendship to a purely professional level:

> At a certain period in my existence I truly believed that good fortune had smiled upon me, for I was asked to make a film with my friend, the great Polish actor Cybulsky. Once seen, his face was never forgotten. He was the only man I knew who could uncork a bottle of vodka by smacking his hand against the bottom – this he would do time after time as the bottles were passed hand-to-hand along our table, much to the pleasure of his guests. Cybulsky will always be remembered, which is more than can be said for a great majority of others actors I have known . . .

Early in 1990 the singer-actress Jacqueline Danno asked me to assist her with an exposition commemorating General de Gaulle's centenary. I had supplied her with a dossier and voice-over appertaining to several female artists who had kept Britain and America going throughout the war, including Jane Froman, Gracie Fields and Vera Lynn. Jacqueline's exposition proved so popular in France that she was invited to take it to Warsaw and I asked her if, whilst there, she would be able to make a few discreet inquiries about Cybulsky.

By the end of the month I had several contacts in Poland, including Ryszard Straszewski, who had produced Cybulsky's last film, *Szyfry* (*The Enigma*) and Hanna Dabrowska, who had witnessed several of Marlene's performances in Warsaw. I also spoke, over the telephone, to a representative of the Komiter Kinematografii (Polish Film Society), who had been assigned to the team of 'minders' for Marlene's tour of Poland in 1966 when the country had been more oppressed than it is today.

Marlene visited Poland three times. None of these visits was mentioned by her biographers, no doubt because of a severe lack of information. The first two were widely covered by the Polish press. There had been subtle hints at a romantic involvement between herself and the young actor. The third and final visit had taken place in strict secrecy and had ended with one of the greatest tragedies of her life. The relationship between Marlene and Cybulsky, however, was only brought out into the open because of a song . . .

'I wrote the German words to "Ich werde dich lieben" and 'Sch, kleines baby",' she told me, after I had singled out her little-known talent as a songwriter. 'And some of the words to "Lili Marlene".' 'There was also a very beautiful song called "Mutter hast dur mir vergeben",' I said. 'It's the kind of song that grows on you the more you hear it, even though I don't understand a single word of German.'

'Your German is lousy,' she said, and not for the first time. 'The song means, *Mother, did you forgive me? Will you ever forgive me, Mother, for what I've done to you?* But it wasn't a German song, originally, and it was the favourite song of a very good friend of mine. His name was Zbigniew – Zbigniew Cybulsky. When I sang it for the first time, I sang it to him in Polish and he cried . . . God, how he cried! Then when I returned to New York, I sat down and wrote out the German words. Cybulsky's most famous film was on the television here, not so long ago. *Cendres et diamants* . . . that was the French title.'

'*Ashes and Diamonds*', I repeated. 'It's a wonderful film.'

'It's more than wonderful,' Marlene enthused. 'And if you've seen the film, you'll realize just how talented he was, and what a terrible, terrible waste it was to have to die like that.'

Hailed as the only indisputed major actor force ever to have emerged from behind the Iron Curtain, Zbigniew Cybulsky had been born near Cracow in 1927, the son of a civil servant. During the Nazi occupation of Poland he had gone underground in order to receive an exemplary education because his family had wanted him to become a lawyer. In 1952 he had rebelled against his family by joining an avant-garde repertory group, the following year founding the Bim-Bom Theatre in Cracow.

The young actor was noticed by Andrzej Wajda, then as now the most famous film director in Poland, and offered a minor role in *A Generation*, the first in a trilogy of outstanding films about the Polish Resistance. As Rostek, he had displayed a moody mien not unlike that of James Dean, his Western counterpart, though Cybulsky could never be accused of emulating Dean, whose films he never saw until 1960. Similarly wayward he certainly was. During a scene in *A Generation*, he balanced a dagger on his chin whilst forcing his head back as far as possible, starting a dangerous craze which quickly spread across Poland. In another scene, after a fierce argument with the director, he leapt on to a speeding train rather than use the stuntman provided. So far as Marlene was concerned, this scene would prove tragically ironic, a few years later.

Cybulsky's next few films may have been successful in Poland, but they had little or no impact on the West. Then in 1957 he had made *Der achte Wochentag*, written by Marek Hlasko and directed by Alexander Ford – the erotic love-making scene, set against the grim Polish landscape, had resulted in the film being banned in Poland, in spite of its success in Germany and at the Cannes Film Festival.

In 1958 came *Ashes and Diamonds*, one of the finest films ever to come out of Poland, and the most successful. Cybulsky portrayed Maciek, a young maverick Resistance fighter turned hired killer, described by one critic as 'a Hamlet in windcheater and dark glasses'. There was a great deal of actor-character similarity. Like Maciek, Cybulsky was a complex, hard-living individual. Like James Dean and Marlon Brando he was wayward, hard to handle, and like the former he was extremely neurotic – this aspect of his psyche came over so wonderfully well in the film, as did his fascination for things macabre. His death by machine-gun at the end of the film was described by the film buff Parker Tyler as 'the most eloquent death by violence ever staged in any motion picture'.

Cybulsky's performance as a confused young man was the most stunning I had ever seen from a man since James Dean's *Rebel Without a Cause*. The film's musical score also meant a great deal to Marlene. During the one love-making scene the song is 'J'ai perdu ma jeunesse', a popular number from the Thirties which had been sung by Damia and Adrian Lamy. Marlene had sung it herself to French troops during the war but after 1958 she never sang it again.

Marlene and Cybulsky had first met in Paris in 1961, when they had been to see Edith Piaf at the Olympia. The actor had stayed in the city long enough to play a cameo role in *Le thé à la menthe*, and Marlene had helped him with his lines. They had visited Britain during the autumn of 1963, where Cybulsky had scored a hit at the Edinburgh Festival. Always edgy and unsure of himself, and never seen in public without his dark glasses, he had spent most of his time 'getting drunk and learning dirty songs' with Kenneth Tynan, seeing Marlene privately.

On 16 January 1964 Marlene flew from Paris to Warsaw. She was not entirely sure what her reception would be like: the majority of her films, with cuts, had been shown in Poland though she was not generally regarded as a chanteuse – basically, her greatest selling point was the close bond which she shared with everyone who had suffered under the Nazi jackboot and Poland, of course, had suffered more than most. Two hours after touching down in the capital, she held a press conference at the Hôtel Eurpejski. She had especially asked for Cybulsky to be there but for some reason the actor failed to turn up. According to her memoirs, he had never heard Marlene sing on the stage and by his own admission he was terrified of meeting her on home territory. Although Cybulsky had never cared much for public or media opinion – the fact he was openly bisexual in a Communist country which frowned upon such things gives a clear indication of this – he was well aware that any 'friendship' between a man of thirty-seven and a woman of sixty-three would do considerably more than raise just a few eyebrows. Even so, he attended every one of her recitals at the Congress Hall and there were six within a period of seventy-two hours. He accompanied her on her visit to the Old Town, carrying the wreath which she placed on the monument commemorating the Ghetto war murders.

Marlene also went with him to the Actors' Club – a visit that culminated in her giving an impromptu if rather inebriated performance of 'Mutter hast du mir vergeben?' perched on Cybulsky's shoulders, singing for the students outside the university in sub-zero temperatures, wearing one of the actor's famous windcheaters. Of her fifteen or so songs for her actual concert performances, only 'Allein in einer grossen Stadt' was sung in German and she refrained from singing 'Lili Marlene' and 'In den Kasernen'.

When the time came for Marlene to leave Warsaw, she broke

down and wept in the airport lounge. She eventually gave a little speech in English, adding, 'I don't want to say goodbye – just let this be au revoir, until the next time.' Cybulsky was conspicuous by his absence, although nothing would ever prevent him from seeing her now that his career had taken off in the West. They met secretly in Sweden when Marlene played a handful of engagements there and he played opposite Harriet Anderson in Jörn Donner's *To Love* and his visits to Paris became more and more frequent.

When Marlene arrived in Warsaw for the second time, on 27 February 1966, Cybulsky was waiting for her at the airport. Still good looking, he had put on weight and this had caused him a few problems in his last film, *Mexico Soon!* in which he had played a swimming coach. Although still the biggest film star in Poland, as well as the richest, his personal life had never been short of turbulence – his marriage was on the rocks and he was in the early stages of alcoholism. Being with him probably reminded Marlene of her ordeal with John Gilbert during the Thirties but the substantial age-gap brought out her mother instinct. She did not stop Cybulsky from drinking, though having him with her most of the time did temporarily curb the habit. He was also allowed the rare privilege of being allowed to sit in on her rehearsals and, when he asked her to sing his favourite songs – 'Déjeuner du matin' and 'Mutter hast du mir vergeben?' – she consented.

As with her previous visit, there were six recitals in Warsaw, but these were followed by five in Gdansk and two in Wroclaw – all in a period of ten days. Her farewell show took place in Warsaw, where Cybulsky rushed on to the stage to present her with a bouquet of flowers – still wearing his tinted spectacles and windcheater. Marlene kissed him on both cheeks and acknowledged him as 'my good friend, the greatest talent in all Poland'. She ended her recital with the Polish version of 'Mutter hast du mir vergeben?', and there was not a dry eye in the house. The next day the actor waved her off as she boarded the plane for Paris.

During the next few months – his friends alleged because he was pining for Marlene – Cybulsky's state of well-being deteriorated to such an extent that his entourage feared he would end up destroying himself altogether in an endless binge of sex and alcohol. Even so, his career seemed to take on a new dimension with films such as *Full Steam Ahead!* and *Jowita*, with Barbara

Lass. Exactly who told Marlene about Cybulsky's renewed crisis is not known, but she decided to brook no delay in going to see him. During the first week in January 1967 she booked in at the Hôtel Metropol in Wroclaw. Her stay culminated this time with one of the saddest events ever to befall Poland:

> Our train for Warsaw was scheduled to leave at midnight, and Cybulsky personally saw to the couchettes. We said our farewells, and though his heart was aching he gave me his word that he would catch up with me as soon as he had finished working on his film. In fact, he changed his mind and decided to travel on the same train. He arrived late at the railway station and tried to board the train whilst it was pulling out. Then he slipped and fell, only to be crushed by the wheels . . .

Ryszard Straszewski informed me that Marlene had not been on the train at the time of the accident. My other source in Warsaw told me she had and that when she had asked about the delay an official had told her that something had been wrong with the line, hence the shunting backwards and forwards whilst station staff had fought to free Cybulsky's mangled body from under the wheels. 'The authorities wished to avoid a scandal by not having a famous actress weeping hysterically on the station platform,' I was told. 'We gave her extra blankets and something hot to drink and told her to get some sleep.'

Zbigniew Cybulsky was thirty-nine years of age when he died and if his days as 'the new James Dean' had been firmly placed behind him, no doubt because he was the better actor and no longer the mere symbol of a wayward generation, then he had also been on the threshold of a new career in England and the United States. He had also been contracted verbally to make a film with Marlene, which perhaps gives one cause to doubly lament his passing. A few hours after his death, as the train was drawing into the station at Warsaw, Marlene was told what had happened. She broke down and wept, though by the time she left the train she was suitably composed to be able to smile at the handful of waiting reporters. These had been forewarned not to ask her any questions and all were good to their word. It is not known if she actually visited Cybulsky's widow, though this would seem unlikely. Neither did she send flowers to his funeral. This would only have fuelled the scandal that the Polish authorities had striven to avoid in the first place. She did, however, have a few words to say to the press who turned up at the airport to wave her off. With tears in her eyes she said, 'The memory of my last visit to Poland will for ever remain one of the most beautiful experiences of my life – but not this one.'

'Cybulsky was the kindest, the most beautiful man in the whole world,' she told me, her voice breaking. 'He was so beautiful that each time I see his photograph I cry. I would have given anything to bring him back . . . and maybe one day I will speak more about him. All that I can tell you now is that I have always held myself responsible for what happened to him. It was all my fault. All my goddamned fault. Cybulsky was the kind of man any woman would have died for. Cybulsky was a god . . .'

One year after Cybulsky's death, his great friend and former mentor Andrzej Wajda offered a eulogy in the form of the film *Everything for Sale*, which starred Malgorzata Potocka, now one of Poland's top producers. Considering that his in-house star had helped him to achieve his own very high standing in the film world, it was the least he could have done.

Another 'god' who had once wanted to die with Marlene passed away on New Year's Day 1972, at a time when she was thinking of Cybulsky and planning a concert in Warsaw to honour the fifth anniversary of his death. This was her great friend and former lover Maurice Chevalier, whom she had never stopped loving since her *Morocco* days.

Marlene and Chevalier had met for the last time in New York only a few months before when he had been there to launch the English-language edition of his memoirs, *I Remember It Well*. Then he had told her of the new 'feminine hand' in his life, the thirty-eight-year-old ex-Bluebell dancer named Odette Meslier whom he had first met in a revue in 1952.

Marlene was in Paris when she heard that Chevalier had been rushed to the American Hospital de Neuilly with suspected kidney failure, and later transferred to the Hôpital Necker to be placed on a dialysis machine. She was also told that because of his advanced age there could be no question of a transplant. It was simply a matter of time.

'Chevalier lived very, very alone. I visited him often at his big house outside Paris. I flew over from America when I found out he was ill, and that man at the house tried to stop everyone from seeing him. That's when I went to the hospital – the one he died in, to see the doctors. But Chevalier had given orders that I should not be allowed to see him because he didn't want me to be worried.'

'So why didn't you go to his funeral?' I asked.

Marlene seemed to groan. Talking about one of the great loves of her life, so soon after discussing Cybulsky, was obviously very painful. 'I went to the funeral of Gary Cooper, and I went to the funerals of Piaf and Cocteau. After that I told myself that there would be no more until my own. That didn't mean that I was uncaring, or not thinking about him. I went back to America and cried in private – for Chevalier, and the others.'

12

'I Wish You Bluebirds in the Spring'

Most of the composers and songwriters of today are dreadful – they wouldn't know a song if it hit them in the face!

The nightmare of *I Wish You Love*, Marlene's only television spectacular, began late in the summer of 1972. Although she had always seemed relaxed and content within the closed confines of the recording studio, she had never liked doing television work. Since beginning her concert tours, she had also loathed cameras and, in particular, close-up shots taken in the middle of a song. The few television appearances she had made during her visit to Berlin in 1960, principally to sing 'Sag mir wo die Blumen sind?', had been exceptional only because she had wanted to make a statement aimed at the Berlin Wall, Hitler, the war, and everything she had hated about Germany. The 1963 Royal Variety Show had also been a worthwhile commitment because she had helped to raise £50,000 for the Variety Artists' Benevolent Fund. In her own words, she only accepted Alexander Cohen's extremely lucrative offer to film one of her live performances for posterity because she needed the money.

At the end of 1965 she had begun working on a volume of memoirs, provisionally entitled *Tell Me, Oh Tell Me Now!*, aided by a twenty-nine-year old Australian journalist called Hugh Curnow. The couple had met backstage at Sydney's Theatre

Royal, and she had been very impressed by the piece he had written about her show. Curnow spent several days showing her around Sydney. Such was his devotion that he insisted upon accompanying her to New York, then on to Paris. At this stage in their friendship Marlene learned, to her horror, that Curnow had a wife and children. Some time later he returned to Australia, though he and Marlene remained close. In 1968, whilst covering a story on a storm-tossed oil-rig, Curnow was killed in a helicopter crash. Marlene's learnt of this onlt three hours before her première at the Adelaide Festival of Arts but in spite of her grief she did not cancel her show. A few months later she paid back the advance for *Tell Me, Oh Tell Me Now!* and this left her financially unstable. She had just managed to stay afloat with the enormous fees commanded for her recitals. In poor countries such as Poland, however, she had always worked cheaply. Not so for her contract with Alexander Cohen – the fee for her fifty-odd minutes' television special was a staggering $290,000, the highest any artist had ever been paid for a one-off performance.

Marlene then announced her conditions. The recitals would take place in a British theatre as opposed to a New York one and she would give two performances. This way, the best versions of her songs could be edited to make it appear as if there had been just the one. Initially, she was delighted by the way in which her team were handling things. The New London Theatre had been scheduled to open in August 1972 although, when she arrived in October for the preliminary rehearsal, the building was still unfinished and she was greeted with the clamour from dozens of cement mixers and drills. Not only this, the actual auditorium was in a state of chaos with most of the seats waiting to be fixed into position.

'I thought about walking out and telling them all to go to hell. But what could I do? They told me the invitations had been sent out and that I would be singing before a privileged audience, whatever that was supposed to mean. I later found out that *nobody* was paying to see me. Even so, I couldn't let them down – not even the ones who wouldn't have come in the first place if they'd have had to pay. And even the cameras were more interested in them than they were in me. But I didn't sing for them. I sang for the people who would want to watch the show when they put it out on the television. I mean, that's what it was for!'

Initially, Marlene hit the roof about the stage. She had previously detailed the set requirements but these had been ignored. Therefore she gave instructions for the set to be taken down and reconstructed – a team was brought in to work on it throughout the night. There was a further problem the following afternoon when Marlene arrived at the theatre only to find the orchestra missing. Needless to say she lost her temper and, if one report is to be believed, her heated exchange with Cohen almost caused her to abandon the project altogether.

'So many things kept going wrong that I went to see the producer, and this time I really meant business. Then I told myself, "Marlene, you've never cancelled a show in your life. Don't let them win one over on you now." '

Only hours before the first performance, Marlene expressed her disapproval – for the umpteenth time – of the backdrop. This was a curious mélange of petals and she asked that it be substituted with a massive line drawing of her face, a design used for the publicity posters during her subsequent tour and for the covers of her programmes. She further expressed severe disapproval over the positioning of the orchestra, although nothing could be done about this. Stan Freeman had arranged his musicians stage-right, in the wings, which meant that Marlene could only just hear the backing through the gigantic speakers which were stacked behind the side curtains. The microphone too was of a type she had never handled before, causing yet another headache.

Incredibly, the finished film, though 'doctored' considerably, represented one of her finest performances. It began with a long drum-roll similar to the one that had been used as a fill-in whilst she had changed costumes during her earlier recitals, only this time and henceforth there would be no break at all in her programme. With the drum-roll came the dancing spotlights after which Marlene seemed to materialize, dressed in one of the tight-fitting Jean-Louis gowns, surmounted by the now legendary swansdown cape which, during Cole Porter's 'I Get a Kick out of You' she swept to and fro constantly about her frail form. There then followed 'a few songs from my records and films', and the well-aired anecdote about von Sternberg and *The Blue Angel*. One by one her songs whipped up the audience's enthusiasm until, shedding her cape, she emerged from behind the curtain looking more vulnerable than before. She sang 'When the World Was Young' – in retrospect perhaps the most autobiographical of all her songs. The lyrics fit her like a perfectly tailored glove:

> It isn't by chance that I happen to be
> A femme-fatale, the toast of Paris,
> I love what I do, I love what I see!
> But where is the young girl
> That used to be me?

The announcement for 'Lola-Lola' was anticipated, though not the tears which she shed during her next two songs. She repeated the last line of 'I Wish You Love' four times (once for each of her grandsons) adding to its very special magic. The emotion of Charles Merrywood's simplistic but hauntingly evocative song about the soldier coming home from the war was almost too much to bear:

> White grass 'neath the stones,
> Where lies my dear Mary,
> The war's over, seems we won . . .

After the song a nosegay was tossed on to the stage by an admirer. Marlene picked it up, crooned through three verses of 'Honeysuckle Rose' and tossed it back into the audience. Reaching out, as if wishing to embrace them in her arms, she sang 'La vie en rose'.

'Lili Marlene', which of course could never have been left out – even if Marlene had wanted it to be – was transformed into a masterly *symphonie en miniature* and was one part of the film which pleased her. Whilst she sang the now portentous lyrics, some thirty black-and-white photographs were projected on to a screen behind her, depicting her wartime activities and including a picture of her comforting a wounded soldier. The penultimate song. 'Where Have All the Flowers Gone?' was almost too much for her. Her voice broke whilst she was announcing the title and as the song ended the stage was suddenly bombarded with flowers – there really is no other way of describing what happened. Marlene certainly had not been expecting it: it had not been part of the deal, she later said, which explains why in one of the two finished films she stopped the cameras to tell an anecdote about one of her Hollywood 'epics' until the stage had been cleared.

'I'd just sung "Where Have All the Flowers Gone?" and all of a sudden it was as though I was being attacked. Before I went on to the stage, somebody told the audience to throw flowers – I loved it when they did, but in the past it had always been a spontaneous gesture, not something which had to be rehearsed. All I wanted to do was to sing my songs. Why couldn't they have been satisfied with that instead of trying to do something new?'

'And would you ever do another television spectacular, if you were asked to?' I posed.

'Never!' Marlene bawled. 'Not for all the money in the world! It was one of the most horrible experiences of my life! I swore then that I would never appear on the television again, and I never have!'

The television special ended with 'Falling in Love Again' and once more photographs were projected on to the screen behind her. This time the subject was her Hollywood films and her various interpretations of the *femme-fatale*. Marlene disliked this too, even though she had agreed to let it happen in the first place.

Three weeks after the show had been broadcast, an article appeared in the *Daily Mail* that ultimately led to a series of unpleasant courtroom battles. Written by the American journalist, Rex Reed, under the heading: DIETRICH'S AMAZING INQUEST ON HER OWN TELEVISION SPECTACULAR the article used words such as 'incompetent', 'inartistic' and 'lacking in financial provision', all claimed by Reed to have been used by Marlene in their interview. The ensuing fight between her and Alexander Cohen went on for several years, and began after an enlargement of Reed's piece appeared in the *Los Angeles Times*. Cohen, who had already refused to pay Marlene the $100,000 balance for her show, successfully sued her for damages. Even so, on 3 April the *New York Post* reported: 'Dietrich is entitled to full pay for her one-woman television show even though she bad-mouthed it, the State Appellate Division has ruled.' The article then concluded that according to the court's decision, Cohen would be forced to pay Marlene whatever he owed her. The producer protested over this and took out a libel suit for defamation of character. On 9 May a meeting of his and Marlene's lawyers decreed that if Cohen dropped his original law suit Marlene would accept $50,000, 'even if this had to be payable in instalments', and the matter ended. Even so, more than sixteen years later Marlene was still chomping at the bit. Enemies, it would seem, were never forgiven.

After her television special, Marlene was still sufficiently friendly with Alexander Cohen to accept an offer to do an introduction at the Tony awards, although she very soon regretted this. Her speech was a long one. Because she was unable to memorize it, she asked Cohen to prepare a series of cue-cards, thirteen in all. These caused havoc during rehearsals for the ceremony. To begin with, they were stacked one on top of the other, vaudeville-fashion. Marlene disagreed with this, finding it impossible to concentrate: from then on every one of Cohen's suggestions was angrily rejected. She was about to opt out of the ceremony altogether when someone suggested that thirteen men should be positioned in the orchestra pit, hidden from the spectators, to hold up each card in sequence. The ploy worked, though Marlene swore never to attend another awards ceremony.

Marlene's nightmare would be repeated when, towards the end of May 1973 she gave a series of recitals in Southport – an anxious time that was witnessed by Jeanne and myself. Within our hotel room there had been a mild argument over what to wear for what *I* had predicted would be an auspicious occasion. We had brought two sets of clothes with us because earlier that week we had turned up at a Dorothy Squires concert, in Jeanne's words, 'looking like a couple of dogs' dinners', only to find everyone else in denims and tee shirts.

My wife was four months pregnant and worried that her condition might show more in a long dress. I assured her that there was nothing to worry about, though half-way to the theatre she did point out that I was wearing odd socks and this necessitated a rush back to the hotel. When we arrived at the theatre a crowd had gathered already, and a military band was playing. Moreover we had to walk on a red carpet between two rows of immaculately uniformed guardsmen. Had I not changed my socks, it could have been one of the most embarrassing moments of my life. I mention this because the next day my feet would cause me an even greater humiliation, yet one which would bring Marlene towards me, many years later.

During the afternoon, Jeanne and I had been passing the theatre car park on our way to the pleasure beach when a little crowd, gathered about an ice-cream stall, had suddenly rushed off in the direction of the stage door. By the time we had caught up with them Marlene had been getting into her car. She was wearing a mid-blue trouser-suit and what appeared to be a taxi driver's peaked cap. Camera poised, I had advanced towards the scene, clicking away. The great star had seemed to snarl at me, though neither of her companions prevented me from taking my pictures.

Within the theatre foyer the Mayor of Southport greeted everyone personally, advising them not to touch the paintwork around the bar area, where liveried waiters served complimentary glasses of champagne. I wondered how Marlene would react, having to work in yet another unfinished theatre. Though the plans for the building had been on the architect's drawing board for almost a year, work had not started on the site until November 1972. Had Marlene been aware of the rush involved to get the theatre ready for her première, I am certain she would have cancelled, particularly so soon after her débâcle with Alexander Cohen. The Southport show was a combination of the television performances and the *Dietrich in London* album, with two numbers that had appeared in neither. I was so impressed by her entrance that I wrote in my journal:

The theatre was in total darkness. The orchestra played 'Falling in Love Again', and she was there – the Lorelei, the Great Marlene, the Blue Angel who never seems to get old. Blonde and still incredibly beautiful, she looked so fragile, especially when she shed her fabulous furs. But, once seen, Marlene is never forgotten!

If Marlene had experienced certain difficulties during the filming of her television special, then no problems could be edited out of a live performance. During the next sixty-five minutes the audience witnessed the depth of her anxiety. During her first song, 'I Can't Give You Anything but Love', her acute nervousness was felt in every corner of the auditorium. She announced, 'I'm here to open a beautiful new theatre, and as usual everything goes wrong! I'm waiting for someone back there to tell me why – it's been one hell of a day!'

Marlene had arrived at the theatre at two o'clock, to check out the set and order last-minute adjustments to the lighting. Joe Davis had done her proud here, lighting her from the footlights so that she would not perspire unduly and feel uncomfortable. Walking on to the stage, however, she had been confronted with the din from the auditorium of the workmen hammering the seats into position – most of the carpeting, still wrapped in polythene, had been in a locked van within the car park.

Now, after the first song, there was a lengthy pause and she turned to face the wings. Then she moved right away from the microphone, giving everyone the impression that she was going to walk off the stage. The spasmodic applause encouraged her to introduce her next song, a real horror called 'Boomerang Baby'. She said, 'It's a song I brought back from Australia. Perhaps I shouldn't have bothered, huh?' The humour returned but a touch for 'Jonny'. 'You'll have to excuse me for singing it in German,' she cooed. 'You see, no English words were ever written to it. I think they must have been trying to tell me something!'

Five songs followed. Then, divested of her furs she returned to the platform just as William Blezard's orchestra was beginning 'When the World Was Young' and tried to detach the microphone, only to discover that it was stuck. Stopping the music, she turned aside and called for help. This instruction was misinterpreted – the microphone was suddenly sucked back into the stage and this made her laugh. 'I wanted to sing with it in my hand!' she said, somewhat suggestively. 'Send it up again!' The microphone then took off like a rocket, soaring to a position two feet above Marlene's head but, even if the audience applauded wildly, she was no longer amused. When the microphone was eventually restored to its original position, she still could not detach it. In desperation she walked to the front of the steps and squinted up at the projection box. 'Isn't there anybody out there who knows what he's doing?' she yelled. A young technician, wearing scuffed denims and a tee shirt, materialized from behind the curtain. Grabbing the microphone, he slapped it into her hand. But she called him back for what must have been the longest and perhaps most humbling moment of his life and, passing the microphone back to him, she asked him to test it. The young man counted from one to three, handed it back with a clumsy bow, and was rewarded by a pat on the head. 'Thank you, dear,' she said. 'At least you seem to know what you're doing!'

The rest of the recital went without hitch. Marlene broke down half-way through 'Go 'Way from my Window', and again during 'Marie-Marie'. Then, before 'Falling in Love Again', she announced, apologetically, 'I want to thank you all for coming to the opening of this new theatre. There have been mistakes, but it isn't your fault. We are pioneers – that is why things go wrong!' Then, to a standing ovation she took a deep bow and, several curtain calls later, she was gone from sight.

Because it had been a very special occasion, after the show we decided to visit one of Southport's classiest restaurants. Though the establishment was virtually empty, several tables had been pushed together in the middle of the room and a card marked RESERVED had been positioned next to a massive floral display. 'For Miss Dietrich', one of the waiters remarked. Twenty minutes later a dozen laughing, tuxedoed gentlemen of varying ages filed past us and took their seats. I observed by turning around that every place had been filled. One of the musicians saw me, smiled, and said, 'She isn't coming. She says she isn't hungry. But if you really want to see her, be outside the stage-door at three tomorrow afternoon – and don't let on, otherwise she'll leave the theatre by a secret entrance.'

This time there was no crowd in the car park, though there was still the conglomeration of lorries, cement mixers, piles of bricks and sacks of rubbish. It had rained during the morning and there were puddles everywhere. At three, on the dot, Marlene appeared wearing the blue trouser-suit and taxi-driver's cap. I wanted to tell her how much I admired her but she ignored me – she was too busy negotiating the short flight of steps leading down to the car park. Then, a catastrophe! Trying to avoid a puddle, her shoe came off. Ever gallant, I rushed towards her to offer what help I could, and she saw the camera. 'Oh, it's you again!' I halted in my tracks as a woman with a pony tail assisted her with her shoe – this was her daughter Maria. Then Marlene herself looked me straight in the eye. 'It was the mud that did it! God, what a place!'

I stepped back into a puddle, drenching not just my own feet but my wife's as well. Then as the car moved off, its rear wheel drove through another puddle and saturated me even more. Marlene must have said something to the driver, for the car stopped for her to wind down the window. 'Okay,' she said. 'If you're so desperate to photograph me, go ahead!' I took several pictures, thanked her, and that was that – or so I thought. Sixteen years later, Marlene remembered our first 'meeting':

> 'You were there, David. You saw what the place was like. The theatre wasn't finished. There were cement mixers all over the place – there was no carpet in the dressing room. The sink didn't have a plug, and the paint was wet. It was terrible! Then my car nearly knocked you over, and I asked the driver to stop . . .'
>
> 'I think you're just having me on.'
>
> Marlene chuckled. 'All those puddles, and a man rushing at me with a camera? Sure I remember you! And I'll never forget that goddamn theatre – it was a lousy place!'

Immediately after this particular conversation I contacted the theatre in question. The current manager explained the difficulties of refurbishing and reopening a theatre on schedule though his suggestion that Marlene should have deferred her performance seemed unfair. After all, she was in the middle of a hectic tour. I then spoke to Donald Sykes, the man who had been house engineer in 1973. He had a very interesting tale to tell – not that I would dare print exactly what he had thought of Miss Dietrich! 'Just say that she was difficult and astute, and that she never missed a cue,' Donald said. 'The sound system was imported – she refused to use ours. She ordered a carpet to be laid. This had to run between her dressing room and the wings and it was to prevent the hem of her gold lamé dress from getting dirty. She asked for the carpet to be vacuumed half an hour prior to her performance. Then she told us to sweep and mop the stage. A table was requisitioned. This had to be thirty inches high and not an inch out either way – she even measured it. She used this for her cue cards, so that she wouldn't forget the order of her songs. That's what she kept looking at – the table and her daughter. She also asked for a pair of scissors to be placed on the table, next to the cue cards. We never found out what these were for and I was too afraid to ask! And the microphone? Yes, there was a hitch, but we managed to sort it out and she wasn't too difficult about that. Her show was perfect – perhaps the only fault was that it wasn't long enough. But she wasn't easy to get on with, not at all, though afterwards she did sign all our programmes. You said that her astuteness was due to her being a perfectionist? At the time, I put it down to old age . . .'

Marlene herself told me the 'secret' of the scissors. In order to perfect that legendary shuffling walk of hers, at least later in life, she always wore a flimsy rubber sheath under her dress, and the dress itself had been stitched up after she had put it on, at Southport. 'The scissors were there in case of an emergency, in case I had to be snipped out of the dress in a hurry. And they were the same ones that Piaf had used to cut her hair after Cerdan's death.'

The next two years were, in effect, a painful journey for Marlene, which I have no desire to linger over unduly. Her concerts throughout the world were largely triumphs of mind over matter. She gave two sell-out recitals at L'Espace Cardin, in Paris. The highlight of these was her superb rendition of Jacques Brel's 'Ne me quitte pas . . .' and 'Bitte geh' nicht fort', which with Burt Bacharach's 'Kleine treue Nachtigall' was her last commercial recording in 1974.

Soon after the Paris concerts, she appeared at the Queen's Theatre in London, where she tripped over a length of cable and fell backwards, badly bruising her legs but finishing the show all the same. She sang in a special show at Covent Garden, which was witnessed by my friend Terry Sanderson. He told me, 'Marlene had finished and was taking a curtain call when she saw this man place his dinner jacket on the edge of the stage. She picked it up, put it on over the Jean-Louis gown, and finished her calls!' The price she had to pay in Washington a few weeks later, however, was very high. Her orchestra, directed by Stan Freeman, had been positioned in a pit six feet below the stage. During the première she leaned forwards to shake Freeman's hand and almost fell. The next evening, to make things easier for her, he stood on top of his piano stool – this gave way and she was hauled into the pit on top of him. This time the show could not go on – her left leg had a gash stretching from her knee to her buttock and she was immediately flown to Houston, Texas, for extensive skin-grafts. These were not successful and when she arrived in London for a season at the Grosvenor House she had to be pushed around in a wheelchair. Sympathy was sorely lacking when the tabloids on both sides of the Atlantic lampooned her with a series of caricatures, adapting one of her most celebrated songs to make it 'Falling Off Stage Again'. And as they had done with Judy Garland a few years before, many people only went to her shows to witness if she could stand up on her feet. This cynical section of the public must have been disappointed therefore to find that her performances were as good as, if not better than, before.

One problem occurred on the night of the première which in retrospect she could have probably done without. Her friend, Kenneth Tynan, had been invited backstage after the performance and at the last moment informed Marlene that Princess Margaret was waiting to see her. Marlene gave the excuse that she was very tired, and that in any case she had nothing to wear, to which the Princess is alleged to have remarked, 'I don't care where it is, I will see her!' Marlene compromised by being 'received' in denims and an old shirt and no one complained.

Over the next few months Marlene continued to be plagued by ill health. She almost suffered serious injury whilst singing in Boston when an ex-GI who had seen one of her concerts during the war leaped up on to the stage and tried to grab her until he was manhandled away by two bouncers. A few weeks later she fell in her Paris apartment and broke her leg (the newspapers reported her *right* leg, though Marlene told me that it was the other one).

There was worse to come. On 22 September 1975 Marlene began a season at the newly built Her Majesty's Theatre in Sydney. The first night was a sell out but, as the week progressed, ticket sales dwindled considerably. By the beginning of the second week, she was playing to a sixty-per-cent capacity. This had nothing to do with Marlene's actual performance but with the fact that as she had refused to hold a press conference, few critics had bothered reviewing her show until the end of the first week. Quite simply, many theatregoers in Sydney did not even know that she had arrived in their city. Consequently, once Marlene had remedied the situation by giving the media their 'pound of flesh', the audience for the evening of 29 September was a good one. The curtain rose and as usual there were the usual false overtures meant to whip up the audience's excitement, but instead of materializing into the spotlight, all people saw was 'a hank of hair from behind a curtain, followed by a glimpse of clutching hands'. At once, the curtain was brought down. That small group of people whom Marlene ranked alongside Hemingway's parasites had not been disappointed – they applauded, sarcastically. The next morning she was diagnosed as having a broken femur in her left leg and an ambulance rushed her to St Vincent's Private Hospital. Surgeons put her in a plaster cast that covered her entire leg from waist to ankle. It was then disclosed that after breaking her leg in Paris a steel pin had been inserted into her hip and that a sharp twinge from this had caused the fall in Sydney.

Her departure from Australia was a feast for the media – wrapped in a sheepskin, she was hoisted by a forklift truck on to the plane bound for New York. On her arrival, she learned to her distress that Rudolf Sieber had suffered a stroke. Needless to say, she went straight to the UCLA hospital in Los Angeles, where she was told that her husband had little time left – he had already lost his speech. Maria, however, insisted that her mother return to New York for further treatment, and as usual when asked to do something, Marlene's self-confessed Prussian spirit obeyed. The hospital, it turned out, was one of the worst experiences of her life, for the doctors there put her into traction:

> My hospital room was filthy, and incapable of cleaning it myself, I brought in my friends to do the job. The food was disgusting, and I was worried for the patients without families who were forced to eat frozen stuff . . . every day they gave it a different name, and they never thawed it out properly. So why didn't I go to the Walter Reed Hospital for the ex-military, as was my right? That is the mystery . . .

Marlene's hospital treatment weighed heavily on her bank balance – the fees for the New York hospital alone were $300 per

day – and naturally she began thinking about her future. She
realized that in order to survive in the luxury to which she had
become accustomed, she would have to keep on performing, or
make another film. Billy Wilder did offer her *Fedora*, his
adaptation of the actor-turned-writer Tom Tryon's best-selling
novel, *Crowned Heads*. The role would have been perfect for her –
it told of the ageing film star who stays young by allowing her
beautiful daughter to take her place. For obvious reasons, Marlene
turned the film down and the part was given to Hildegard Knef,
who excelled in it. Marlene then began making plans to tour
Scandinavia and there was talk of a number of engagements in
Poland. She still missed Cybulsky.

None of these ambitions was fulfilled due to Marlene's fragile
health. The woman whom Art Buchwald had described as 'a
modern Florence Nightingale whose most important purpose in
life is to bring comfort to the sick and encouragement to the
wounded' was forced to face up to the fact that she herself needed
looking after and that the resources were not always there to do
so. She attempted to secure an undisclosed amount of reparation
money from Germany, claiming that her husband had been
deprived of his property by Hitler. She hoped that this money
would enable him to be installed in the Motion Picture Country
Home, where at least he would be allowed to die with some
comfort. His companion, Tamara, had died in a lunatic asylum in
1968, since which time he had been cared for by his housekeeper,
Eva Wiere. The money, however, was not forthcoming. What
Marlene had overlooked was the fact that Rudolf, like herself, had
left Germany before Hitler had come to power. As a last resort,
Marlene was forced to rent out her Park Avenue apartment but
even then Rudolf was not moved out of his ranch for his closest
friends, including Eva Wiere, declared that being surrounded by
Tamara's personal effects was the only thing keeping him alive.
During the last week of May 1976, Marlene returned to Paris. She
had barely settled in her apartment when she received a call from
California to say that Rudolf had died.

Marlene did not attend her husband's funeral – the combination
of illness, fragility and a desire to avoid the tittle-tattlers of the
tabloids prevented her from doing so. The chief mourners were
Walter Reisch, Hans and Varya Kohn, an antiques dealer named

Peter Gorian, Eva Wiere and, of course, Maria. Marlene did make a monumental effort to secure Rudolf's diaries because she was worried that they might fall into unscrupulous hands. Some sources suggested that Marlene was suffering from a guilt complex, but she did not destroy the diaries. Instead, she placed them in a bank vault and resumed her own memoirs. *Marlene Dietrich's ABC* had been published in New York by Doubleday in 1962 and had caused little stir. The new volume, *Nehmt nur mein Leben*, attracted an advance of $250,000 from the German publishers, Bertelsmann and Goldmann, but this amount was doubled by offers from *Die Sterne* and Simon and Schuster. Once again, Marlene found herself financially secure.

Her memoirs, however, were pretty unrevealing, which did not come as a great surprise to her intimate friends, but did come as a great relief to many acquaintances. Then, in November 1976 she suffered another tragedy when Jean Gabin died, almost without warning. Marlene is alleged to have told a friend, 'Now I have been widowed for a second time.'

13

'Go 'Way from My Window, Don't Bother Me No More'

I only wish that I could live for ever, for Maria's sake . . . because, you know, I only live for my daughter. She's such a remarkable, intelligent woman.

By the time Marlene got around to singing and recording 'Just a Gigolo' in 1978, it had been covered so many times that most of the music-hall fraternity had forgotten who had introduced it in the first place. Written by Léonora Casucci, and arranged by André Mauprey and Jean Lenoir, it had been recorded by Damia in 1930, two years after she had performed it in a revue at the Apollo in Paris. Its original title was 'C'est mon gigolo', and the French words were superior to the rather banal English ones. For Marlene, it had been an all-important swan song, for she had sung it in the film of the same name, directed by David Hemmings, in 1978, and just a few weeks after Damia's death. I remembered that Marlene's brief scenes for the production had been shot privately over a three-day period at the Eden Hotel, far from the set and from the glare of publicity which she had come to hate. David Bowie, perhaps the unlikeliest of co-stars, had told a British journalist that he had felt very distressed when informed that he would not be meeting his idol 'in the flesh'. The same ruling had applied to the other stars of the film – Curt Jurgens, Kim Novak and Maria Schell.

Marlene's role in *Just a Gigolo* was her most unusual since portraying Erika von Schlütow in *A Foreign Affair* – she played the mysterious, heavily veiled Baroness von Semering, a filthy-rich widow in charge of a legion of handsome young studs. The critic and biographer, Alexander Walker, had described the film, correctly so, as 'a West German evocation of the economic and moral chaos of the Weimar Republic in which her art had flourished'.

I asked Marlene if she had felt at all sad, making the film and recording the song so soon after Damia's death. 'Why should I?' she barked. 'She was old – she'd had a good run for her money.'

Many people anticipated that *Just a Gigolo* would be the first film in what should have been Marlene's twilight career. This was not to be, for until the end of 1989 she remained a virtual recluse in her avenue Montaigne apartment. Then, the director of the Moulin-Rouge approached her to make a speech to commemorate the famous music-hall's centenary:

'I wouldn't have done it, if it hadn't been for you. All this talk of your friend Mistinguett – I simply had to do it, didn't I? Why didn't you go to the Moulin-Rouge whilst you were here, in Paris? If you could have called at my apartment on the eighteenth instead of the twenty-second, we would have met again. I was preparing a speech for the celebration on the nineteenth. You could have helped me with the tape. Then again, the tone of your voice the other day. Do I take it that you don't approve of the Moulin-Rouge?'

'I don't consider it a music-hall any more,' I replied. 'It's all tits – and German and American tourists. In my opinion the entertainment's second-rate.'

'And the Folies-Bergère isn't?' she quizzed. 'You went there, for God's sake!'

In its hey-day the Moulin-Rouge had been the very pinnacle of the French entertainment scene. Paul Derval, who had taken over the theatre during the Thirties, had radically changed the musical revue by introducing nudes – fine for the yen-and-dollar tourist industry, but decidedly harmful to the strong traditions nurtured by the café-concerts. Even so, according to Roger Normand, Marlene had seen and been delighted by Frédéric Rey, the Austrian-born nude adagio-dancer, soon after visiting Paris for the first time. Had she taken up Michel Guyarmathy's offer to star in her own revue at the Folies-Bergère, Rey would have partnered her.

At around this time, towards the end of 1989, Marlene began showing interest in my career. Marlene had never cared for the chanteuse Barbara until I sent her a tape of one of her concerts. Then she had read of her charitable deeds, particularly her work for AIDS sufferers and children. When I wrote '*Les hommes bafoués*' for Barbara to music by Chopin, the singer called it 'a gathering of storm clouds over scorned lovers'. Marlene asked for a copy of the cassette. Chopin was her favourite composer, she said. Another talent who had died tragically young.

> I asked her her opinion of my song and she replied,
> 'The song is okay, but I don't like the subject. There were two moving lines. "*Je devine anodine, pour bercer leurs nuits, Leurs nuits fachées de peur.*" And I'm glad you persuaded me to see your singer. She was terrific.'

One week later, Marlene rang and there was quite a lot of background noise and rattling of papers. What I heard next knocked me sideways, for she had inserted the cassette of 'Les hommes bafoués' into her machine, and she now pronounced her own German and English lyrics over my arrangement!

> I would like to meet a man
> Who doesn't just talk about love,
> A man who only says to me,
> 'Are you going to give it to me,
> Whether I want it or not?'
> There, right smack into my face!
> A man who treats me just like any other woman,
> Who says to me: 'When?'

The fact that Marlene was anti-gay surprised me, bearing in mind that her rise to fame had occurred during the Berlin decadence of the Thirties. It was an undeniable fact that Marlene was revered more by the gay community than by anyone else. In January 1991, Terry Sanderson, the good friend of mine who supplied me with the weird but wonderful Wildebeest-Maclon album (detailed on page 280), wrote a moving and extremely efficient tribute to Marlene. This was published under the heading 'The Gay Man's Apparent Need for Goddesses as Icons' in that month's edition of *Gay Times* and I was so impressed that I sent a copy to avenue Montaigne. Terry had told me, 'I once stood outside her Paris apartment. I don't know why – I knew she wasn't coming out, I just wanted to be there!' It was, of course, adulation at its most profound:

> One sad smile from Marlene was worth a thousand gushing showbiz insincerities. She was in a class of her own. I followed her around the country, studying every aspect of her theatrical magic. Others had pledged their particular allegiance to Judy Garland. In France, Edith Piaf had the same effect. These goddesses are not worshipped entirely for their camp value, but for their appeal to the histrionic and vulnerable part of our [gay] character. We are told that this is because they are strong, independent spirits who in their personal lives experienced great traumas. I have no explanation for this apparently cruel desire to see our heroines suffer – I cannot say why they are our heroines in the first place, and yet I cannot deny the lengths I would go to in order to be in the front row of a Dietrich concert. I did things for Marlene that I would never have done for anyone else . . .

I wondered what Marlene's reaction would be, after reading my friend's article, and I was more than a little worried that she would take it the wrong way. I rang her and explained that it must have made for a pleasant change, sending her a nice article after all the rubbish which had appeared in the press. Marlene did not think so.

> 'The gay thing? I suppose it is interesting from the point of view that I appreciate all the good things your friend said. But people saying good things gets boring after a while, sweetheart. I like to

hear the bad things because that gives me the opportunity to voice my opinion.'

Marlene did not like female impersonators, though she did admire the one-off by the magician Paul Daniels. A photograph had appeared in the *Daily Star* with the caption TV PAUL'S MARLENE DIE-TRICK! I sent Marlene a copy of the cassette. Lola-Lola, crooning 'Falling in Love Again', suddenly falls into the barrel upon which she is sitting. Later in the sketch she is awarded a 'Cecil' by 'Joan Collins' (the actress Carmen Silvera) 'for her outstanding performance in the film *Bush Christmas*'.

'Me falling into the barrel, it was funny,' she said. 'And the man who did it only did it for a laugh. Did I ever tell you about the female impersonator who did me falling off the stage, in Australia? Now that was bad taste . . .'

The play *Falling in Love Again*, written by Laurence Roman and based on Martin Flossman's *Marlene*, opened and closed at Exeter's Northcott Theatre with virtually no publicity at the end of 1990. Marlene was very angry, so angry that I was forewarned of her bad mood by Norma Bosquet. Allen Sadler of the *Stage* described the Dietrich character as 'subject to bouts of self-doubt, and yet obstinate and arrogant, a petty calculating cold fish, generous but often unfeeling, but retaining a wide-eyed appreciation of business opportunities'. Again, her anger had nothing to do with the content of the play, but with the fact that someone was playing her whilst she was still alive.

'They can do whatever they like when I'm dead. Until then, I don't want to hear of anyone playing my life.'

The play *Privates on Parade*, recounting the adventures of a British Army concert-party during World War Two – and including an impersonation of Marlene by the actor Colin Baker – fared slightly better.

She gruffed, 'Well, I guess the theatres must pay the people to see things like that. The Austrians tried to put on a show which was so bad that my German lawyer seized the script. But you have to have a good reason to go that far. What about the American you told me about?'

'His name's Jim Bailey,' I explained. 'He did a whole show of Judy Garland in London recently, alternating it with a whole show of Barbra Streisand. He looks and sounds like her. And now I hear he's planning a show on you – a copy of the one you did for Alexander Cohen in 1972. He'll probably be wearing a copy of the Jean-Louis gown that you sold.'

'Well, thank God these people never last long,' she sighed.

These emulations were to go on and on – few of them acceptable, most of them tacky, such as the one in Berlin, included in a programme to commemorate the first anniversary of the demolition of the Wall. An impersonator by the name of Patachou put on a recital at a seedy night club – an event that deeply offended not just Marlene but the real Patachou who was, of course, her favourite French singer after Piaf.

In August 1990, Marlene sent me a list of titles for our album *Marlene: My Favourite Songs*. This had to be changed when, for copyright reasons, we were not allowed to use all the songs. It became *The Essential Marlene Dietrich*, and it sold better than either of us had expected, as the record company had a policy of steering clear of previously unpublished material. There is an enormous cost involved in transcribing old songs from the original 78 rpm recordings so as to eliminate surface noise and bring them into line with the quality expected of modern compact discs. Marlene's choice, typed out in order of preference by her friend Mrs Colpet, was most interesting:

1 'Bitte geh' nicht fort'
2 'Je tire ma révérence'
3 'Déjeuner du matin'
4 'Marie-Marie'
5 'Luar do sertão'
6 'Die Antwort weiss ganz allein der Wind'
7 'Wenn der Sommer wieder einzieht'
8 'Und wenn er wieder kommt'
9 'Allein in einer grossen Stadt'
10 'Go 'Way from My Window'
11 'Frag nicht warum?'

12 'I Wish You Love'
13 'Such Trying Times'
14 'I've Been in Love Before'
15 'Das hobellied'
16 'Lazy Afternoon'
17 'Das lied ist aus (Warum)'
18 'Miss Otis Regrets'
19 'One for My Baby'
20 'Annie Doesn't Live Here Any More'
21 'Die Welt war jung'
22 'Mit Dir, mit Dir da möcht ich Sonntags angeln geh'n'
23 'Ja, das haben die Mädchen so gerne'
24 'Nach meine beene ist ja ganz Berlin verrückt'

The Gulf War affected Marlene badly. Having experienced two world wars, both of which had scarred her one way or another, she clearly believed that she would end her days without being forced to witness, albeit from a safe distance, yet more strife and human sacrifice. The fighting in the Middle East coincided with the release of *The Essential Marlene Dietrich* and this resulted in a last-minute change to the tracks so that the French version of 'Where Have All the Flowers Gone?' with beautiful lyrics by Francis Lemarque, could be included,

'Òu vont les fleurs?' is now issued in Britain for the first time and serves to remind us of Marlene's paramount importance as an authority on the human condition and an ambassador for world peace. To the French and the Americans in particular she remains an institution, a potent symbol of all that is intensely patriotic. For her tireless work during the last war, and for her indomitable courage, she was awarded the Congress Medal of Freedom and the prestigious *Légion d'Honneur*. As a singer and as a dear friend, Marlene is unique. This is because everything she does or has done reflects her love of the human race. Like Martin Luther King, she is without equal. There will only ever be one Marlene Dietrich.

The text on the album cover was of course much longer and,

though I expected her to dissect it the way she had everything else that I had written, Marlene's only regret about our album was that I had been unable to use 'Marie-Marie'. We spoke about this on 8 February 1991, the day of the cease-fire in the Gulf War.

'I got another part of your beautiful script this morning, and I wanted to know if it's been printed up yet? No? Well, I want you to change "the last war" to "the Second World War". Because "the last war" is now, David. In spite of the news this afternoon, the fighting is not over yet. The headline today – I have it here, is, US TANKS TRAPPED – IRAQUIS IN FIERCE BATTLE! ALLIES REJECT BAGHDAD'S CEASE-FIRE PLEA! That means that they won't cease the fire, which was what I was hoping. As long as this son-of-a-bitch is still alive, we are in trouble . . .'

I could only agree. 'They're saying that Saddam's own people will deal with him when they catch him. But we can't risk that, can we? It's something we'll have to do for ourselves. We have to get rid of him in order to feel safe.'

'You see, so far they've only talked about trying to free Kuwait. And now that they have freed it, the French think the war's over. The Americans don't, and that's a good thing. They have to get rid of that son-of-a-bitch, that terrible man. I read in today's newspaper what they'd found in Kuwait City, in the jails and the laundries. They found all those poor people who had been tortured by the Iraquis. Oh, God . . .'

In June 1991 Jeanne and I visited Paris, and during the first day of our stay left a package containing books, notes, and two chapters from the typescript of this book with the receptionist at the avenue Montaigne. The next afternoon Marlene left a message with our hotel, telling us that it would be all right to drop in on her at any time. We went there at once, and met Ramon, whom she always called her 'factotum', for the first time.

Marlene had asked me to give him a handwritten note, complete with my signature and 'code'. According to Ramon, Marlene screwed it up and flung it aside, adding angrily that she had never heard of me. In fact, Marlene had never seen the note because Ramon had heard her yelling at someone over the phone, and had been afraid of entering her bedroom. The phone calls had been to my hotel, where she had proceeded to tear a strip off the receptionist there, accusing him of never passing the message on to me in the first place!

After a subsequent meeting with Ramon, the young man invited us to go for a drink with him at the drugstore on the Ronde-Point of the Champs-Elysées – a chance remark about Jeanne's asthma had convinced him that we were genuine friends of Marlene. Several weeks earlier he had been given the task of photocopying some of my letters and other documents, and he had been sitting with her when she had telephoned the hospital during my wife's illness. We spoke about Marlene, naturally, though I was cautious not to give away too much about our friendship. Ramon told me that she had offered him a shoulder to cry on when his father died, and that she herself had wept on his shoulder upon hearing the news of the recent death of the controversial French entertainer Serge Gainsbourg, famous in Britain for 'Je t'aime moi non plus', his recording with Jane Birkin which had been banned by the BBC.

> 'I'm going to miss Gainsbourg,' she had told me. 'He always went to a great deal of trouble to make himself look a mess when he appeared on the television, unshaven, smoking like a chimney and drinking. I admired that because he was making a statement, whilst challenging everyone to criticize him. He was an ugly man, but beautiful inside where it matters. A talent like Gainsbourg only comes along once in a lifetime.'

Ramon also told me about Marlene's 'excursion' to the Théâtre des Champs-Elysées – all the way across the road from her apartment in the avenue Montaigne – to see Vladimir Ashkenazy. 'It was an almighty headache from start to finish,' he said. 'I lost count of how many times she had me crossing that street, changing her mind every five minutes about the seating arrangements. And then, afterwards, she played hell with me because she couldn't get the cassettes she wanted.'

Two weeks after our return to England, on 30 July 1991, Marlene rang me. 'From now on, David, I want you to address all letters and packets to me as SIEBER. S-I-E-B-E-R! That's my name from now on, my married name. That's the name I pick out from all the fan mail. Then I want you to cross out my other name – the one written next to my telephone number. Just write the name SIEBER next to it, and hide it. Something strange is happening here. I can't tell you what it is, sweetheart, but I don't feel safe any more.'

Less than twenty-four hours after that call, Marlene was subjected to her most harrowing ordeal since the Ardennes: two men wearing masks barged into her bedroom and took a number of photographs of her lying on the bed. It took her a week to tell me what had happened and even then I detected that she was still shaking. And not for the first time was I reminded of Marlene's vulnerability – a fragile, elderly lady living hundreds of miles from her relatives and most of her friends.

'Somebody broke into my bedroom. It was last Wednesday, just a week ago. I thought I was safe here, you know, but now I only feel so very shocked. Thank God I didn't have a heart attack. There was a stranger standing in the doorway, then a flashlight. What did it say in the British newspapers?' I explained, very little: two masked men had barged into Marlene's bedroom and taken photographs which they had tried to sell to a German magazine. The editor had then handed them over to the police and out of gratitude Marlene had agreed to give her first interview in twenty years. This made her laugh, in spite of all she had been through.

'I agreed to give an interview – after a break in! Aye-aye-aye! Let me tell you exactly what happened. The thieves were let in by somebody downstairs, and must have known how to get to my diaries – otherwise they wouldn't have found them. One man took the photographs, the other stole the diaries. Then he went to the Paris office of *Bunte* magazine and said, "I have this, and I want to sell it!" The man at *Bunte* – he's called Burda – called the headquarters of the magazine in Munich. He told them that he had the diaries and the photographs. Munich said buy, and Paris bought. Then he put a man on the plane with the diaries and photographs . . . and the negatives. Then the *Bunte* man opened my diaries and do you know what is in my diaries, David?'

'Your private thoughts?' I suggested.

Marlene laughed again. 'My diaries! "Monday morning, Norma came, I received the bill for the rent." Next page, "Norma came, paid the rent and made the photocopy." Next page, "Received a letter from Maria. I answered the letter." My diary only states facts. It doesn't say anything intimate – anything they hoped they could sell. So, when the man in Munich saw what was in my diaries, he saw that he couldn't buy. Who wants to know when I pay my rent, for God's sake! Then he looked at the photographs. They are so bad that nobody would pay for them – and he then wanted to play Jesus Christ, so he told Burda to call *Bunte*'s New York office and contact my grandson. He told Peter that he had the diaries and the negatives, and Maria and Peter flew to Munich to get them back. They were unprintable, but as they had already paid the money *Bunte* said they would have to do the article. They did this to whitewash themselves and show what wonderful people they were – what wonderful, honest reporters they have! They couldn't use photographs of me, so they used photographs of my daughter. They took them whilst she was in their office getting my things back. Then they put everything into the mouth of Maria – how I look now, everything . . . that I'd slept with so-and-so, everything. It's a pity you don't speak any German, though it is a stupid article. The text isn't interesting at all. Get the magazine for the pho-to-graphs, honey! Stephanie of Monaco is on the cover, Number Thirty-Two. It says she is thinking of death.'

'I think the thieves were on drugs – it's something Norma said. They were hoping to get a lot of money for the diaries, and you know what drug addicts are like. They'll do anything. They'll kill their mothers and fathers. They'll stop at nothing! And you know, honey, only I could have stood this – to have a stranger come in here and photograph me in bed. I still cannot believe what happened.'

There were some discrepancies between Marlene's version of the burglary and what was actually reported in *Bunte* – not least of all the date of the break-in. She told me that it had happened on 31 July, the day after she had instructed me to henceforth address all mail to Madame Sieber. The British and French newspapers which covered the story also quoted this date. The *Bunte* reporter, Günther Stamp, said that he first met the person responsible for the theft on 11 July 1991. 'I have photographs of Marlene Dietrich. They were taken recently, and she does not object to my selling them to you,' he is alleged to have said. Needless to say, Stamp had refused to handle any 'hot' property and had demanded something in writing. He wrote, 'I then saw the picture of the old lady in bed, and recognized a Dietrich with an angry expression.' On 15 July, Stamp and the unnamed man had met again in a Paris café, and this time he had been offered nine red-brown diaries and the ultimatum: buy the lot, or forget the deal. Stamp bought the package, solely so that he could return Marlene her property, and the matter should have ended there.

The article in the 7 August edition of *Bunte* reported that the burglary had taken place on 22 July, and that Maria Riva had been informed – she and her son Peter had arrived in Munich the next day to collect the diaries and photographs. The article ended:

> On 24 July, Maria and Peter meet the reporter and say MD has diaries back. Photos/negatives no longer exist. MD has burnt them. 'There is another man there (in the apartment), an old friend of Marlene's. We put the prints and the negs in the incinerator – the prints burnt but not the negs. M asks why don't YOU burn them? The friend produces another match . . .' The next day, 24 July, Marlene writes to *Bunte*. 'My daughter has told me that I have to thank you. I cannot express my thanks in words, etc . . .'

> When I questioned Marlene as to whether in fact there had been *two* burglaries, she said simply, 'The first one – the one that is mentioned in *Bunte* – was a set-up. And I still am missing my 1980 diary.'

I believe her then, and I believe her now. The 1980 diary turned up, in *Bunte*, on 14 May 1992. And if the burglary *had* taken place on 22 July, all I can say is that she sounded remarkably cheerful when she called me early the next morning – we laughed and joked for some time over Madonna, and even sang one of her old songs together. Then we discussed a piece she was writing for *Spiegl*.

> 'This article will be a good one,' she enthused. 'I mean, it would be – I wrote it myself. *Spiegl* is a decent magazine. I answered all their questions and they paid me very, very well – twenty thousand dollars. And that made me think. David, will you try and find my old British agent? I was told he'd gone to live in Florida, but when I tried to get in touch, his telephone had been disconnected. He has a book that I wrote a few years ago, a very secret book which contains a few ideas of mine about writers. I want it back so that I can give it to my daughter. Maria would make a fortune out of it. And you know that I only live for Maria.'

Towards the end of 1991, when she was still recovering from

the shock of the burglary, Marlene was further distressed by some of the newspaper reports concerning alleged love affairs, most of which she had denied to me. We discussed this on 11 November, two days after the death of Yves Montand: Marlene had listened to my interview, broadcast live on French radio from outside his Paris apartment.

'I don't mind people writing about my love affairs, if they really happened. But when journalists start inventing people I hardly knew, I get angry. It's no secret that he had an affair with a chorus-boy. He did have a fling with Marilyn Monroe ... the photographs were in all the newspapers, and in any case he always spoke about these things honestly. Even Signoret forgave him. His love affairs were much more important. You're a very innocent man, dear, if you don't know the world. Look after your wife, sure, but don't be afraid of having love affairs as well!'

A few days later, in preparation for what everyone assumed would be Marlene's ninetieth birthday, an article appeared in the *Daily Mail* under the heading: MARLENE DIETRICH AT 90 – A PRISONER OF HER THREE-ROOM APARTMENT? The piece, spread over two full pages and including a picture taken of her during the early eighties, had been penned by William Langley following an interview with her former secretary, Bernard Hall. According to Hall, Marlene's ever-shrinking world no longer comprised three rooms or even one, but merely a bed which she hardly ever left: lying upon this she was surrounded by her worldly goods – books, files, stationery, fan mail and her two telephones. Hall also talked about her eccentricities: that she often called out for groceries and take-away meals that she did not need, that sex was just a 'more or less acceptable accessory', but that the thing that concerned her the most was her own legend. Further information was supplied by the French writer Alain Bosquet who, though not giving away any secrets, did test their friendship by speaking to a newspaper in the first place. And yet, the article did not shock her.

'The last I heard of Bernard Hall, he was very sick. For many years he was a good friend of mine. Find me his address, and I'll get in touch with him. As for Alain Bosquet, he's Norma's husband and I suppose he should have known better, though on the face of it I don't find the article bad. It could have been worse.'

'And your birthday,' I asked. 'Are you going to do anything special? Will your family be coming to see you for Christmas?'

'I always spend Christmas alone,' she replied. 'And you've seen all the papers? They claim that I'll be ninety years old. Ha-ha-ha! As for my birthday – why should it be different from any other day? My daughter sent me a cable this morning. And do you know what it said? THERE MUST BE NO BIRTHDAY FUSS. That is what Maria thinks, so it must be right. All these stories that you read in the newspapers! Just wait until I die, then you'll see what will happen. People will come forward – people I don't even know. And they'll all say the same thing: "I knew her!" "I slept with her!" It's going to be terrible for my daughter. She will have to go through all of that, and that's why she's been preparing herself for my death – for years. There'll be all the money to sort out, and my funeral. There's all the furniture in this place to get rid of. Maria's going to have to be very, very brave. But she'll do it because she's intelligent. My daughter is a brilliant woman, David. I'm telling you that because it's necessary for you to know that there are more important things in this world than birthdays.'

Marlene's (ninety-*first*) birthday was celebrated all over the world, though less so in Britain than anywhere else. *Around the World in Eighty Days, Blonde Venus* and the much-hated *Rancho Notorious* were shown on British television and the radio came up with a selection of her Berlin recordings from the late Twenties and early Thirties. I rang her on the actual day, as did her close friend Sacha Briquet. Apparently she spent most of the day alone. However there were scores of cards, all unopened.

A few days before Christmas 1991, Jeanne's father had a stroke and died less than forty-eight hours later. She rang me that night: again she cried. Then she said:

'Maybe this is going to sound a little harsh, sweetheart, but perhaps it was for the best that your father-in-law died. I mean, he could have ended up like Max Colpet. Remember how I told you about when he had had a stroke for the first time? He went to the hospital, and he was cured. He came out feeling better, in fact, than he had ever felt before. But if the stroke had gone wrong, his doctors told him that he could have become lame. It's much better to be dead than to have to spend the rest of your life like that.'

We then spoke about the book which Bernard Hall was allegedly writing. My agent had checked this out, and the script was thus far described as harmless enough. Marlene believed me.

On 8 January 1992, I received news from New York confirming that Maria was writing a biography of her mother, and that its contents were 'dynamite'. When I informed Marlene about the book – and she really did not know about it until then – she collapsed. This worried me no end, though less than an hour later she called back and said, 'I told Maria about the book just now, and she laughed herself sick. There is no book!'

By 13 January, the British newspapers overflowed with so-called exclusives on the Riva book. I was roped into the controversy when one particular publication referred to Marlene's reaction to the book, 'as reported by her British author friend'. Marlene put me straight over this.

> 'You are the only British author that I know, so I knew at once that you would never speak to the newspapers about me. It's very important that you know how much I trust you . . .'
>
> At this stage in our conversation, she broke down and cried.
>
> 'I had to tell you, David. It was my duty. I believe you! I believe you . . .' she sobbed, time and time again.

Marlene's last three months were distressingly devoid of peace of mind. And yet she proved a good deal tougher than most of her friends expected. My admiration for her was profound. She rang every day, sometimes as often as six times in any one day, to report the latest event. Then on 27 April 1992, during what would be our last major conversation, she read me the letter that she had received that very morning which explained that, during one of my visits to her apartment, I had been 'bugged'. Once again, she wept.

> 'It isn't true. You've never recorded anything here. I know that. I'm very upset. The newspapers are all wrong, and they're all full of such shit. The man who wrote the letter says that he was here with you, in my apartment, and that you recorded our conversation. And in case anyone mentions this after I'm dead, I just wanted everyone to know that he's a liar.'

Marlene's voice sounded very weak, though this had nothing to do with the letter. She was recovering from falling out of bed, and an injury which had necessitated six stitches, put in without anaesthetic because she had refused to leave the apartment to go to hospital. The doctor who tended her wound assured her that because of her advanced age recovery would be slow, but hopefully complete. As for our conversation, it ended with her asking me to write a letter to Maria, expressing my own opinions about the newspaper reports and assuring her daughter that, no matter what happened, I would always be on Marlene's side.

Very early on the morning of Friday 1 May, the telephone rang but all I heard was a French news broadcast, playing extremely loudly in the background. Assuming that it could have only been Marlene, and worried that she had been taken ill, I called back. Her response was both confusing and upsetting.

> 'I don't want to talk to you, so I've sent a letter. We wanted it all, you and I, and we got it all, didn't we?'

I never received the letter, which was printed in a German magazine a few weeks later.

That night I couldn't sleep. What had Marlene meant – that she never wished to speak to me again? Then the next day it dawned on me. She had said 'I don't want to talk to you!' – and curtly so – twice before: once when she had been entertaining her close friend Louis Bozon, and again when she had been interrupted in the middle of writing an important letter. Jeanne told me not to fret – and she is usually right in these things. I therefore decided that I would wait until Marlene called me, as I had often done in the past.

On Monday 4 May, at 7.45 p.m. precisely – ironic, for during the early days of our friendship she had always called at this time – the phone rang:

> 'I have called to say goodbye. I am telling you that I love you, and that now I may die . . .'

I never spoke to my beloved friend again.

Time and time again I called her number – the line was always busy, I later learned, because she had left the receiver off the hook.

After calling me she had called Maria in New York, but her husband, William Riva, was ill and she was unable to leave for Paris straight away. Peter Riva, her son, arrived at the avenue Montaigne early the next morning to be met by a very distraught Norma Bosquet. Marlene was in a terrible rage: since saying goodbye to her closest friends she had refused to allow anyone inside her bedroom.

Peter took over the proceedings. He carried her into the living room, and placed her on the sofa so that she could be surrounded by her most treasured personal effects, photographs and books – there was the picture of Jeanne and myself which she had asked for, and a copy of *The Piaf Legend* was next to the television set: the photograph of this later appeared in magazine articles all over the world. Marlene seemed content. Peter then gave orders for her old bed to be taken out of the apartment and organized a mechanical replacement. The ex-housekeeper, Angèle, then helped him to tidy the bedroom. Marlene was fed a bowl of soup and fell asleep at once.

The following afternoon, Peter Riva and Norma Bosquet, accompanied by her solicitor, Jacques Kam, set off for the Mairie of the VIIIth arrondissement. Their quest: to hold an audience with a ruling magistrate in the hope that he would grant a perpetual medical-surveillance order. Whilst they were there they received a tearful call from Madame Tahon, the housekeeper.

Marlene was gone.

Epilogue

'Allein in Einer Grossen Stadt'

Just wait, when I die. Just wait how they're all going to come forward. And they're all going to say, 'I knew her!' Just wait till I die . . . all the stories that's going to come out . . .

Marlene was coiffed, made-up and embalmed, then dressed in her favourite Balenciaga outfit of black jacket, trousers and frilled blouse – she had once worn this to impersonate Tallulah Bankhead and had even retained the maroon designer carrier bag. And for some time, in anticipation of this moment, she had kept a full-sized French tricolour in her apartment – a personal gift from de Gaulle, given when he had presented her with the *Légion d'Honneur*. This was draped over her body as she lay upon the sofa and no Frenchman worthy of his name would have dreamed of removing it when, later that evening, she was taken to the funeral home at Nanterre, just outside Paris.

In an official statement, Jacques Kam said that she had died of old age. 'She was lucid and conscious to the end,' he added. Peter Riva told the press, 'Maria Magdalena Dietrich died on a very beautiful spring day in Paris.' I have no clear indication of the identity of the man who broke the news to me at 3.45 p.m., British time, twenty-five minutes after it had happened, but the sad event was confirmed to me a few minutes later by Peter Riva. I was

231

beyond tears. I had just lost the old lady who had told me – and more than once – that outside her family I was her next of kin.

The woman who had said, 'When I do it, it will be quick and painless – and if I thought I was becoming a burden on my family, then of course I would do it. I've had a good life. If only we all had the right to choose the way we want to die.'

And the woman who had also said, 'I only wish that I could live for ever, for my daughter's sake. For you know that I only live for Maria . . .'

In truth, Marlene could not have stage-managed a better moment for leaving us. It was the eve of the 45th Cannes Film Festival, and the organizers had chosen her photograph – the famous one from *Shanghai Express* where her hands are clasped above her head and her exquisite expression is framed by plumes – as the official poster. The caption read DIETRICH ETERNELLE. In London, too, *The Blue Angel* was about to open in the West End. Before the opening of the Festival, there was a moment's silence, after which Gérard Depardieu said, 'Stars never die'. They then relayed Marlene's favourite song through the loudspeakers: her version of Jacques Brel's 'Ne me quitte pas', which she had sung in German.

The tributes, of course, were legion and only in Britain did the sludge take over from the accolades. The better eulogies were delivered by friends and admirers who predeceased Marlene. The late Kenneth Tynan, whose tribute had first appeared in 1967 in *Playbill* had enthused.

> Her voice tells you that whatever hell you inhabit, she has been there before, and survived. Her style looks absurdly simple – an effortless act of projection, a serpentine lasso whereby her voice casually winds itself around our most vulnerable fantasies. But it is not easy. It is what remains when ingratiation, sentimentality and the manifold devices of heart-warming crap have been pared away. Steel and silk are left, shining and durable.

The *Guardian* printed the reminiscence of the late musicologist Alan Dent, wherein he had borrowed lines from Tennyson: 'clothed in white samite, mystic, wonderful'. Elsewhere the only worthwhile tribute from a living authority came from Gilbert Adair of the *Independent*, whom I gratefully thank:

> She was the cinema's most sheerly legendary star, the mystique of whose languorous eroticism far exceeded the confines of her (by no means undistinguished) filmography; and it is quite possible that, had the camera not recorded the trace of her presence, bemused future generations would have wondered whether, like some mythical beast, a phoenix or a unicorn, she had existed at all ... She was a statue in celluloid, a figurine of light and shadow, as immaterial as a hologram ... Her appeal, which is still calculated to catch a cinema audience collectively by the throat, was utterly opposed to that of 'the girl next door'. No one ever lived next door to Marlene Dietrich ... For, in the case of Marlene Dietrich, the cinema – a medium defined by Cocteau, yet again, as revealing Death at work – also demonstrated that it could be the petrified fountain of youth and beauty.

The French, naturally, were positively overwhelmed by news features and magazine articles written around Marlene's friendship with Jean Gabin, *Paris-Match* had their photograph across the cover, many more inside, and a reproduction of a telegram which she had sent him from Beverly Hills. Unsigned and dated 27 November 1941, it read: SHIT AND MORE SHIT MY ANGEL. Under the heading *L'hymne á l'amour de Marlene à Gabin* the magazine also printed several of her love letters to the actor. Elsewhere, the magazine showed pictures of her cluttered apartment and a photograph of her draped body lying upon the sofa. Someone even took a photograph of what was inside her refrigerator.

In the week-end magazine *VSD (Vendredi-Samedi-Dimanche)* the French copied the British tabloids, albeit more tastefully, by allowing Marlene's former secretary, Odette Miron-Boire, to give an insight into her seventeen years with Marlene. 'You would think that I had engaged her as a companion, the way she fussed over me,' Miron-Boire confessed. 'There was always a cup of coffee waiting for me when I arrived each morning, and she flatly refused to let me tackle the housework.' Miron-Boire then went on to discuss, at length, Marlene's culinary skills and extraordinary generosity, and not one word about her love life. Sacha Briquet, commenting on the former, said, 'Her kitchen was sacred – much more so than the cinema or the stage.'

Louis Bozon, who like myself had endured Marlene's morbid but highly amusing sense of humour more than once, had said his adieu on the Sunday before I had. Writing in a French magazine, he repeated what she had told him:

Maria won't be here when I die, so what you must do is this. You must shove my body into a dustbin bag and dump it in the trunk of your car. At least that way I'll be assured that nobody will photograph me when I'm dead. Then you can return to my apartment and wait for my daughter. Poor Maria's going to have a lot of problems when I die.'

Alas, if only some of the others could have nurtured the kindness of a Bozon, or an Adair. Some of the tabloids wrote willy-nilly without even bothering to substantiate their stories. Others simply wrote smut. Hugo Vickers of the *Daily Telegraph*, whilst attempting to counter Peter Riva's statement that Marlene had not left her bed for five years, repeated the equally mistaken anecdote, 'Marlene could sometimes be seen early in the morning, draped in Indian shawls, walking a tiny dog.'

One item which caused a great deal of controversy was a photograph of a fur-clad old lady, sitting in a wheelchair outside what appeared to be Marlene's apartment. I knew that this could not possibly have been Marlene, and so did Peter Riva. (I spoke to him on the eve of her funeral.) This photograph had accompanied a number of articles in publications around the world, each of which had bought it in good faith. After all, hardly anyone had seen Marlene for years, so few people knew what she had looked like. Shortly before her death, two photographs had been snapped through her fourth-floor bedroom window by a man on an extending crane of the type used for lopping tree branches: one had shown the back of her head, the other half of her face. In the nick of time she had shielded herself with a writing-pad.

On the eve of Marlene's funeral I was contacted by the producer of *Hard News*, the Channel Four media watchdog programme who by this time had been alerted to the fact that the photograph was indeed a fake. Quite by chance, their programme was televised the day after Marlene's funeral, on the very day that the *Sunday Times* published a lengthy account of her private life which she had been trying to stop. 'The papers have been mourning the death of Marlene Dietrich,' the announcer said. 'And no one more than the *Sunday Times*. As with most colour supplements, today's was printed some time ago. The press was actually rolling a profile of Marlene as news came in of the star's sad departure. Caught out by the demise of the Divine Dietrich, they had to spend £10,000 changing the presses, but we can still see what they didn't get around to changing by the curious use of the present tense.' The announcer then went on to explain about the photograph of the old lady in the wheelchair, suggesting that it did not look at all like the ones of Marlene which had just been printed in *Bunte*, and adding Peter Riva's anecdote, 'My grandmother hadn't been out of her bed for five years, let alone out of her apartment.' The programme ended with Marlene's own prepared attack on the press, which she had asked me to record just before her birthday. Accompanied by her favourite photograph – the one I had used on our album – and followed by my favourite song, 'Où vont les fleurs?' it really was an attack from beyond the grave:

> Just wait when I die. Just wait how they're all going to come forward. And they're going to say, 'I knew her!' Just wait till I die, what's going to happen – all the stories that's going to come out. You have to be prepared for that when you're famous!

Quality magazines such as *Bunte* and *Paris-Match* continued to serve up slices of Marlene's life for some time – with varying degrees of accuracy and authenticity, concentrating on affairs real or invented with Gabin, von Sternberg, Frank Sinatra, Yul Brynner and Hemingway. Marlene had been right all along, and I could almost hear her complaining, as she had before: 'If you believe everything you're going to read in the newspapers, then you'll tell yourself that if she spent that much time screwing, then how the hell did she get around to spending any time with her career?'

Only her funeral was reported, by and large, with any degree of respect. The greatest mystery of all, however, was why she was being buried in Berlin in the first place. Since 1930 and *The Blue Angel* she had visited Germany four times, and always with reservation: to search for her missing sister, Elizabeth; to attend her mother's funeral, when she had insisted on wearing her American uniform; to tour the country with Burt Bacharach; and finally in 1965 to record the *Berlin-Berlin* album. She hated the Germans and each time I mentioned them she would exclaim, 'Nazis! Nazis!' And as with many of her friends, she had always told me that she would be buried in Paris. The event had been arranged between her and General de Gaulle and there was a well-aired anecdote: 'When I die, I would like to be buried in Paris. I would like to leave my heart in England – and in Germany, nothing.' Her favourite spots were Milly-la-Forêt, where Cocteau had been buried, and the park at Marnes-la-Coquette, not far from Chevalier. According to her family, Marlene had changed her mind after the demolition of the Berlin Wall, insisting that she would now like to be buried 'at Friedenau, next to my mother'. Her lawyer, Jacques Kam, issued the same statement. I did not believe a single word of this and my opinion was shared by several of her friends and thousands of her French admirers. One journalist told me whilst I was in France, 'They wanted to bury Marlene in Berlin simply so that we French couldn't have her any more. This is going to be the final insult to our own *grande dame*.'

On Thursday 14 May, at a little after ten in the morning, seventeen hundred people filed into the church of La Madeleine, led by a black-clad, headscarfed Maria Riva, her husband William, and members of their family – Michael Riva, his wife and son Mikey; Peter and Sandra with their sons Matthew and Sean; and David and Paul Riva. Almost all of these people had seen little or nothing of Marlene during her years of solitude, and like everyone else they did not see her now: she had left explicit instructions that her simple oak coffin be sealed at Nanterre and not opened under any circumstances. A French government official carried her medals, holding them as though they were sacred relics, and there were representatives of the British and American embassies rubbing shoulders with the German and Russian ambassadors.

All eyes, of course, were on Marlene's daughter, belying her sixty-seven years and from some angles looking remarkably like her mother. Nervously, she planted a kiss on the tricolour-draped coffin. The floral tributes were magnificent and included a wreath of white lilies and pink and yellow roses from President Mitterrand. The largest wreath of all came from the management of the Paris Olympia, just up the road on the Boulevard des Capucines, though I am sure Marlene would have much preferred the simple bouquet of wild flowers that had been placed on her coffin.

There were surprisingly few showbusiness personalities amongst the mourners, mainly because almost every one of her Hollywood contemporaries had predeceased her. James Stewart, too ill to make the flight from California, sent a message. Audrey Hepburn, who had promised to attend, was sadly prevented from doing so because of illness. I saw Charles Aznavour, Roger Normand and the actor Michael Lonsdale, who read the address from *The Apocalypse of Saint John* in both English and French. Louis Bozon, choked with emotion, read *The Flag* by Rainer Maria Rilke, Marlene's favourite poem. The choir sang Bach's 'Wohl mir, dass ich Jesus habe', a hymn to her Lutheran faith that had almost ended after she had witnessed some of the atrocities of World War Two, and this was followed by a dirge-like organ arrangement of 'La Marseillaise'. In his sermon, the pastor of the Madeleine, Père Philippe Brizard said, 'Everyone was impressed by Marlene's sense of duty. Marlene lived like a soldier, and she would have wanted to die like a soldier. She was highly discreet and secretive, preferring to preserve her secret garden. Her secret now belongs to her alone.' Her coffin was then solemnly carried out of the church, ready to be draped in the Stars and Stripes in preparation for her final journey to Berlin, where everyone assumed that she would be buried with her mother, Joséphine. The next day, Maria was photographed by *Paris-Match*, blowing a kiss as Marlene's coffin slowly moved along the conveyor-belt into the hold of a Lufthansa aircraft.

Marlene's great friend and favourite lyricist Max Colpet, himself a harsh critic of Hitler during the early Thirties, hit out against the Germans' hostile attitude towards Marlene in his statement to the *Frankfürter Allgemeine*: 'In countries other than Germany, people would be as proud of such a world-famous star as the Swedish are of the "heavenly" Garbo, the French of Bardot, and the English of Laurence Olivier. Here they hold it against her that during the war she toured with Orson Welles to cheer up the GIs which, since she had become American, was her duty. They will not forgive her for marching with de Gaulle after the Liberation of Paris to the memorial of the Unknown Soldier, at the Arc de Triomphe. This is something she did with honest enthusiasm.'

For twenty-four hours Marlene's coffin, now draped with the bear standard of Berlin, was guarded by the police following a large number of threats from neo-Nazi fringe groups – some of these were photographed during the Friday afternoon, spitting into her empty grave within the Friedenau cemetery. Since the announcement of her death, her films had been screened almost non-stop on television, and the radio stations devoted many hours to playing her recordings, interspersed with interviews from friends and former colleagues. The press, with the exception of the tactless *Bild Zeitung*, who ran the same smut as some of the British tabloids – including an article headed, 'THE ARMY WILL FETCH HER HOME' – were generally kind. One report anticipated a crowd of 100,000 for her funeral and added that a star-studded extravaganza – to be held at the Deutsches Theater with a 'cast' of 600 – was well under way. There was also talk of a memorial plaque being erected outside the house in Schoeneberg where Berlin authorities claimed Marlene had been born, and of naming a street after her. None of these schemes actually materialized and the official excuse – that there had been insufficient time – was scoffed at by her admirers, and prompted a bitter attack from the pro-Dietrich *Tagezeitung*: 'People everywhere will now look upon Berlin and this absurd, shameful spectacle. We will never rid ourselves of the impression that instead of granting this citizen of the world and anti-Fascist her final honour, all we did was kick her up the arse.' Such thoughts were expressed by Berlin's culture senator, Ulrich Roloff-Momin, who blazed, 'I am startled by this outpouring of Fascist thinking at such a sad time. Marlene Dietrich did more for Berlin than Berlin ever did for her, and that is a fact.'

The neo-Nazis, most of whom had not even been born when Marlene had made her last major film, took to the streets of Berlin very early on the Saturday morning, mixing with the 5,000 or so mourners lining the route of the funeral and handing out their propaganda leaflets. During the night three of their members had been arrested after being caught scaling the cemetery wall, yelling that they were going to daub Marlene's grave with filthy slogans and swastikas, as some of them had despoiled the posters of her in Paris the previous week. Part of their spiel read: 'You are reminded that during World War Two, Fräulein Dietrich stated publicly that she expressed much greater sorrow over the bombing of London than that of Hamburg'. By and large, these people were ignored, though this did not convince the police – who had already sent a bill to the senate totalling £35,000 for their services so far – that there would not be further disturbances once the funeral got under way.

Two years before, Marlene had asked me to reproduce the most 'amusing' account of her funeral in this book, so I am sure – or at least I hope I am sure – that she would have been amused by John Sweeney's tongue-in-cheek report in the *Observer*:

The manner of her leaving the world was how Marlene liked to live: stylish, a performance of exhilarating ambiguity, casting puzzles in the air. How better to bemuse her fellow Germans than by having as her hearse not a Mercedes or a BMW or an Audi – but a late Fifties Cadillac? The sleek, black gas-guzzler, with a radiator grille that would frighten a shark off the scent of blood, nuzzled through the streets of Berlin like a treat for chrome fetishists. The procession set off, the Berlin police a little too officious about preventing the mourners and the media from getting close. Half-way along the route, the undertaker driving the Cadillac hit the gas pedal à la James Dean and the hearse lurched off like a supercharged drag-racer, leaving police officers and camera-men panting in its wake. It was a moment that Marlene, no lover of authority, would have savoured . . .

All along the route to Friedenau, fans tossed tiny posies of violets into the back of the Cadillac, proudly flanked by an authoritative escort of eight police motor cyclists. Violets, it is alleged, were once the symbol of lesbianism in the Berlin of the

Twenties. Not so to Marlene, who had been told by Edith Piaf that violets were the 'flowers of *le petit peuple* in the galleries', the working class men and women who had helped to make them both famous and who ultimately wept the genuine tears during their final journeys. Even so, Berlin's gay community were there, at the cemetery gates, to give her a rousing send-off which she would have appreciated, in spite of her later aversion towards homosexuality. These were the people who had bought her records and watched her films just the same as everyone else, but who had gone one step further by adopting her as their patron saint. And if some people considered the sudden outburst of applause to be out of keeping with the solemnity of the occasion. Maximilian Schell thought otherwise. He shouted, 'Welcome home, Marlene. I think you must have liked that, eh?'

Within the cemetery came the final insult to Marlene – as if they had not done enough already – for the German authorities had decided not to bury her with her mother. 'There isn't enough space,' was the announcement. Admirers were reminded of the fact by the message, '*Marlene's Mutter Liegt Nicht Hier. Sondern Dort Um Die Ecke*' ('Marlene's mother does not lie here. She's around the corner'), which the gravedigger had chalked on the tarpaulin covering the empty grave, twenty yards from that of Joséphine von Losch.

After reading the 23rd Psalm, the German pastor Gottfried Wiarda said, 'Marlene has come home. Here her life began more than ninety years ago, and here we are laying her to rest as she requested.' Maximilian Schell added, scarcely concealing his anger when someone in the crowd shouted that Marlene had been a traitor, 'Her last wish, to be buried here, shows just how much of her heart was still in her old home. Marlene was a Berliner.' He then went on to read another of her favourite poems, and one adored by her mother: Ferdinand Freilgrath's haunting *Love as Long as You Can*:

> Oh love, as long as day may dawn,
> The hour will come,
> You'll stand beside a grave and mourn
> Whoever gives his heart to you.
> Oh, show him all the love you own,
> And fill his waking hours with joy,

And never make him feel alone.
And watch your tongue as best you can –
A wicked word is quickly spoken.
'Oh God, I didn't mean it so!'
The other goes away, heart-broken,
Then you kneel down beside the grave
And say: 'Look at the woman who
Is weeping here to see you go!
Forgive me, please, for hurting you!
Oh God, I didn't mean it so!'
But he can't see and he can't hear you,
He can't be welcomed back, somehow.
The mouth that kissed you oft before
Can't say that all's forgiven, now . . .
He did forgive you, long ago,
But many hot tears fell, my friend,
About you and your bitter word . . .
Oh, he's at rest, he's reached the end!

Throughout this moving interlude, Maria Riva clutched at a tiny bunch of lilies-of-the-valley but, as Marlene's coffin was slowly lowered into the ground, she sank to her knees, crossed herself, and blew one last kiss. This time the emotion was too much for her and she had to be supported by members of her family as she staggered away from the graveside.

There was a large wreath from the German Liberal Party Alliance 90 that read, 'You were the other Germany'. The actress Hildegarde Knef, who had been the first to welcome Marlene back into her homeland during her 1960 tour, kept it simple: 'Adieu Marlene'. The European Film Institute, however, got it exactly right by inscribing their tribute, 'Angels don't die'.

If my book serves to present Marlene Dietrich as a good, honest, courageous and moral human being to just one tiny portion of the population of this world, then I have not worked in vain.

My wife and several intimate friends insist that I will get over my great loss, but I do not think so. Even now, when the phone rings I half expect to hear her voice:

'David? It's Marlene. . . .'

Appendices

Au dernier moment
~~QUAND TOUT EST PERDU~~

Paroles :
Roger NORMAND
Sablons 23-78

Musique :
Daniel JANIN
Cha. 32-28

I.

~~Quand tout est perdu~~, Au dernier moment,
Il y a toujours,
Un petit moment,
Où l'on espère...
~~Quand tout est perdu~~, Au dernier moment,
Dans l'oeil des amants,
On lit bien souvent,
Une prière, et
Comme un chien battu,
Qui ne saurait plus,
Un enfant déçu,
Implorant sa mère...
~~Quand tout est perdu~~, Au dernier moment,
Les yeux des amants,
Cherchent éperduement
Dans leur colère...s'ils
Vont se blesser...ou
Bien s'adorer...ou
Recommencer...
~~Quand tout est perdu!~~
Au dernier moment.
....

Au dernier moment
~~Quand tout est perdu,~~
On veut se haïr,
Et de longs moments,
On se déteste...
~~Quand tout est perdu~~, Au dernier moment,
Plus de souvenirs,
Mais des mots méchants,
Rien que des restes...et
Chacun sans pudeur,
Piétine son coeur,
Renie son bonheur,
Bafoue ses caresses...
~~Quand tout est perdu~~, Au dernier moment,
C'est là bien souvent,
Qu'en un seul instant
On se découvre...et
De ce cri de haine, on
Fait un "je t'aime"
~~plaqour épandu...~~
Au dernier moment.
....

Le cri admirable,
Fait d'irréparable,
Devient formidable....
~~Quand tout est perdu!...~~
Au dernier moment.

AU DERNIER MOMENT

Je certifie que cette
chanson, écrite
pour=
Marlène
Dietrich.
a été travaillée par elle,
déclarée à la S.A.CEM,
mais n'a, jusqu'alors
bénéficié d'aucune
édition publique, et
qu'elle n'a pas d'Éditeur.

A ce jour.
24-5-92
Barbe Roger
dit
Roger Normand

The working copy of the lyric sheet of 'Au dernier moment', authorized by Roger Normand. Marlene said: 'It would have been the greatest song in my second career, but singing it brought me great pain.'

The Songs of Marlene Dietrich

The following titles represent the recorded output of Marlene Dietrich between the years 1928 and 1991, including authors, composers, orchestras, etc. Tape recordings and live performances of songs not recorded in the studio are also included: in the event of the latter, these are usually the first time they were taped on stage.

1 Orchestra Walberg, director Peter Kreuder
2 Orchestra Burt Bacharach
3 Piano Marlene Dietrich
4 Orchestra Michel Emer
5 Orchestra Bert Grund
6 Orchestra George Smith
7 Orchestra Friederich Hollander
8 Orchestra Victor Young
9 Orchestra/Upright Stan Freeman
10 Orchestra Jimmy Carroll
11 Piano Mischa Spoliansky
12 Piano Friedrich Hollander
13 Piano Udo Lindenberg
14 Orchestra Buddy Cole
15 Orchestra Gordon Jenkins
16 Orchestra Charles Magnante
17 Orchestra Percy Faith

Song	Author/Composer	Backing	Year	Other Details
'Allein in einer grossen Stadt' 1	Wachsmann-Colpet	1	1931	Berlin recording
'Allein in einer grossen Stadt' 2	Wachsmann-Colpet	1	1933	Paris recording
'Allein in einer grossen Stadt' 3	Wachsmann-Colpet	2	1960	
'Alle Tage ist kein Sonntag'	Colpet	2	1954	
'All of me'		2	1954	Café de Paris
'All right, okay you win!'	Gerald-Calhoun	2	1959	Rio de Janeiro
'Angel'	Hollander-Robin		1937	Film: *Angel*
'Annie Doesn't Live Here Any More'	Young-Burke-Metzl	17	1951	
'Another Spring Another Love' 1 & 2	Shayne-Paris	2	1957	
'Assez' 1	Walberg-Stern-Tranchant	1	1933	For Polydor
'Assez' 2		1	1933	For Ultraphone
'Au dernier moment'	Normand-Génin	2	1962	
'Auf der Mundharmonika'	Spolianksy-Gilbert	2	1964	
'Aus der Jugendseit'	Colpet	2	1954	
'Awake in a dream'	Hollander-Robin	3	1936	Film: *Desire*
'Back Home in Indiana'	MacDonald-Hanley	4	1957	Film: *The Monte Carlo Story*
'Baubles, Bangles and Beads'		2	1954	
'Berlin-Berlin'	Kollo	5	1965	
'Besides'		9	1954	With Rosemary Clooney
'Bitte geh' nicht fort'	Brel-Colpet	2	1964	'Ne me quitte pas'
'Black Market'	Hollander	15	1949	Film: *A Foreign Affair*
'Blonde Women'	Hollander-Connelly	7	1930	Film: *The Blue Angel*
'Blowin' in the Wind'	Dylan	2	1964	
'Boomerang Baby'		9	1972	Live: New Theatre, London
'Boys in the Backroom'	Hollander-Loesser	16	1939	Film: *Destry Rides Again*
'Candles Glowing'	Bader-Harrison	5	1965	
'C'est si bon'			1962	With Louis Armstrong
'Cherché la rose'	Salvador	2	1962	Sung in French
'Cherché la rose'	Salvador-Colpet	2	1962	Sung in German
'Come Rain or Come Shine'	Arlen-Mercer	17	1952	

Song	Author/Composer	Backing	Year	Other Details
'Czy mnie jeszcze pamietasz'	Nieman-Grau	2	1966	Warsaw, sung in Polish
'Dark Town Strutters' Ball'		2	1955	Las Vegas
'Das alte lied'	Hollander-Liebmann		1940	Live: USA radio
'Das hobellied'	Kreutzer		1943	Sung in German
'Das lied ist aus (Warum)'	Stolz-Reisch	2	1954	Live: Café de Paris
'Das war in Schöneberg'	Kollo-Bernauer-Schanzer	5	1965	
'Das Zillelied'	Kollo-Pflanzer	5	1965	
'Dat's Nice, Donna Fight!'	Showalter	10	1953	With Rosemary Clooney
'Der Kleine trommelmann'	Simeone-Onorati	2	1964	'Little Drummerboy'
'Die Antwort weiss ganz allein der Wind' 1 & 2	Dylan-Bradke	2	1963	'Blowin' in the Wind'
'Die Welt war jung'	Philipe-Gérard/Colpet	2	1962	'Le chevalier de Paris'
'Du hast ja keine Ahnung wie schöhn du bist Berlin'	Gilbert-Schönfeld	5	1965	
'Durch Berlin fliesst immer noch die Spree'	Gilbert		1965	
'Ein Roman'	Kaper	5	c1940	Live USA radio
'Emporté par le vent'	Dylan-Delanöe	2	1964	'Blowin' in the Wind'
'Es gibt im Leben manchesmal Momente'	Bromme-Steinberg	5	1965	
'Es liegt in der Luft'	Spoliansky-Schiffer	11	1928	Potpourri from the revue
'Everyone's Gone to the Moon'	King	9	1965	Acetate, London
'Falling in Love Again' 1	Hollander-Connelly	7	1930	Film: *The Blue Angel*
'Falling in Love Again' 2	Hollander-Connelly	8	1939	
'Les feuilles mortes'	Prévert-Kosma		1946	Tape recording
'Fur alles tun auf diese welt'	Colpet-Seeger		1964	'Turn, Turn, Turn'
'Get Away, Young Man'	Darby		1952	Film: *Rancho Notorious*
'Girl on the Telephone'			1955	Café de Paris
'Give Me the Man'	Robin-Hajos		1930	Film: *Morocco*
'Glochen läuten'	Olias-Bader	5	1966	'Candles Glowing'
'Golden Earrings'	Young-Livingstone-Evans		1947	Film: *Golden Earrings*
'Good for Nothin''	Engvick-Wilder	10	1952	With Rosemary Clooney
'Go 'Way from My Window'	Niles-Dietrich	2	1964	'I'm Looking Out the Window'

Song	Author/Composer	Backing	Year	Other Details
'Guy What Takes His Time'	Rainger	10	1952	Film: *Rancho Notorious*
'Gypsy Davey'	Darby		1952	Film: *Manpower*
'He Lied and I Listened'	Hollander-Loesser	5	1941	Live: Queen's Theatre
'Honeysuckle Rose'	Waller-Razaf	2	1964	
'Hot Voodoo'	Coslow-Rainger		1930	Film: *Morocco*
'I Am the Naughty Lola' 1	Hollander-Connelly	7	1930	Film: *The Blue Angel*
'I Am the Naughty Lola' 2		2	1955	English/German
'I Can't Give You Anything But Love'	McHugh-Fields	2	1964	Queen's Theatre, London
'Ich bin die fesche Lola' 1	Hollander-Connelly	7	1930	Film: *The Blue Angel*
'Ich bin die fesche Lola' 2	Hollander-Connelly	2	1960	
'Ich bin von Kopf biss Fuss auf liebe eingestellt' 1	Hollander	7	1930	Film: *Der Blaue Engel*
'Ich bin von Kopf biss Fuss auf liebe eingestellt' 2	Hollander		1960	
'Ich hab noch einen koffe in Berlin' 1	Siegel-Pinelli	2	1956	Film: *I Am a Camera*
'Ich hab noch einen koffe in Berlin' 2	Siegel-Pinelli	2	1960	
'Ich weiss nicht zu wem ich gehore' 1	Hollander	7	1930	
'Ich weiss nicht zu wem ich gehore' 2	Hollander	2	1960	
'Ich werde dich lieben'	Welch-Dietrich	2	1964	'Theme for Young Lovers'
'I Couldn't Be so Annoyed'	Robin-Whiting		1930	Film: *Blonde Venus*
'I Couldn't Sleep a Wink Last Night'	Adamson-Metzl		1943	'Ich hab' die Ganze nacht geweint'
'I Fall Overboard'	Hollander-Loesser		1940	Film: *Seven Sinners*
'If He Swing By the String'	Addison-More	2	1963	Film: *Tom Jones* (not MD)
'If It Isn't Pain, It Isn't Love'	Robin-Rainger		1935	Film: *The Devil is a Woman*
'I Get a Kick Out of You'	Porter	9	1972	Live: Queen's Theatre, London
'Illusions' 1	Hollander	15	1947	Film: *A Foreign Affair*
'Illusions' 2	Hollander	12	1949	
'Illusions' 3	Hollander	13	1987	With Udo Lindenberg
'I Love the Man I'm Near'	?	?	c1950	
'I May Never Go Home Anymore' 1 & 2	Roberts-Brooks	2	1957	

Song	Author/Composer	Backing	Year	Other Details
'I'm in No Mood for Music'	Hollander-Loesser	2	1941	Film: *Manpower*
'In den Kasernen'	Gérard-Kock		1964	
'I Refuse to Rock n'roll'		2	1955	Film: *Meet Me in Las Vegas*
'It's the Same'	Forrest-Wright	10	1953	With Rosemary Clooney
'I've Been in Love Before'	Hollander-Loesser	8	1939	Film: *Seven Sinners*
'I've Grown Accustomed to Her Face'	Lerner-Loewe	2	1959	Live: Rio de Janeiro
'I Will Come Back Again'	Vannah-Giltman	2	1959	Live: Rio de Janeiro
'I Wish You Love'	Trenet	2	1959	Théâtre de l'Etoile, Paris
'Ja das haben die Mädchen so gerne'	Schönfeld-Gilbert	5	1965	
'Ja so bin ich'	Stolz-Reisch	1	1933	
'J'aurais toujours une chambre à Berlin'	Siegell-Pinelli	2	1962	'Ich hab noch einen koffe in Berlin'
'Je sais que vous êtes jolie'	Christiné-Poupon		c1940	USA radio
'Je tire ma révérence' 1	Bastia	2	1944	possibly with Michel Emer
'Je tire ma révérence' 2	Bastia	7	1959	Théâtre de l'Etoile
'Jonny' 1	Hollander	1	1929	
'Jonny' 2	Hollander	1	1931	Jazz version, Ultraphone
'Jonny' 3	Hollander	2	1931	For Polydor
'Jonny' 4	Hollander	2	1960	
'Johnny, When it's Your Birthday'	Hollander	2	1959	Tape recording
'Just a Gigolo'	Cassucci-Mauprey		1978	Film: *Just a Gigolo*
'Kinde heut' abend da such ich mir was aus' 1	Hollander-Liebmann	7	1930	Film: *Der Blaue Engel*
'Kinde heut' abend da such ich mir was aus' 2	Hollander-Liebmann	2	1960	
'Kisses Sweeter Than Wine' 1 & 2	Campbell-Newman	2	1957	Kentucky Bluebird
'Kleine treue nachtigall'	Bacharach-Colpet	2	1964	Café de Paris
'Knocked 'em in the Old Kent Road'		2	1955	With Rosemary Clooney
'Land, Sea and Air'		14	1954	
'Laziest Gal in Town'	Porter		1950	Film: *Stage Fright*
'Lazy Afternoon' 1	Hollander	7	1939	Acetate

Song	Author/Composer	Backing	Year	Other Details
'Lazy Afternoon' 2	Hollander	6	1954	Café de Paris, London
'Leben ohne liebe kannst du nicht'	Spoliansky-Gilbert	11	1931	Film: *Nie wieder Liebe*
'Légende des étoiles'	Walberg-François	1	1933	Polydor, Paris
'Les jeux sont faits'	Emer	4	1957	Film: *The Monte Carlo Story*
'Let's call it a day'	de Sylva-Henderson-Brown		c1940	USA radio
'Let's Do It'	Cole Porter		?	No other details
'Liebe Leierkastenmann'	Kollo		1965	
'Liebeslied'	Gold-Perry	5	1961	Film: *Judgment at Nuremberg*
'Lili-Marlene' 1	Leip-Schultz	2	1943	Sung in German
'Lili-Marlene' 2	Leip-Schultz		1944	Sung in French
'Lili-Marlene' 3	Leip-Schultz	16	1944	English lyric: Connor
'Lili-Marlene' 4	Leip-Schultz	2	1955	New York, Columbia, England
'Lili-Marlene' 5	Leip-Schultz	2	1960	Sung in German
'Little Joe the Wrangler'	Hollander-Loesser		1939	Film: *Destry Rides Again*
'Lola-Lola' (English)	Hollander	2	1960	Live: Queen's Theatre, London
'Lonesome Road'	?	2	1960	Live: Titania Palast, Berlin
'Look Me Over Closely'	Gilkyson		1954	
'Love Me'	?	17	1952	USA radio
'Luar do sertao'	Cearense	2	1959	Live: Rio de Janeiro
'Makin' Whoopee!'	Kahn-Donaldson	2	1959	Live: Rio de Janeiro
'Marie-Marie' 1	Bécaud-Delanoë	2	1959	Sung in French
'Marie-Marie' 2	Bécaud-Colpet	2	1960	Sung in German
'Marie-Marie' 3	Bécaud-Colpet	2	1962	Sung in English
'Mean to Me' 1	Ahlert-Turk		1942	English version
'Mean to Me' 2	Ahlert-Turk-Metzl		1943	'Sei Lieb zu Mir'
'Mein Blondes Baby' 1	Kreuder-Rotter	1	1931	Berlin recording
'Mein Blondes Baby' 2	Kreuder-Rotter	1	1933	Paris recording
'Mein Blondes Baby' 3	Kreuder-Rotter	2	1960	
'Miss Otis Regrets'	Porter-Metzl		1951	'Mein Mann ist verhindert'
'Mit Dir, mit Dir da möcht ich sonntags angeln gehn'	Kollo-Rideamus		1965	

Song	Author/Composer	Backing	Year	Other Details
'Moi, je m'ennuie'	Walberg-François		1933	Live: Holland
'Moon River'	Mancini	1	1962	'Muss i denn'
'Must I Go?'	Traditional		1943	Sung in English
'Must I Go?'	Traditional		1951	
'Mutter hast du mir vergeben?' 1	Grau-Nieman-Dietrich	2	1964	Recorded in Warsaw. Original title: Czy mnie jeszcze pamietasz
'Mutter hast du mir vergeben?' 2	Grau-Nieman-Dietrich	2	1964	Elektrola recording
'My Baby Just Cares for Me'			1964	Live: Warsaw
'My Blue Heaven'	Whiting-Donaldson	2	1964	Live: Queen's Theatre, London
'Nach meine beene ist ja ganz Berlin verrückt'	Kollo-Hardt	5	1965	
'Near You' 1 & 2	Goell-Craig	2	1957	
'Nice and Easy'		2	1962	
'Nimm dich in acht vor blonden frauen'	Hollander-Rillo	7	1930	Film: *Der Blaue Engel*
'No Love, No Nothing'	Robin-Warren		1954	Café de Paris
'One for My Baby'	Arlen	2	1959	Live: Rio de Janeiro
'On ne lutte pas contre l'amour'	Boyer-Spoliansky	1	1933	'Leben ohne lieve kannst du nicht' Film: *Calais-Douvre*
'Où vont les fleurs?'	Seeger-Lemarque	2	1959	'Where Have All the Flowers Gone?'
'Paff der Zauberdrachen' 1 & 2	Lipton-Oldörp	2	1963	Puff
'Peter' 1	Nelson-Hollander	7	1929	German version
'Peter' 2	Nelson-Hollander	1	1933	German version
'Peter' 3	Nelson-Hollander	10	1956	Sung in English
'Peter' 4	Nelson-Hollander	2	1960	German version
'La plus bath des javas'	Georgius-Tremolo		1944	Paris
'Quand l'amour meurt'	Crémieux-Millandy	1	1931	Film: *Morocco*
'Qu'est ce que vous voudrez?'			c1940	USA radio

Song	Author/Composer	Backing	Year	Other Details
'Qui j'aime?'	Hollander-Boucher	1	1933	'Ich weiss nicht zu wem ich gehore', Film: *Tumultes*
'Rien ne va plus!'	Emer	4	1957	Film: *The Monte Carlo Story*
'Sag mir wo die Blumen sind?'	Seeger-Colpet	2	1963	'Where Have All the Flowers Gone?'
'Sans me parler'	Prévert-Kosma	2	1962	'Dejeuner du matin'
'Sch, kleines baby!'	Siegel-Dietrich	2	1964	'Hush Little Baby!'
'Sentimental Journey'		9	1972	Queen's Theatre, London
'Shir hatan'	Sahar	2	1964	Sung in Hebrew
'Solang noch Untern Linden'	Kollo-Wolff	5	1965	
'Something I Dreamed Last Night'		17	1952	
'Still war die Nacht'	Debout-Colpet	5	1966	'This World of Ours'
'Strange Thing I Find You'	King-Clifford		1942	Film: *The Lady is Willing*
'Such Trying Times'	Addison-Moore	2	1963	
'Surabaya Jonny'	Brecht-Weill	9	1967	Live: Montreal
'Surrey With the Fringe on Top'	Rodgers-Metzl-Hammerstein		1948	'Schlitternfahrt'
'Sweet as the Blush of May'	Skinner		1941	Film: *The Flame of New Orleans*
'Sweet Rosie O'Grady'	Nugent	2	1958	Live: Las Vegas
'Symphonie'	Alstone-Tabet-Bernstein	16	1944	Sung in French
'Taking a Chance on Love'	Latouche-Metzl-Fetter		1943	Sung in German
'This Evening Children'	Hollander	7	1930	'lost' until 1958
'This World of Ours'	Debout-Colpet	2	1964	
'Three Sweethearts Have I'	Rainger-Robin		1936	Film: *Desire*
'Time for Love'		17	1954	From the radio series
'Time on my Hands'	Adamson-Metzel-Youmans		1943	Sung in German
'Too Old to Cut the Mustard'		10	1952	Sung in German
'Treue liebe'	Colpet	2	1954	
'Und wenn er wiederkommt'	Gérard-Colpet-Maeterlinck	2	1964	
'Untern Linden-Untern Linden'	Kollo-Schanzer	5	1965	With Rosemary Clooney

Song	Author/Composer	Backing	Year	Other Details
'Vie en rose' 1	Piaf-Louiguy		1950	Film: *Stagefright*
'Vie en rose' 2	Piaf-Louiguy		1954	Café de Paris, London
'Vie en rose' 3	Piaf-Louiguy		1954	With Bing Crosby
'Voyages de noces'	Valtav-Rochette	2	1959	Live: Monte Carlo
'Warum tut liebe weh'	Colpet	2	1964	'A Little on the Lonely Side'
'Wenn der Sommer wieder einzieht'	Cavanagh-Metzl	2	1964	
'Wenn die beste Freundin'	Spoliansky-Schiffer	11	1928	Revue: Es liegt in der Luft
'Wenn die Soldaten' 1 & 2	Trad: arranged Pronk	2	1964	
'Wenn du Einmal eine Braut hast'	Hirsch-Heye	5	1965	
'Wenn ich mir was wunschen dürfte' 1	Hollander	7	1930	
'Wenn ich mir was wunschen dürfte' 2	Hollander	13	1987	With Udo Lindenberg
'Wer wird denn weinen'	Hirsch-Rebner	2	1960	
'What Am I Bid for my Apples'	Hajos-Robin		1930	Film: *Morocco*
'Where Have All the Flowers Gone?'	Seeger	2	1963	
'White Grass 'neath the Stones'	Merriwood	9	1972	New Theatre, London
'Within the Ruins of Berlin'	Hollander	7	1948	Film: *A Foreign Affair*
'Wo die Wiesen sind'		5	1965	
'Wo hast du nur die schönen blauen Augen her'	Erwin-Katscher	5	1965	
'Wo ist der Mann'	Kreuder-Colpet	1	1933	
'You Do Something to Me'	Porter	8	1939	
'You Go to My Head'	Coots-Gillespie	8	1939	
'You Little So-and-So'	Coslow-Rainger		c1940	USA radio
'You're the Cream in My Coffee'	de Sylva-Brown-Henderson	2	1959	Live: Rio de Janeiro
'You've Got that Look'	Hollander-Loesser	9	1939	Film: *Destry Rides Again*
'Das zerbrochene Ringlein'	?	?	1954	No other details

The Films of
Marlene Dietrich

DER KLEINE NAPOLEON   Union-Film 1923
Director: Georg Jacoby
Script: Georg Jacoby, Robert Liebmann
Cast: Napoleon Bonaparte: Egon von Hagen; Jerome Bonaparte:
Paul Heidemann; Georg von Melsungen: Harry Liedtke;
Charlotte: Antonia Dietrich; Kathrin: Marlene Dietrich.
Also starred: Jacob Tiedtke, Loni Nest, Alice Hechy, Kurt
Vespermann, Paul Biensfeld, Kurt Fuss, Marquisette Bosky,
Wilhelm Bendow

TRAGÖDIE DER LIEBE   Joe May Films 1923
Director: Joe May
Script: Adolf Lantz, Lee Birinski
Sets: Paul Leni
Costumes: Ali Hubert
Production Asst: Rudolf Sieber
Cast: Ombrade: Emil Jannings; Manon de Moreau: Mia May;
Musette: Erika Glassner; the judge: Kurt Vespermann; Lucie:
Marlene Dietrich

DER MENSCH AM WEGE   Osmania Films 1923
Director/Script: Wilhelm Dieterle
Sets: Herbert Richter-Luckian
Cast: the Human Angel: Wilhelm Dieterle; Schuster: Alexander
Granach

Also starred: Marlene Dietrich, Emile Unda, Wilhelm Völker, Heinrich George

DER SPRUNG INS LEBEN Oskar Messter Films 1924
Director: Johannes Guter
Producer: Oskar Messter
Script: Franz Schultz
Sets: Rudi Feldt
Cast: circus acrobat: Xeni Desni; her partner: Walter Rilla; student: Paul Heidemann; a ringmaster: Leonhard Haskel
Also starred: Marlene Dietrich, Frida Richard, Hans Brauswetter, Kathe Haak, Olga Engl

DIE FREUDLOSE GASSE Hirschal-Sofar Films 1925
Director: G.W. Pabst
Script: Willi Haas
Sets: Hans Sohnle and Otto Erdmann
Cast: Josef Rumfort: Jarro Furth; Grete Rumfort: Greta Garbo
Also starred: Marlene Dietrich (unbilled), Loni Nest, Max Kohlhase, Silvia Torf, Asta Nielsen

MANON LESCAUT U F A 1926
Director: Arthur Robison
Script:
Arthur Robison and Hans Kyser
Sets/costumes: Paul Leni
Cast: Manon Lescaut: Lya de Putti; Des Grieux: Vladimir Gaidarov; Maréchal des Grieux: Eduard Rothauser: Marquis de Blis: Fritz Greiner; Michéline: Marlene Dietrich
Also starred: Trude Hesterberg, Frida Richard, Lydia Potechina, Hubert von Meyerinck, Emilie Kurtz

EINE DU BARRY VON HEUTE Felsom Films 1926
Director: Alexander Korda
Script: Alexander Korda and Robert Liebmann
Sets: Otto Friedrich Werndorff
Cast: Toinette: Maria Korda; Sillon: Alfred Abel; Count Rabbatz: Alfred Gerasch; Cornelius: Friedrich Kayssler; Padilla: Jules von Szöreghy; Darius: Hans Albers; a coquette: 'Marlaine' Dietrich
Also starred: Karl Platen, Jean Bradin, Hans Wassmann

MADAME WÜNSCHT KEINE KINDER   Fox-Europa 1926
Director: Alexander Korda
Script: Bela Balazs and Adolf Lanz
Sets: Otto Friedrick Werndorff
Production Asst: Rudolf Sieber
Cast: Elvane Parizot: Maria Korda; Paul le Barroy: Harry Liedtke
Also starred: Marlene Dietrich, Trude Hesterberg, Maria Paudler

KOPF HOCH, CHARLY!   Ellen Richter 1926
Director: Willi Wolff
Script: Willi Wolff and Robert Liebmann
Sets: Ernst Stern
Cast: Charly: Ellen Richter; John-Jacob Bunjes: Michael Bohnen;
Edmée Marchand: Marlene Dietrich; Ditmar: Anton Pointner
Also starred: Blandine Ebinger, Toni Tetzlaff

DER JUXBARON   Ellen Richter 1927
Director: Willi Wolff
Script: Willi Wolff and Robert Liebmann
Sets: Ernst Stern
Cast: Baron: Reinhold Schünzel; Hugo Windisch: Henry Bender;
Zerline Windisch: Julia Serda; Sophie: Marlene Dietrich; Fränze:
Trude Hesterberg
Also starred: Teddy Bill, Colette Brettl, Albert Pauling

SEIN GRÖSSTER BLUFF   Nero Films 1927
Director: Harry Piel
Script: Henrik Galeen
Sets: W.A. Herrmann
Cast: Henry/Harry Devall: Harry Piel; Madame Andersson: Toni
Tetzlaff; Tilly: Lotte Lorring; Mimikry: Albert Pauling; Yvette:
Marlene Dietrich
Also starred: Fritz Greiner, Charly Berger

CAFÉ ELECTRIC   Sascha Films, Austria 1927
Director: Gustav Ucicky
Script: Jacques Bachrach
Sets: Arthur Berger
Cast: Göttlinger: Fritz Alberti; Erni: Marlene Dietrich; Ferdl:
Willi Forst; Erni's friend: Anny Coty

PRINZESSIN OLALA   Super-Films 1928
Director: Robert Land
Script: Robert Land and Franz Schultz
Sets: Robert Neppach
Cast: Prince: Hermann Böttcher; Boris: Walter Rilla; Chamberlain: Georg Alexander; Xenia: Carmen Boni: Hedy: Ila Meery; Chicotte de Gastoné: Marlene Dietrich; René: Hans Albers

ICH KÜSSE IHRE HAND, MADAME   Super-Films 1929
Director/Script: Robert Land
Sets: Robert Neppach
Cast: Jacques: Harry Liedtke; Laurence Gerard: Marlene Dietrich; Adolf Gerard: Pierre de Guingand; Tallandier: Karl Huszar-Puffy
Title song: music Ralph Erwin, lyrics Fritza Rotter, sung by Richard Tauber

DIE FRAU NACH DER MAN SICH SEHNT   Terra-Film 1929
Director: Kurt Berhhardt
Script: Ladislas Vajda
Sets: Robert Neppach
Cast: Stascha: Marlene Dietrich; Karoff: Fritz Kortner; Mrs Leblanc: Freda Richard
Also starred: Oska Simar, Uno Henning

DAS SCHIFF DER VERLORENEN
MENSCHEN   Glass-Wegeroff 1929
Director/Script: Maurice and Jacques Tourneur, assisted by Max Glass
Sets: Franz Schroedter
Cast: Ethel: Marlene Dietrich; Captain Fernando Vela: Fritz Kortner; Morian: Gaston Modot
Also starred: Robert Irvine, Vladimir Sokoloff

GEFAHREN DER BRAUTZEIT   Strauss-Film 1929
Director: Fred Sauer
Script: Walter Schlee, Walter Wassermann
Sets: Max Heilbronner
Cast: Evelyne: Marlene Dietrich; Baron van Geldern: Willi Forst; Yvette: Lotte Lorring
Also starred: Bruno Ziener, Elza Temar, Ernst Stahl-Nachbaur

DER BLAUE ENGEL/
THE BLUE ANGEL   Erich Pommer UFA 1930
Director: Josef von Sternberg
Producer: Erich Pommer
Script: Robert Liebmann
Sets: Otto Hunte, Emil Hasler
Cameramen: Hans Schneeberger, Gunther Rittau
Cast: Lola-Lola: Marlene Dietrich; Professor Rath: Emil Jan-
nings; Guste: Rosa Valetti; Mazeppa: Hans Albers
Also starred: Kurt Gerron, Ilse Fürstenberg, Edouard von
Winterstein, Reinhold Bernt, Hans Roth
Songs: 'Nimm dich in acht vor bonden frauen' ('Blonde women),
'Ich bin die fesche Lola' ('I am the Naughty Lola'), 'Kinde heut'
abend such ich mir was aus' ('This Evening Children), 'Ich bin von
Kopf bis Fuss auf Liebe eingestellt' ('Falling in Love Again')

MOROCCO   Parmount 1930
Director: Josef von Sternberg
Script: Jules Furthman
Sets: Hans Dreier
Photographer: Lee Garmes
Costumes: Travis Banton
Cast: Amy Jolly: Marlene Dietrich; Tom Brown: Gary Cooper;
Kennington: Adolphe Menjou
Also starred: Albert Conti, Ulrich Haupt, Francis McDonald,
Juliette Compton, Eve Southern
Songs: 'Quand l'amour meurt', 'Give Me the Man', 'What Am I
Bid For My Apples?'

DISHONOURED   Paramount 1931
Director: Josef von Sternberg
Script: Daniel H. Rubin
Photographer: Lee Garmes
Costumes: Travis Banton
Cast: X-27: Marlene Dietrich; Head of Secret Service: Gustav
von Seyffertitz; Lieutenant Kranau: Victor McLaglen; Kevrin:
Lew Cody
Also starred: Warner Oland, Barry Norton, Wilfred Lucas

SHANGHAI EXPRESS   Paramount 1932
Director: Josef von Sternberg
Script: Jules Furthman
Costumes: Travis Banton
Art director: Hans Dreier
Photographer: Lee Garmes
Cast: Madeleine (Shanghai Lily): Marlene Dietrich; Captain
Donald Harvey: Clive Brook; Hui Fei: Anna May Wong; Henry
Chand: Warner Oland; Mrs Haggerty: Louise Closser Hale
Also starred: Eugene Palette, Lawrence Grant, Gustav von
Seyffertitz, Emile Chautard

BLONDE VENUS   Paramount 1932
Director: Josef von Sternberg
Script: Jules Furthman
Costumes: Travis Banton
Photographer: Bert Glennon
Art director: Wiard Ihnen
Cast: Helen Faraday: Marlene Dietrich; Edward Faraday: Herbert
Marshall; Nick Townsend: Cary Grant; Johnny: Dickie Moore
Songs: 'Hot Voodoo', 'You Little So-and-So', 'I Couldn't Be So
Annoyed'

SONG OF SONGS   Paramount 1933
Director: Reuben Mamoulian
Script: Sam Hoffenstein, Leo Birinski
Photographer: Victor Milner
Costumes: Travis Banton
Cast: Lily Czepanek: Marlene Dietrich; Waldow: Brian Aherne;
Baron von Merzback: Lionel Atwill; Frau Rasmussen: Alison
Skipworth.
Song: 'Jonny'

THE SCARLET EMPRESS   Paramount 1934
Director: Josef von Sternberg
Script: Manuel Komroff
Photographer: Bert Glennon
Costumes: Travis Banton
Art directors: Hans Dreier, Peter Ballbusch

Effects: Gordon Jennings
Cast: Catherine the Great: Marlene Dietrich; Alexei: John Lodge; Grand Duke Peter: Sam Jaffe; Empress Elizabeth: Louise Dresser
Also starred: C. Aubrey Smith, Marie Sieber

THE DEVIL IS A WOMAN   Paramount 1935
Director/Photographer: Josef von Sternberg (assisted by Lucien Ballard)
Script: John Dos Passos, S.K. Winston
Costumes: Travis Banton
Art director: Hans Dreier
Cast: Concha Perez: Marlene Dietrich; Antonio Galvan: Cesar Romero; Don Pasqual: Lionel Atwill
Also starred: Edward Everett Horton, Alison Skipworth
Songs: 'If It Isn't Pain, It Isn't Love', 'Three Sweethearts Have I'

DESIRE   Paramount 1936
Director: Frank Borzage
Script: Edwin Justus Mayer, Waldemar Young, Sam Hoffenstein
Producer: Ernst Lubitsch
Photographer: Charles Lang
Art director/costumes: Travis Banton
Cast: Madeleine de Beaupré: Marlene Dietrich; Tom Bradley: Gary Cooper; Mr Gibson: William Frawley
Also starred: John Halliday, Akim Tamiroff, Alan Mowbray, Ernest Cossart
Song: 'Awake in a Dream'

THE GARDEN OF ALLAH   Selznick/United Artists 1936
Director: Richard Boleslawski
Producer: David O. Selznick
Script: W.P. Lipscomb, Lynn Riggs
Photographer: W. Howard Greene
Art directors: Sturges Carne, Edward Boyle, Lyle Wheeler
Special effects: Jack Cosgrove
Costumes: Ernst Dryden
Cast: Domini Enfilden: Marlene Dietrich; Boris Androvsky: Charles Boyer; Count Anteoni: Basil Rathbone
Also starred: Tilly Losch, C. Aubrey Smith, Maria Riva, Joseph Schildkraut, Alan Marshall, John Carradine

I LOVED A SOLDIER   Paramount 1936
Director: Henry Hathaway
Script: John van Druten
Producer: Benjamin Glazer
Photographer: Charles Lang
With Marlene Dietrich, Charles Boyer, Walter Catlett, Akim
Tamiroff. Not completed

KNIGHT WITHOUT   AlexanderKorda/United Artists 1937
ARMOUR
Director: Jacques Feyder
Producer: Alexander Korda
Script: Lajos Biro, Arthur Wimperis
Photographer: Harry Stradling
Sets: Lazare Meerson
Music: Miklos Rosza
Costumes: George Benda
Cast: Alexandra: Marlene Dietrich; Fotheringill: Robert Donat
Also starred: Basil Gill, Robert Clements, Irene Vanburgh, David
Tree

ANGEL   Paramount 1937
Director: Ernst Lubitsch
Script: Samson Raphaelson
Costumes: Travis Banton
Photographer: Charles Lang
Art directors: Hans Dreier, Robert Usher
Cast: Maria Barker: Marlene Dietrich; Frederick Barker: Herbert
Marshall; Anthony Halton: Melvyn Douglas
Also starred: Edward Everett Horton, Ernest Cossart, Laura Hope
Crews
Song: 'Angel'

DESTRY RIDES AGAIN   Universal 1939
Director: George Marshall
Producer: Joe Pasternak
Script: Felix Jackson, Gertrude Purcell, Henry Meyers
Photographer: Hal Mohr
Costumes: Vera West
Cast: Frenchy: Marlene Dietrich; Tom Destry: James Stewart;

Boris Callahan: Misha Auer; Lilybelle Callahan: Una Merkel; Kent: Brian Donlevy; Wash Dimsdale: Charles Winninger
Songs: 'The Boys in the Backroom', 'Little Joe the Wrangler', 'You've Got That Look'

SEVEN SINNERS   Universal 1940
Director: Tay Garnett
Producer: Joe Pasternak
Script: Harry Tugend, John Meehan
Photographer: Rudolph Mate
Costumes: Irene
Cast: Bijou: Marlene Dietrich; Bruce: John Wayne; Little Ned: Broderick Crawford; Sasha: Mischa Auer; Dr Martin: Albert Dekker
Also starred: Anna Lee, Oscar Homolka, Billy Gilbert
Songs: 'I Fall Overboard', 'The Man's in the Navy', 'I've Been in Love Before'

THE FLAME OF NEW ORLEANS   Universal 1941
Director: René Clair
Producer: Joe Pasternak
Script: Norman Krasna
Photographer: Rudolph Mate
Costumes: René Hubert
Cast: Claire Ledux: Marlene Dietrich; Robert Latour: Bruce Cabot; Charles Giraud: Roland Young; Zolotov: Mischa Auer
Also starred: Andy Devine, Laura Hope Crews, Frank Jenks, Eddie Quillan, Franklin Pangborn
Songs: 'Sweet as the Blush of May', 'Salt o'the Sea', 'Oh Joyous Day'

MANPOWER   Warner Brothers 1941
Director: Raoul Walsh
Executive producer: Hal B. Wallis
Script: Jerry Wald, Richard Macaulay
Photographer: Ernest Haller
Art director: Max Parker
Costumes: Milo Anderson
Cast: Fay Duval: Marlene Dietrich; Hank McHenry: Edward G.

Robinson; Johnny Marshall: George Raft: Jumbo Wells: Alan Hale; Dolly: Eve Arden; Omaha: Frank McHugh
Songs: 'He Lied and I Listened', 'I'm in No Mood for Music'

THE LADY IS WILLING   Columbia 1942
Director/producer: Mitchell Leisen
Script: James Edward Grant, Albert McCleery
Photographer: Ted Tetzlaff
Dance director: Douglas Dean
Cast: Elizabeth Madden: Marlene Dietrich; Corey McBain: Fred MacMurray; Buddy: Aline MacMahon
Song: 'Strange Thing, and I Find You'

THE SPOILERS   Universal 1942
Director: Ray Enright
Producer: Frank Lloyd
Script: Lawrence Hazard, Tom Reed
Photographer: Milton Krasner
Costumes: Vera West
Cast: Cherry Mallotte: Marlene Dietrich; Alex McNamara: Randolph Scott; Roy Glennister: John Wayne; Helen Chester: Margaret Lindsay
Also starred: Richard Barthelmess, Harry Carey

PITTSBURGH   Universal 1942
Director: Lewis Seiler
Producer: Charles K. Feldman
Script: Tom Reed, John Twist, Kenneth Gamet
Photographer: Robert de Grasse
Costumes: Vera West
Cast: Josie Winters: Marlene Dietrich; Pittsburgh Markham: John Wayne; Cash Evans: Randolph Scott

FOLLOW THE BOYS   Universal 1944
Director: Eddie Sutherland
Producer: Charles K. Feldman
Costumes: Vera West
The film starred George Raft and Vera Zorina. Marlene was one of many guest stars appearing as themselves

KISMET   MGM 1944
Director: William Dieterle
Producer: Everett Riskin
Photographer: Charles Rosher
Script: John Meehan
Costumes: Irene/Karinska
Cast: Jamilla: Marlene Dietrich; Hafiz: Ronald Colman; Mansur:
Edward Arnold; Caliph: James Craig
Songs: 'Tell Me, Tell Me Evening Star', 'Willow in the Wind'

MARTIN ROUMAGNAC   Alcina 1946
Director: Georges Lacombe
Producer: Marc le Pelletier
Script: Pierre Véry
Photographer: Robert Hubert
Music: Marcel Mirouze
Art director: Georges Wakhevitch
Cast: Blanche Ferrand: Marlene Dietrich; Martin Roumagnac:
Jean Gabin; Martin's sister: Margo Lion
Also starred: Marcel Herrand, Daniel Gélin

GOLDEN EARRINGS   Paramount 1947
Director: Mitchell Leisen
Producer: Harry Tugend
Photographer: Daniel L. Fapp
Script: Frank Butler, Abraham Polonsky, Helen Deutsch
Music: Victor Young
Dance: Billy Daniels
Costumes: Kay Dodson
Cast: Lydia: Marlene Dietrich; Ralph Denistown: Ray Milland;
Professor Krosigk: Reinhold Schünzel
Also starred: Murvyn Vye, Bruce Lester, Quentin Reynolds,
Dennis Hoey
Song: 'Golden Earrings'

A FOREIGN AFFAIR   Paramount 1948
Director: Billy Wilder
Script: Charles Brackett (producer), Billy Wilder, Richard L. Breen
Photographer: Charles B. Lang Jr

Music: Frederick Hollander
Costumes: Edith Head
Cast: Erika von Schlütow: Marlene Dietrich; Phoebe Frost: Jean Arthur; Captain Pringle: John Lund; Colonel Plummer: Millard Mitchell
Songs: 'Within the Ruins of Berlin', 'Black Market', 'Illusions'

JIGSAW   Tower/United Artists 1949
Director: Fletcher Markle
Photographer: Don Malkames
The film starred Franchot Tone and Jean Wallace. Cameo parts included John Garfield, Henry Fonda and Marlene as a night-club entertainer

STAGE FRIGHT   Warner Brothers 1950
Director/producer: Alfred Hitchcock
Script: Whitfield Cook, James Bridie
Photographer: Wilkie Cooper
Music: Leighton Lucas
Art director: Terence Verity
Costumes: Christian Dior
Cast: Charlotte Inwood: Marlene Dietrich; Eve Gill: Jane Wyman; Smith: Michael Wilding; Jonathan Cooper: Richard Todd; Commodore Gill: Alistair Sim
Also starred: Sybil Thorndyke, Joyce Grenfell, Kay Walsh
Songs: 'La vie en rose', 'Laziest Gal in Town'

A NEW KIND OF LOVE   United Artists 1950
Director: Billy Wilder
Script: Erich Maria Remarque, Billy Wilder
Tests were made with Maurice Chevalier as Marlene's co-star but the project was abandoned when Chevalier was prevented from entering America by the McCarthy witch-hunt

WITNESS FOR THE   Small/Hornblow/United Artists 1958
PROSECUTION
Director/script: Billy Wilder (assisted by Harry Kurnitz)
Producer: Arthur Hornblow Jr
Music: Matty Malneck
Costumes: Edith Head

Cast: Christine Vole: Marlene Dietrich; Sir Wilfrid Robarts; Charles Laughton; Leonard Vole: Tyrone Power; Miss Plimsoll: Elsa Lanchester
Also starred: Henry Daniell, John Williams
Song: 'I May Never Go Home Any More'

NO HIGHWAY IN THE SKY   20th Century-Fox 1951
Director: Henry Koster
Script: R.C. Sheriff, Oscar Millard, Alec Coppel (based on novel by Nevil Shute)
Photographer: Georges Perinal
Costumes: Christian Dior
Cast: Monica Teasdale: Marlene Dietrich; Mr Honey: James Stewart; Marjorie Corder: Glynis Johns; Elspeth Honey: Janette Scott
Also starred: Jack Hawkins, Ronald Squire

RANCHO NOTORIOUS   Fidelity/RKO 1952
Director: Fritz Lang
Producer: Howard Welsch
Photographer: Hal Mohr
Script: Daniel Taradash
Costumes: Don Loper
Cast: Altar Keane: Marlene Dietrich; Frenchy Fermont: Mel Ferrer; Vern Haskell: Arthur Kennedy
Also starred: Gloria Henry, Lloyd Gough
Songs: 'Get Away, Young Man', 'Gypsy Davey', 'Legend of Chuck-a-Luck'

AROUND THE WORLD   Mike Todd/United Artists 1956
IN EIGHTY DAYS
Director: Michael Anderson
Producer: Mike Todd
Script: James Poe, S.J. Perelman
Music: Victor Young
Costumes: Miles White
The film starred David Niven and Cantinflas. There were many cameo appearances and Marlene played 'a saloon girl'

THE MONTE CARLO STORY   Titanus/United Artists 1957
Director/script: Samuel A. Taylor
Producer: Marcello Girosi
Photographer: Giuseppe Rotunno
Costumes: Elio Constanzi
Cast: Marquise Maria de Crevecoeur: Marlene Dietrich; Count
Dino della Fiaba: Vittorio de Sica; Mr Hinkley: Arthur O'Connel;
Jane Hinkley: Natalie Trundy
Songs: 'Le jeux sont faits', 'Rien ne va plus!', 'Back Home in
Indiana'

TOUCH OF EVIL   Universal International 1958
Director/script: Orson Welles
Costumes: Bill Thomas
Photographer: Russell Metty
Music: Henry Mancini
The film starred Orson Welles, Charlton Heston and Janet Leigh.
Marlene was given a cameo part as a fortune-teller

JUDGMENT AT NUREMBERG   Roxlom/United Artists 1961
Director/producer: Stanley Kramer
Script: Abby Mann
Photographer: Laszlio
Music: Ernest Gold
Costumes: Jean-Louis
Cast: Dan Haywood: Spencer Tracy; Madame Berthold: Marlene
Dietrich; Ernst Janning: Burt Lancaster; Colonel Tad Lawson:
Richard Widmark; Hans Rolfe: Maximilian Schell; Irene
Hoffman: Judy Garland; Rudolf Peterson: Montgomery Clift
Song: 'Lili Marlene'

THE BLACK FOX   Steloff-Image/Heritage Films 1962
Director/producer: Louis Clyde Stoumen
Music: Ezra Laderman
Marlene narrated Stoumen's script

PARIS WHEN IT SIZZLES   Paramount 1964
Director: Richard Quine
Script: George Axelrod

Photographer: Charles B. Lang Jr
Music: Nelson Riddle
Costumes: Christian Dior
The film starred Audrey Hepburn and William Holden. Marlene
and Noël Coward were included amongst the 'walk-ons'

JUST A GIGOLO   Leguan 1978
Director: David Hemmings
Script: Joshua Sinclair, Ennio de Concini
Photographer: Charly Steinberger
Music: Günther Fischer
Costumes: Max Maga, Ingrid Zore
Cast: Baroness von Semering: Marlene Dietrich; Paul von
Prsygodsky: David Bowie; Hermann Kraft: David Hemmings;
Prince: Curd Jurgens
Also starred: Kim Novak, Sydne Rome, Maria Schell
Songs: 'Just a Gigolo', 'Jonny', 'Revolutionary song', 'I Kiss Your
Hand Madame', 'Don't Let It Be Too Long'

Marlene Dietrich:
My Favourite Albums

The following are albums that have been released in Britain, France, Germany and the United States over the last twenty-five years. Selected by Marlene herself, they contain around seventy per cent of her commercial output. Some of the albums have been deleted and are regarded as collectors' items.

MARLENE SINGT
BERLIN-BERLIN Polydor, Germany 238 102
Sleeve notes/compilation by Marlene Dietrich: 'Solang noch Untern Linden', 'Du just ja keine ahnung wie schön du bist Berlin', 'Durch Berlin fliesst immer noch die spree', 'Mit dir, mit dir da möcht ich Sonntags angeln gehn', 'Nach meine Beene ist ja ganz Berlin verrückt', 'Ja, das haben die Mädchen so gerne', 'Wenn ein mädel einen herrn hat', 'Lieber leierkastenmann', 'Das war in Schönberg', 'Untern Linden-Untern Linden', 'Das zillelied', 'Wenn du einmal eine braut hast', 'Es gibt in leben manchesmal moment', 'Wo hast du nur die schönen blauen augen her', 'Berlin-Berlin'.

WIEDERSEHEN MIT MARLENE Elektrola, Germany 83 220
Recorded live during the German tour of 1960: 'Ich bin von Kopf bis Fuss auf Liebe Eingestellt', 'Ich bin die fesche Lola', 'Wer wird den weinen', 'Mein blondes Baby', 'Peter', 'Allein in einer grossen stadt', 'Wenn ich mir 'was wüschen dürfte', 'Johnny wenn du Geburtstag hast', 'Marie-Marie', 'Lili Marlene', 'Ich weiss nicht zu wem ich gehöre', 'Ich hab' noch einer Koffer in Berlin', 'Kinder,

heut' abend'. The British release of this album, *Marlene Dietrich Returns to Germany*, was supplemented with 'Sag mir wo die Blumen sind'.

THE ESSENTIAL MARLENE DIETRICH   EMI, England 5621
Sleeve notes/compilation by David Bret and Marlene Dietrich: 'Ich bin von Kopf bis Fuss auf Liebe eingestellt', 'Quand l'amour meurt', 'Give Me the Man', 'Leben ohne liebe kannst du nicht', 'Mein blondes Baby', 'Allein in einer grossen Stadt', 'Peter', 'Lola-Lola', 'Wer wird denn weinen', 'Johnny', 'Lili Marlene', 'Déjeuner du matin', 'Où vont les fleurs?', 'Wenn die Soldaten', 'In den Kasernen', 'Wenn der sommer wieder einzieht', 'Und wenn er wiederkommt', 'Die Welt war jung', 'Blowin' in the Wind', 'Where Have All the Flowers Gone?', 'Ich werde dich lieben', 'Der Trommelmann', 'Auf der Mundharmonika.

DIETRICH IN RIO   CBS, United States RM52077
Live at the Copacabana Palace, 17 August 1959: 'Look Me Over Closely', 'You're the Cream in My Coffee', 'My Blue Heaven', 'The Boys in the Backroom', 'Warum', 'Je tire ma révérence', 'Well all right', 'Makin' whoopee', 'I've Grown Accustomed To Her Face', 'One For My Baby', 'I Will Come Back Again', 'Luar do sertão'.

DIE NEUE MARLENE   EMI, England, CLP 1885
'Wenn die Soldaten', 'Die Antwort weiss ganz allein der Wind', 'In den Kasernen', 'Und wenn er wiederkommt', 'Sag mir wo die Blumen sind', 'Auf der Mundharmonika', 'Der Trommelmann', 'Wenn der Sommer wieder einzieht', 'Ich werde dich Lieben', 'Paff der Zauberdrachen', 'Ssch, kleines Baby', 'Mutter hast du mir vergeben?'.

DIETRICH IN LONDON   PYE, England NPL 18113
Live at the Queen's Theatre, 1964: 'I Can't Give You Anything but Love', 'Laziest Gal in Town', 'Shir hatan', 'La vie en rose', 'Jonny', 'Go 'Way from My Window', 'Allein', 'Lili Marlene', 'Warum', 'Lola-Lola', 'I Wish You Love', 'Marie-Marie', 'Honeysuckle Rose', 'Falling in Love Again'.

LILI MARLENE   CBS, United States 32375
The songs here, with the exception of the title track, appeared under English titles though sung in German and were originally issued on a set of 7″ 45 rpm records: 'Lili Marlene', 'Lieb zu mir' ('Mean to Me'), 'The Hobellied', 'Ach Fräulein Annie wohnt lange nicht mehr hier' ('Annie Doesn't Live Here Any More'), 'Du liegst mir im Herzen' ('You Have My Heart'), 'Schlitternfahrt' ('The Surrey with the Fringe on Top'), 'Time on My Hands', 'Taking a Chance on Love', 'Mein Mann ist verhindert' ('Miss Otis Regrets'), 'Muss i denn' ('Must I go'), 'Du hast die Seele mein' ('You Have Taken My Soul'), 'Ich 'hab die Ganze nacht geweint' ('I Couldn't Sleep a Wink Last Night').

DIETRICH AT THE CAFÉ   Sony, England MDK 47254
DE PARIS
Introduced by Noël Coward: 'The Boys in the Backroom', 'Laziest Gal in Town', 'Lola-Lola', 'Jonny', 'Lili Marlene', 'La vie en rose', 'Lazy Afternoon', 'Falling in Love Again', 'Look Me Over Closely', 'No Love No Nothing'. Supplementary tracks, some from live performances with applause edited out: 'Warum', 'One for My Baby', 'Makin' Whoopee', 'I've Grown Accustomed to Her Face', 'Too Old to Cut the Mustard/Dot's Nice Donna Fight' (with Rosemary Clooney); 'Baubles, Bangles and Beads/A Guy that Takes His Time', 'Peter'.

LILI MARLENE   Polygram, France, 840169/1
The first thirteen songs on this album represent the 1964 live performance at the Queen's Theatre in London, 1964. The remaining tracks are 'Moi, je m'ennuie', 'Allein in einer grossen Stadt', 'Mein blondes Baby', 'Peter', 'Bitte geh' nicht fort' ('Ne me quitte pas'), 'Kleine treue Nachtigall'.

L'ANGE BLEU   Chansophone, France 102-4
Succès et Raretés 1928/33. Compilation/sleeve notes by Jacques Primack: 'Wenn die beste Freundin', 'Falling in Love Again', 'Nimm dich in acht vor Blonden Frauen', 'Blonde Women', 'Ich bin die fesche Lola', 'Ich bin von Kopf bis Fuss aufe liebe eingestellt', 'Wenn ich mir was wünschen dürfte', 'Kinder heute abend da such ich mir was aus', 'I Am the Naughty Lola', 'This Evening Children', 'Peter', 'Jonny' (Polydor version), 'Jonny'

(Ultraphone), 'Leben ohne liebe kannst du nicht', 'Quand l'amour meurt', 'Give Me the Man', 'Assez' (Polydor), 'Assez' (Decca), 'Moi, je m'ennuie', 'Ja so bin ich', 'Allein in einer grossen Stadt', 'Mein blondes Baby', 'Wo ist der Mann'.

MARLENE DIETRICH   Decca, England AH131
'Lili Marlene', 'Symphonie', 'You Do something to Me', 'You Go to My Head', 'I've Been in Love Before', 'Illusions', 'Black Market', 'You've Got That Look', 'The Boys in the Backroom', 'Falling in Love Again'.

THE MARLENE DIETRICH
COLLECTION   Déjavu, England 2098
This contains the tracks from the previous album plus Marlene's 1965 London recordings: 'Another Spring Another Love', 'This World of Ours', 'If He Swing by the String', 'Near You', 'Candles Glowing', 'Kisses Sweeter than Wine', 'Such Trying Times'.

Marlene also asked me to thank Terry Sanderson for bringing to her attention the extraordinary *MARLENE DIETRICH LIVE:* Volume One, a non-profit first for all Dietrich deamon clubs and Roy's Marlene-watchers everywhere! (Wildebeest-Maclon, USA 5290): 'Hot Voodoo', 'You Little So-and-So', 'I Couldn't Be Annoyed', 'Quand l'amour meurt', 'Awake in a Dream', 'Falling in Love Again', 'I've Been in Love Before', 'Symphonie', 'La vie en rose', 'Ein Roman', 'Let's Call It a Day', 'No Love No Nothing', 'It Must Have Been Something I Dreamt Last Night', 'Lieb su mir', 'Das alte lied', 'Ich weiss nicht su wem ich gehöre', 'Je sais que vous êtes jolie', 'La vie en rose' (with Bing Crosby), 'Warum', 'Love me'.

Index